AFTER THE WEST WAS WON

AFTER THE WEST WAS WON

Homesteaders and Town-Builders in Western South Dakota, 1900–1917

BY PAULA M. NELSON

University of Iowa Press Iowa City

University of Iowa Press, Iowa City 52242
Copyright © 1986 by the University of Iowa
All rights reserved
Printed in the United States of America
First paperback printing, 1989

Book and jacket design by Sandra Strother Hudson
Typesetting by G&S Typesetters, Inc., Austin, Texas
Printing and binding by Thomson-Shore, Inc., Dexter, Michigan

Library of Congress Cataloging-in-Publication Data

Nelson, Paula, 1951–
    After the West was won.

    Bibliography: p.
    Includes index.
    1. City and town life—South Dakota—History—
20th century.   2. Frontier and pioneer life—South
Dakota.   3. South Dakota—History.   I. Title.
F656.N45 1986   978.3′031   86-11405
ISBN 0-87745-156-7 cloth, ISBN 0-87745-250-4 paper

*On the title page: A farm woman in the garden with
her hoe, Timber Lake area, Dewey County, 1915.*

*Except as noted, all photographs are reproduced
courtesy of the South Dakota State Historical
Society.*

TO MY MOTHER,
who has always had faith
and
to the memory of my father,
who would have been pleased

CONTENTS

Acknowledgments   *ix*

Introduction   *xi*

1. Merely the Pioneers   *1*

2. The Last Great Frontier   *13*

3. Fifty Miles to Water, One Hundred Miles to Wood   *25*

4. Threshers Came Right after Dinner   *41*

5. Sociability Is What We Need in This Country   *61*

6. The Best and Most Progressive Town   *81*

7. Happy Homes, Fine Residences, and Good Schools and Churches   *101*

8. We've Reached the Land of Drouth and Heat   *119*

9. Let the Good Work Go On   *143*

10. To Overcome the Drawbacks and Failure   *155*

11. Conclusion   *169*

Notes   *179*

Bibliography   *207*

Index   *215*

ACKNOWLEDGMENTS

I wish to thank a number of people who helped me with the research and writing of this book. The personnel of the South Dakota Historical Resource Center in Pierre have been very cooperative over the years. Their friendliness and encouragement during my two visits to Pierre were much appreciated. Rosemary Evetts, the librarian, and Bonnie Gardner, the curator of photographs, deserve special thanks. Their interest and enthusiasm made my work pleasurable, and their willingness to work with my sometimes sketchy requests allowed me to pursue new avenues of inquiry without repeated trips to Pierre.

At the University of Iowa, where this book began as a doctoral dissertation in the history department, I would like to thank three members of my dissertation committee: my advisor, Professor Malcolm J. Rohrbough, and Professors Stephen J. Pyne and Linda K. Kerber. Professor Rohrbough, especially, spent considerable time and effort on the project and I would like to extend a warm thank-you to him. I would also like to acknowledge the Department of History's assistance in granting me a dissertation research fellowship to finance a trip to Pierre, and for its extension of financial aid, which allowed me to teach while completing the dissertation.

The staff of the interlibrary loan department of the University of Iowa Libraries also deserve recognition for their assistance in locating the many obscure privately printed sources necessary for the successful completion of my dissertation. Through them I was also able to order a number of South Dakota newspapers on microfilm from the Center for Research Libraries in Chicago. The Center's long-term loan

x

ACKNOWLEDGMENTS

system helped my work immeasurably. I would also like to thank my skilled word processor, Mary Strottman. Her competence, flexibility, and good humor took a tremendous burden from my shoulders.

I also owe a number of personal debts that I would like to mention here. I would like to acknowledge my late grandmother, Hilda Berntson, of Hector, Minnesota, and my dear friend, Emma Shellenberg, of Marshall, Minnesota, rural women who reached maturity during the era described in this book. Through their stories and by their example they have shown me the very best in rural life and values. My husband, Stephen C. Krumpe, deserves special thanks. He provided a wealth of advice, encouragement, and editorial skill when I needed it most. Without his love and commitment I never could have written this book.

My greatest debt is reflected in the dedication.

INTRODUCTION

In 1893 the city of Chicago hosted the World's Columbian Exposition, a celebration of the quadricentennial of Columbus' discovery of America and the opening of the westward march across the North American continent. With conscious irony, Frederick Jackson Turner used the occasion to proclaim the passing of the American frontier. In the midst of the Exposition's celebration of technology, science, and progress, Turner sounded the knell for the frontier, a powerful and deep-seated symbol in American tradition, ideology, and myth. Turner noted that the 1890 census had revealed for the first time that there was no discernible line of frontier settlement in the United States. "And now," he said, "four centuries from the discovery of America, at the end of a hundred years of life under the Constitution, the frontier has gone and with its going has closed the first period of American history."[1] For Turner this closing meant the end of America as it had existed for three centuries, a colony and a nation shaped by the hopes and dreams of rebirth in the wilderness. In a practical sense, the frontier had provided people with opportunities for material success, but Turner chose not to emphasize that aspect. Instead, he wrote about the spiritual growth that the frontier had induced. As Harold Simonson interprets it: "The myth proclaimed that on the open frontier a person could be reborn; he could have a second chance. Freed from the heavy accretions of culture, the frontiersman again could experience the pristine harmony between himself and nature, or to prove his superiority, he again could battle nature's inscrutable ways, and through strength and resourcefulness, triumph over them."[2]

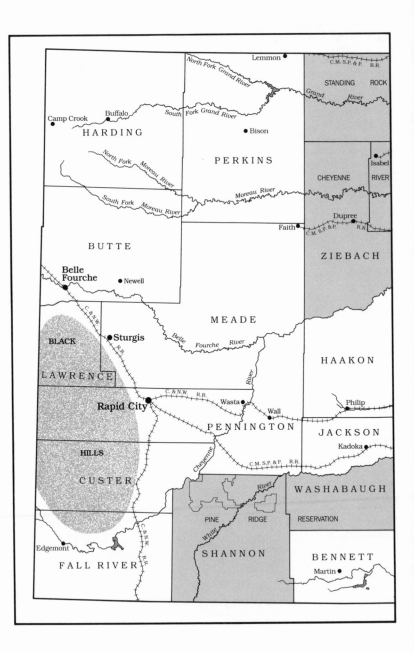

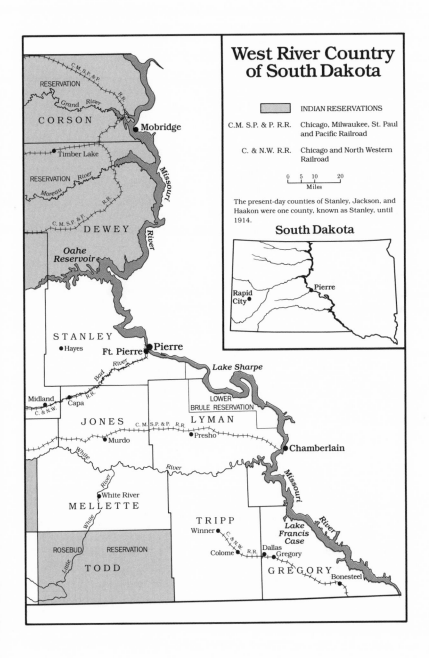

West River Country of South Dakota

INDIAN RESERVATIONS

C.M. S.P. & P. R.R.   Chicago, Milwaukee, St. Paul and Pacific Railroad

C. & N.W. R.R.   Chicago and North Western Railroad

0   5   10   20
Miles

The present-day counties of Stanley, Jackson, and Haakon were one county, known as Stanley, until 1914.

South Dakota

Rapid City

Pierre

RESERVATION

C.M.S.P.&P. R.R.

Grand River

CORSON

Mobridge

Timber Lake

RESERVATION   River

Moreau   R.R.

C.M.S.P.&P. R.R.

DEWEY

Missouri River

Oahe Reservoir

STANLEY

Hayes

Ft. Pierre   Pierre

Bad River   R.R.

Lake Sharpe

Midland   Capa

C. & N.W.

JONES

C.M.S.P.&P. R.R.

LYMAN

LOWER BRULE RESERVATION

Murdo

Presho

Chamberlain

White River

River

White River

MELLETTE

White River

Missouri River

TRIPP

Winner

Lake Francis Case

Colome

C.&N.W. R.R.

Dallas   Gregory

ROSEBUD   RESERVATION

Little River

TODD

GREGORY

Bonesteel

Notwithstanding Turner's epitaph, the power and lure of the frontier myth survived the frontier's demographic demise. In the years following Turner's address, hundreds of thousands of latter-day pioneers poured into the interior of the Great Plains. While Turner and other academic nostalgics worried about the future direction of the nation in the context of the closed frontier, a new migration poured westward to fill in the vast regions that remained unsettled after the West was supposedly won. They came fortified with nineteenth-century notions of progress, success, and the opportunities provided by free land and were supported by twentieth-century technology. They believed that they were the luckiest of Americans, for they had the great opportunity to write the final chapter of a three-century-long epic of conquest. The settlers of the last frontier sensed that their migration was the last chance America would have to tame a new country and civilize a wilderness.

This is the story of one place involved in the last great frontier migration: the plains of western South Dakota. Called the "west river country" by the people who lived there because of its location west of the Missouri River, the area was settled by 100,000 newcomers between 1900 and 1915.[3] Like earlier generations of settlers, the early waves had subdued the indigenous Indian population and developed an exploitative economy based on natural, rather than man-made, resources. And as was the case on earlier frontiers, these initial waves of migratory exploiters were followed by much larger waves of permanent agricultural settlers. Ambitious, hardworking people with great faith in their ability to establish a flourishing society of farms and towns, they fully intended to duplicate the successes of earlier pioneers. But by the standards of previous frontiers, they failed, and their failure added a bitter twist to the frontier dream. These people had to confront the possibility that the frontier myth of opportunity might be a fantasy, that a second chance might be only an opportunity for a second failure, that nature could not always be conquered. As the recognition of failure became clear, many settlers felt betrayed and conquered. Daniel Boone had become Sisyphus. The boundless frontier of myth, where all things were possible, lay behind them, and before them lay only the closed frontier with its limited expectations, "*no exceptions and . . . no escape.*"[4] They did not submit without a hard fight. The struggle these settlers waged to realize their dreams matched

or exceeded the heroic epics of earlier times on other frontiers.

The people who settled western South Dakota pursued a different kind of frontier experience from those who had followed the frontier dream before them. These latter-day pioneers were both blessed and cursed with twentieth-century baggage. By 1900 the West had become a myth, an adventure yarn that appealed to people who wanted to partake of a legend but not necessarily to make a home in it. The technology of transport and communication available at the time allowed many to travel west and homestead as a vacation, lighting only briefly on the land before returning to a modern urban world. Technology had also eased the burdens of work in long-settled regions, especially in towns and cities, and settlers drawn from such places had few pioneer skills. Many chose not to learn them; hard work under difficult conditions had not been part of their frontier dream.

West river settlers were different, too, because of the place they inhabited, a land of uncertain rainfall, temperature extremes, and wind. A generation before, pioneers in Nebraska and Kansas had learned that the Great Plains could be an unfriendly and unpredictable place to build a future. Few people moving to western South Dakota seemed to understand the lessons of that earlier experience. They continued to believe that their efforts would turn out differently, that they were exceptions, that they could escape the lessons of the land. The fact that they could not became clear in the drought of 1910–1911, when crops were baked and dreams desiccated. In several counties, from a third to half the people left their new homes and continued their search for success and happiness in the settled world. Those who remained rebuilt a life on changed assumptions and diminished expectations.

This is a story, then, of dreams and ambitions thwarted. It is also a story of heroism and success of an unexpected kind. The drought forced the people who remained in the west river country to readjust economically, socially, and psychologically. This process created a people with strong character, combining pride and humility, optimism and cynicism, independence, self-reliance, and an element of defensiveness as well. As residents of a marginal, "problem" area, they had constantly to defend their country and their choice to remain. They learned to work harder and live with less, and they saw their ability to do so as a great moral victory. Pioneers in the west river country had to redefine success not only as material wealth, which remained in short supply, but also as spiritual wealth born of trial and endurance. This self-image, developed during hard times on the last frontier, was reinforced by the difficult decades of the twenties and thirties. It continues to shape the character of the region today.

AFTER THE WEST WAS WON

1. MERELY THE PIONEERS

A sturdy sod house near Belvidere in Stanley County in 1906.

It is said that Nature makes the man to fit his surroundings. If that be the case, then a description of the land partly, at least, describes the people. Our homeland was proportioned on a big scale. There seemed to be nothing small, nothing limited, in our domain. Our home . . . was one of great plains, large rivers, and wooded mountains. So wide were the prairies that the sun seemed to rise out of one distant edge and in the evening to set in the opposite distant edge. The weather was extreme. The winter was cold with sleet and ice and the temperature often below zero. The winds were so strong they made us feel their strength. The summers were hot and violent with color. . . . We grew used to strength, height, distance, power.

Luther Standing Bear,
Teton Sioux or Lakota

It was winter and a cold wind howled across the prairie. A small band of Oglalas had camped near the eastern bank of what would later be known as the Missouri River. They were poor and starving. Their travels in search of buffalo had led them farther west than they had ever gone before. The struggling band could not travel quickly; they did not yet have horses and relied on dogs to pull the material for their small tipis and their belongings from place to place. The people walked from camp to camp, always in search of food.

As the Oglalas shivered with cold and hunger in their tipis, a scout spotted buffalo on the ice of the river just to the west. The men ran to the river, hoping to kill enough to feed their hungry people. The buffalo tried to escape but their hooves slipped on the ice and the hunters killed many. In their pursuit of the animals, they had crossed to the west bank of the great river. The women and children soon joined them and began to process the kill. They set up camp on the unfamiliar west bank, intending to return to their usual territory once they had completed their work and rested awhile. Suddenly a warm chinook wind began to blow, melting the ice. The Oglalas were trapped in the new country. They remained in camp until spring, when they again began to wander, moving away from the river, west to the high plains.

Their new west river home was a rich, rolling grassland marked with occasional buttes and deep canyons where streams cut their beds. It was a land alive with buffalo. Although the Oglalas had not intended to cross the Missouri, the move was a fortuitous one for them and for the other subtribes of the Teton, or western Dakota (called the Lakota be-

Wild, rough country, rocky ridges, brush-tangled coulees, crisscrossed by
trails known only to wild animals that seldom saw any but wilder, warrier
neighbors, in a region so big a good fast crow couldn't wing over it in a
week—that sort of home ground is bound to encourage outlaw tendencies.
It breeds the will to resist, to break away and keep freedom. . . . There
couldn't help being many wild stampedes where thousands of half-tame
cattle were handled on a semi-frontier where virgin soil had never known
the plow; where the rocks, the streams, the butte landmarks with their tall
Indian water signs on the highest point seemed to have existed always;
where the wild life and the forage, down through the centuries, were
changed only by the hand of Mother Nature.

Ike Blassingame,
cowboy for the Matador ranch

cause of their linguistic differences), who soon followed. The Oglala tradition tells of a chance meeting with the Cheyenne, who gave them horses. With horses and with the guns supplied by white traders, the Oglalas became great hunters and warriors, as did the other Lakota bands once they acquired similar tools. The Indians now had the tools and skills necessary to live well from the richness of the grasslands and they did.[1]

The Lakota bands began to cross the Missouri River some time before 1750. French maps from the 1640s place them in north central Minnesota, where they lived in a mixed horticulture and hunting prairie economy. Shortly after this, they began their journey to the south and west, driven by the gun-bearing Cree. In small bands the Lakota and their relatives, the Dakota, moved west. The Dakota found comfortable territory in southwestern Minnesota and eastern Dakota. The Lakota pushed on to the unknown lands beyond. As they drifted, their economy gradually shifted toward the buffalo culture of the plains. Once they crossed the Missouri River, the bison became their staple food as well as their source of tools, clothing, and tipi hides. The women gathered wild plants to supplement the tribe's diet. The tribal economy also depended on trade with other tribes and goods seized in warfare. Because of the demands of nomadism, the Lakota lived in tipis furnished with goods that could be moved quickly and easily. Men engaged in warfare and the hunt. Women processed the meat and other foods, moved and maintained the camp, and cared for the young children. In retrospect, it appears that Lakota society reached its

Land that only a few years ago was considered unfit for agriculture has been tried and found to produce abundant crops, and the fact is evident that stockmen will have to yield to farmers. There is no doubt that the stock interests have been of benefit to the country, but they are to agriculture what the prospector is to mining . . . merely the pioneers.

The Black Hills Journal,
Rapid City, Dakota Territory, July 17, 1885

zenith early in the nineteenth century and maintained its cultural vigor until the decade of the 1870s, when increasing pressure from white settlers forced a confrontation and the ultimate military defeat of the tribe. Until outside forces overpowered it, however, Lakota society represented a successful adaptation to the Great Plains. The Lakota empire ranged from the Platte River north to the Heart and from the Missouri west to the Big Horn Mountains. Within this domain the Lakota reigned supreme over both Indian and white competitors.[2]

The movement of white settlers that ultimately ended Lakota hegemony on the northern plains was prompted by a variety of factors. The rich lands in Oregon, the gold rush to California and later to Colorado and Montana, and the potential of the grasslands for grazing and even farming attracted a large, sustained migration of Anglo-Americans and European immigrants westward across the continent. The United States government, gradually recognizing the inevitability of American migration westward, abandoned its policy of maintaining much of the West as a large preserve for Indian peoples. Instead, the government began concentrating the various tribes on small holdings, or reservations, freeing more territory for roads and forts and for sale to individual settlers.

By the mid–nineteenth century, white settlement began to infringe on Lakota territory from all directions. Throughout the 1840s small wagon trains of farm families trekked westward to Oregon along the Great Platte River Road, located on the southern border of the Lakota homeland. In 1849 they were joined by thousands of miners seeking a

new El Dorado in California. The migrants demanded protection from
the Indian peoples along the way, and the United States government responded by deploying the army to build and garrison forts at strategic locations on the trail. The increased traffic brought important publicity for the lands of the Great Plains. Once labelled the Great American Desert, the plains began to appear more appealing as Americans gained greater familiarity with the region and saw their cattle grazing contentedly on the short grasses.[3]

The mining frontier, however, was the first to impinge directly on Lakota lands. The discovery of gold in Colorado in 1858 brought hordes of miners and merchants to the central plains. The discovery of gold in Montana in 1864 lured thousands more to the northern plains. They demanded supply lines and government protection, and the resulting roads and forts were of necessity located on hunting grounds treasured by the Lakota. This was the first real threat to the Lakota's hegemony. The tribe engaged the army in repeated conflicts until the federal government agreed to close the forts and the Bozeman Trail to the mines. The formal treaty signed by the Lakota in 1868 to end the hostilities, however, did not reflect a Lakota victory. Rather, the Lakota had consented to the concentration of their people in the area that eventually became the western half of the state of South Dakota. They also agreed to accept central agencies from which each band would receive rations and annuities until they could become self-supporting.[4]

The Lakota had little opportunity to adjust to the terms of the 1868 treaty, because the discovery of gold in the Black Hills in 1874 attracted fresh hordes of miners and merchants, who moved into the region swiftly and in brazen violation of federal law. Army patrols, whose mission was to protect tribal rights, ushered them out. The prospectors, undaunted, waited only until the soldiers disappeared from view before retracing their steps back to the Hills and the gold.

The invasion of the Black Hills area by hundreds of miners enraged the Lakota. They began to raid mining parties enroute to the diggings. The federal government, under pressure from the miners and citizens of settled regions nearby who hoped to profit from the rush, tried to force the Lakota to sell or lease the Hills. When they refused to do so, the government gave up its attempts to control access to the area. This decision represented a de facto opening of the Black Hills. The miners would not be protected by army patrols, but neither would their movements be impeded. Anyone brave enough to face possible Lakota attacks was free to enter the goldfields.[5]

The Sioux War of 1876 was a direct result of the gold rush to the Hills. Its most dramatic moment came in June 1876, when large bands of Lakota under Sitting Bull and Crazy Horse annihilated General George Armstrong Custer's command at the Little Big Horn, but hostilities continued through September, and camps of "hostiles" remained in the Powder River country until February 1877. Meanwhile Congress, scandalized by the defeat, voted in August 1876 to halt all appropriations to the Lakota until they signed over the Black Hills. With that kind of leverage, Congress won the point. The agreement signed in October 1876 set new boundaries for the Great Sioux Reservation. The Indians lost hunting rights in Wyoming and Montana, gave up all claims to the Black Hills, and agreed to a reservation boundary set at the 103d meridian, except for lands between the two branches of the Cheyenne River, which they also ceded to the government. The government, in turn, built new agencies for the bands within the redrawn reservation boundaries. Reservation life then began in earnest for the Lakota people.[6]

The opening of the Black Hills and the surrounding grasslands attracted the attention of cattle ranchers eager for new grazing land and new markets. The cattle frontier had begun in Texas after the Civil War when enterprising individuals began to drive herds north to Kansas railheads to connect with the Chicago markets. As new areas of the Great Plains became available for settlement, ranchers moved in and established open-range operations. In Dakota the grass was lush and the markets plentiful. The development of towns in the Black Hills brought miners hungry for beef, and the reservation annuities system provided another opportunity, since the government purchased large quantities of beef for the Lakota. Overhead remained low because few ranchers tried to get actual title to the lands their cattle grazed. Instead they used the free grass and free water of the public domain. Low overhead, together with the natural increase of the herd, promised to lead to big profits with a minimum of risk, as it had in other areas of the Great Plains as the open range pushed northward.

After the Lakota ceded the grasslands near the Black Hills, large cattle outfits from Texas, New Mexico, and Wyoming quickly moved in, bringing the open-range ranching tradition of the Southwest. Names, now legendary, dotted the maps of the west river plains. Hash Knife, Turkey Track, 101, Matador, and other great ranches all claimed grazing areas. Many of these large companies had foreign investors supplying capital for the venture. They ran thousands of cattle on the open range and employed dozens of cowboys, especially at roundup time.

The big outfits shared their range with small ranching entrepreneurs, often family groups, who also recognized the opportunities of the free range. The number of small ranchers increased as the nineteenth century drew to a close, especially after an 1889 agreement between the federal government and the Lakota opened substantial portions of the west river plains to white settlement. The small ranchers built their homes in the shelter of creek valleys. They lived in relative isolation because their livelihood demanded open spaces for cattle to graze. Although the number of small ranchers was relatively few, they, along with the cattle barons and their many cowboys, formed the first American society of the plains west of the river during the last years of the nineteenth century.[7]

A third frontier, that of the farmer, did not directly affect the west river country until 1889. Agriculture had advanced west from the woodlands of the Mississippi valley early in the nineteenth century, crossing the river into Iowa and Minnesota in the 1830s and 1840s. The farmer's frontier moved hesitantly when it first faced the prairies. Americans had been a woodland people, and they adjusted slowly to the tall-grass prairies of the Midwest, developing new agricultural skills and tools to tame them. Once they became familiar with the new environment, however, farmers generally prospered.

By the 1860s the farming frontier pressed into western Minnesota, western Iowa, and the eastern fringes of Dakota on the north and well into Kansas and Nebraska in the central plains. As farmers moved farther from sources of timber, they began to innovate. The sod house, for example, provided cheap housing from a readily available material. During the twenty years from 1870 to 1890, the line of agricultural settlement pushed into Dakota Territory. In a rush known as the Great Dakota Boom, farm families and town-builders brought "civilization" to all of Dakota east of the Missouri River. The population of all of Dakota stood at 12,887 in 1870; by 1890, after statehood, the population of eastern South Dakota alone was 296,249.[8]

Several factors contributed to the interest in Dakota lands. The railroads extended their lines westward, making Dakota easily accessible. Railroad corporations promoted settlement heavily because they needed the business of settlers who would build farms, grow crops, and ship their harvest east by rail. Their literature was designed to lure the most skeptical farmer to this newly opened land of milk and honey. Farmers responded because cheap lands were increasingly scarce east of the Dakota line. Although scientists worried publicly that the drier lands west of the 98th meridian would not be able to support traditional humid-land agriculture, eager settlers had nowhere else to go. They filed claims on and beyond the line of semiaridity, confident of their ability to subdue the land as their predecessors had done on all the agricultural frontiers before them.

While railroad expansion and land hunger were the primary reasons for the boom, other factors contributed as well. Technology and the factory system invented, manufactured, and distributed tools such as the steel moldboard plow to help farm families conquer the grasslands. Constantly improving machinery, like self-binding reapers for grain, eased some of the labor associated with farming. New strains of hard spring wheat seemed well adapted to the soils and climate of Dakota and provided a cash crop for the new settlers. The industrial technology of the late nineteenth century also devised a new milling process that converted the hard wheats into excellent flour with a ready market. With these tools to aid them, settlers filed on 24 million acres of land between 1878 and 1887.

During the years of the boom, 1878 to 1887, the population of Dakota Territory spread over a wide area from the Missouri River on the west and south to the Canadian border on the north. The miners and ranchers occupied the far outposts of the Black Hills. Yankton, the territorial capital, located as it was in the far southeastern corner of Dakota, could not easily serve constituents in Aberdeen, Jamestown, or Deadwood, so in 1883 the residents of the territory voted to remove the capital to Bismarck. The move spurred politicians in the south to campaign for statehood for the half of the territory located below the 46th parallel (the present line between the states of North and South Dakota). It took six years of struggle between single-state and double-state factions locally and intense partisan wrangling in Congress before a bill granting statehood to both North and South Dakota was passed and signed. The two states entered the Union in 1889, and voters chose Pierre as the temporary capital of South Dakota.[9]

By the late 1880s, a number of groups in South Dakota had begun to eye the large Indian reservation west of the Missouri River and to lobby for its opening to white settlement. Because much of the farm-land east of the river was taken up, businessmen and real-estate pro-moters feared a decline in the economy. Black Hills residents, who were isolated from the centers of commerce and political power in the eastern part of the state, hoped that the creation of farms and towns in the grasslands west of the river would bring them into the mainstream of South Dakota life. Ranchers who inhabited the lands ceded by the Lakota in 1877 wanted more land for their open-range operations, al-though businessmen throughout the state generally opposed granting more leases to cattlemen. The open-range cattle industry, they believed, would not attract the large numbers of people South Dakota needed to sustain a booming economy.

While local interests campaigned for their own benefit, eastern hu-manitarians urged a new solution to the "Indian problem" that they believed would aid assimilation of the tribes into American life. The reformers influenced Congress to pass the Dawes Act, which granted individual Indians in the West quarter sections of land from reserva-tion holdings. After the allotment process was completed, the federal government would open any remaining lands to white settlement. Al-though the Dawes Act was not drawn up for the Lakota alone, it pro-vided for the legal breakup of the reservation that Dakota expansion-ists desired.

In 1889 the Sioux Commission managed to overcome Lakota opposi-tion and won an agreement that opened 9 million acres of reservation land to settlement under the Homestead Act. Indian people could take allotments (individually owned acreages) on the ceded lands if they wished rather than relocating to the six reservations created by the act. The government could then open any unallotted land, deemed "surplus," to homesteaders.[10] According to the terms of the agree-ment, the government would charge non-Indians a fee for these lands according to the time of entry, with the money earmarked for the Lakota people. After ten years, however, no fee would apply, and settlers could take up the land for the cost of filing.

Eager, energetic homesteaders would have been well advised to pause for a moment to inspect the natural surroundings of their new homes. The west river grasslands opened to homesteaders in 1890 and in government lotteries after the turn of the century lay entirely within the physiographic province known as the Great Plains, a place noted for its rolling, almost treeless topography and its sun and wind and sky. The westward movement of the agricultural frontier in the second half of the nineteenth century had propelled farm families into increasingly drier lands. Settlers carving out claims during the Great Dakota Boom discovered that rainfall amounts decreased and became less predictable as they moved toward the Missouri River. The 98th meridian, generally considered the line of semiaridity for agricultural purposes, fell near the city of Huron. The Missouri River in Dakota roughly followed the 100th meridian, made famous by John Wesley Powell, who urged a new social and economic structure for lands lying west of it. Farmers taking up land beyond the Missouri would face dramatically different circumstances.[11]

Three factors made the west river grasslands different from the prairie plains east of the Missouri. First, the topography west of the river was more broken. The Great Plains sections of South Dakota featured rolling grassland, buttes, and canyons, and butte and canyon topography predominated. Buttes were always visible, though their composition changed from area to area. Most streams flowed in canyons 200 or more feet deep. The region between the Moreau and White rivers was marked by sharp-crested buttes with their caprocks of white or gray sandstone eroded into large boulders. Tepee buttes appeared in the western portion of the region between the Moreau and the White. Their symmetrical, conical shape, reminiscent of Indian tipis, prompted the name. The northwestern portion of the state, that lying northwest of the divide between the Moreau and Cheyenne rivers, had larger and more distinctive buttes, often capped with white sandstone and occasionally pine trees, especially in Harding County. Buttes of this type formed ridges that ran for miles. The Slim Buttes in Harding County, for example, were thirty miles long and 600 feet high.

Another important topographical feature west of the river was the Badlands country. Small patches of Badlands dotted the northwestern corner of the region. One, known as the "Jump-Off" country, lay at the headwaters of the Moreau. Other areas included the country around the Slim Buttes and Cave Hills in Harding County and the Grand and Moreau river valleys. The most famous area of Badlands was that along the White River. The subtly colored, castlelike spires of rock stretched for more than a hundred miles and created a formidable barrier to communication and transportation. The Great Wall, a sixty-mile-long line of cliffs and pinnacles, marked the northern bluff of the White River. Before highway engineers arrived to reshape the passes, travel across the Wall was limited to one steep wagon trail through Cedar Pass and two or three trails that could be negotiated only on foot or horseback.[12]

Soil composition was the second factor that made west river lands different from those to the east. The soils of the west river region belonged to the Chestnut group, brown soils with less humus than the richer soils east of the river. Large areas of the west river country were covered with Pierre shale, or gumbo, soils. These lands contained a high percentage of clay and were sticky when wet, extremely hard when dry, and difficult to cultivate. Settlers accustomed to richer loams might struggle with the gumbo for years until they discovered the proper tillage techniques and crop varieties.[13]

Finally, the climate of the region west of the river shaped life for those who settled there. It was a region of unpredictable and often extreme weather. Average precipitation and temperature figures were therefore deceiving. Counties on the Missouri River received an average of 21.16 inches of rainfall per year. That amount decreased steadily as one moved west to the state border, where the average fell to 13.66 inches. But more important, moisture amounts fell below this average 40 percent of the time, except in far northwestern South Dakota, where the figure was 60 percent. Occasionally, the area received far more precipitation than average. Rainfall at the Cottonwood Agricultural Experiment Station, for example, which averaged 16.45 inches per year, ranged from 9.95 inches in 1910 to 27.62 inches in 1915. Such extremes of precipitation altered the agricultural potential of the region as much as did the low averages. Mary Hargreaves has pointed out that "the margin between success and failure in dryland agriculture is very narrow." Fifteen inches of moisture is, she writes, "the general standard for successful grain production." Ten inches is the lowest possible amount for any crop at all. Twelve inches will produce a light crop, and fourteen may double the normal yield. Farm families in western South Dakota could not depend on nature to supply enough moisture for their crops.[14]

Temperature, humidity, and wind were also important climatic factors. Temperatures west of the river could go as high as 115 degrees in summer and as low as 57 degrees below zero in winter. Humidities were low year-round compared to the eastern half of the nation, making heat and cold easier for people to bear but also causing increased danger to plants from summer scorching or damaging frosts in late spring or early fall. Winds, too, helped dry the soil. In South Dakota wind velocity averaged eight to ten miles per hour. Extremes were not uncommon, however, occasionally reaching sixty miles per hour on clear, sunny days. Violent thunderstorms in summer and blizzards in winter raked the region. Tornadoes were also an occasional and terrifying hazard.[15]

The west river plains, then, shared the qualities of Great Plains physiography. The land was rolling, marked by buttes and canyons and covered with lighter and less fertile soils than more humid areas. The rainfall was limited and the weather unpredictable. The rolling, almost treeless topography made the region "a vast amphitheatre of earth and sky." People who came to live on the land had to learn its nature and adapt to its special demands. That was especially true for farming people, who had to change the land to make their living from it.[16]

Farmers did come to the west river country, although not in 1890, when the lands were first opened for white settlement. A series of dry years and a national depression, which halted railroad expansion and limited economic growth generally, kept them away. But South Dakota promoters were only temporarily disappointed. After the turn of the century, a variety of economic and social circumstances, coupled with government and railroad promotions, lured thousands of homesteaders and town-builders west. Just as the Lakota had done 150 years before, they crossed the Missouri River to new lands and a new life on the other side.

2. THE LAST GREAT FRONTIER

A young couple stands proudly at the door of their tar-paper shack on the Alkali Divide in Meade County, twenty-two miles east of Sturgis.

The Rosebud opening is but one of a few opportunities left in which cheap homes of a superior character may be secured on the public domain. . . . Practically in a day other [homesteaders] will be located on more than two thousand farms, at a stroke transforming 400,000 acres of unoccupied lands into one of the most densely populated sections of the west. . . . No coming west and growing up with the country is this. One has "growed" immediately upon arrival.

Chamberlain *Register*,
July 7, 1904

Promoters captured the imagination of many a prospective settler when they billed the west river country of South Dakota as "the last great frontier." The slogan deftly characterized the migration to the west river country as the latter days of the continental conquest begun by the English settlers at high tide on the James River in 1607. Coupled with a sense of continuity was an air of defiant heroism. At a time when the nation as a whole had turned decisively toward urban-industrial development, the opening up of the west river country struck a reprise of the mystic chords of America's agricultural and frontier heritage. The lure of the frontier myth combined with economic opportunity to attract a hundred thousand new settlers into the west river country in the first years of the twentieth century. The movement took place more than a decade after the frontier had officially closed and at a time when the dominant demographic shift was from rural areas into established towns and cities. That the last great frontier was a historical hybrid is demonstrated by the vigor with which the federal land bureaucracy, a venerable frontier institution with its roots in the eighteenth century, combined with the railroad, the engine of industrial development, to facilitate mass transit into America's last wilderness.

By 1900 the transformation of the United States from a rural nation of small, independent property owners to a society dominated by the city, the factory, the wage earner, and the machine, was well underway. The workplace for the majority was no longer the farm or the general store in a crossroads town. The office, the factory, and the department

The young man who has the nerve to leave the drudgery of the mill and factory and strike out for himself will succeed in the west. If he works earnestly in his new home, within a few years he will find that he has a place in the community and has a recognized individuality which the factory hand or the small clerk can never know.

Murdo *Coyote,*
January 18, 1907

store, where men and women were employees rather than entrepreneurs, dominated the new world. Workers had the assurance of a weekly wage, but they paid for this security (such as it was) with the loss of independence and individuality. For women, who had not enjoyed much economic freedom under the old system, regimented jobs as clerks and shopgirls afforded greater independence and individuality than they had previously experienced. For both sexes the new employment opportunities associated with urbanization and the factory system provided options unavailable in an agrarian and decentralized society. Because most native-born Americans had grown up in a rural world, however, the opportunities presented by the new order often appeared to be overshadowed by the social evils it created. Their parents very likely had been landowners. The preceding generations may have worked very hard for their living, but they appeared to have controlled their own destinies. Corporations, monopolies, and the wage system had barely touched their lives. The problems of the cities—crime, "new immigrants" at the rate of a million a year, political corruption, slum housing, and labor disputes—were foreign to them. The urban generation of 1900 confronted these changes head-on. For some, they were not attractive.[1]

For those individuals dissatisfied with the economic opportunity or social context of the urban world, a move to the last great frontier provided an appealing solution to the uncertainties of the new order. Many Americans shared a faith in the redemptive powers of the natural world. For them, agriculture was the highest possible calling. They

The land-hunger we can all understand, as we all share it, but what is there in it that inspires men to cross a continent and take their place in a line like that of last night for a chance in a hundred to draw a quarter section? . . . It is partly the same spirit of adventure that sent Jason searching for the Golden Fleece in Greek mythological day, it is made up partly of the greed that sent thousands across the continent in 1849 after the real, red gold in California, but largely it is inspired by the desire for a home interest in the American soul. It is the real land hunger, the feeling that the freest and richest people on the face of the earth have that they hold an inherent right to stand upon their household gods where no man can say to them "nay."

Yankton *Press-Dakotan,*
July 20, 1904

feared the regimented life of the factory and placed their trust in the proven virtues of the farm. Many homesteaders who moved to the west river country saw themselves participating in and completing the great American movement to tame the wilderness and to be purified by it.[2]

Most Americans living at the turn of the century were well schooled in the frontier myth. The movement to the West had been glorified in song and story for much of the nineteenth century. As the frontier came to a close, a variety of popularizers melded history and fantasy in varying proportions to produce a West of romance and adventure for the enchantment of a rapidly urbanizing and industrializing nation. The nationwide tour by Buffalo Bill's Wild West Show gave many people their first glimpse of "real" western costumes and traditions. At the same time, a number of literate, upper-class easterners moved to or vacationed in the West and publicized their exploits, celebrating the rejuvenating qualities they had found in the wilderness. Theodore Roosevelt was the most famous of this group. His adventures as a rancher in North Dakota were well known, and his elevation to the presidency put him in a position of great visibility and power. Further, Roosevelt's presidency coincided with the publication of Owen Wister's novel *The Virginian,* which glorified the cowboy and western life. During those same years, motion pictures, which frequently featured western themes, made their debut. Literature, movies, and charismatic public figures like Roosevelt all played an important role in bringing a certain image of the West into the homes and hearts of the nation.[3]

Along with these sociocultural tensions, a number of more tangible factors drew settlers to western South Dakota. These included the end of the depression of the nineties and a resulting expansion of the economy; the extension of railroads into the northern plains, making the frontier suddenly accessible; the rising cost of farmland in settled regions; and finally the aggressively publicized development of dry-farming techniques, which convinced many that proper methods could overcome any environmental problem on the plains.[4]

In western South Dakota two developments began the rush. First, the federal government announced a series of lotteries for "surplus" Indian lands; second, and more important, the Chicago and North Western and the Chicago, Milwaukee, St. Paul and Pacific railroads each decided to extend their lines from their termini at Pierre and Chamberlain on the Missouri River across the plains to Rapid City. Fierce competition developed between the two lines as they raced west in 1905, each hoping to beat the other to the Black Hills. The combination of the lotteries and the railroad construction, along with the promotions attending each, generated publicity for the west river country and lured prospective settlers by the thousands.

Participation in the government land lotteries is one indicator of the level of interest in homestead lands. In 1904 the federal government announced that with allotments to individual Indians on the Rosebud reservation 60 percent completed, lands in Gregory County (totaling 2,412 claims) would be made available to the general public. The General Land Office in Washington, mindful of the chaotic and sometimes tragic conduct of the Oklahoma land rushes held between 1889 and 1895, decided to institute a lottery for the South Dakota lands. Land Office officials maintained careful control over all aspects of the lottery process to guard against fraud and violence. They named four towns—Bonesteel, Chamberlain, Fairfax, and Yankton—official registration centers. Applicants had to apply in person to enter their names. The only exceptions were soldiers and sailors, who were permitted to register by proxy. The registration offices were open for eighteen days beginning July 5, 1904. After the registration period ended, government officials supervised the drawing of the homestead winners. Winners were informed by mail and had to return to the state to file on the lands. The railroads, of course, did an enormous business as hordes of prospective settlers showed up to register for the 2,412 available claims. Yankton drew the greatest crowds, with 57,434 people filing there. The total number of registrants for the claims in all four centers reached 106,308.

Because of the agreements made with the Lakota, the lottery claims were not free. In setting prices for the newly opened lands, federal land officials decided that the best lands would be entered first, and they charged $4.00 per acre for any lands taken up within the first three months after the opening. Between three and six months after the opening, lands might be entered at $3.00 per acre. After six months the price dropped to $2.50 per acre. Homesteaders could pay for their lands on the installment plan. They could also "commute," or gain title to their homesteads by making full payment after a shorter residency period, usually fourteen months, rather than the standard five years' residence. The General Land Office devised a wide range of rules to cover all potential circumstances. For example, if winning applicants did not appear on the day specified to choose their lands and file on them, their places on the list were forfeited.

During the fall of 1907, the General Land Office oversaw the opening of a second reservation, the Lower Brule. This opening was much smaller, with only 343 homesteads. The same rules used in 1904 applied to this lottery, although the officials in this case decided to base fees on the actual quality of the land rather than the time of entry. Federal regulations also allowed a six-month grace period for establishing residence on the claims, because the entry time fell in late December. Forcing settlers onto new claims in the dead of winter would cause undue hardship, officials realized. Although far fewer people registered for this drawing (4,350 people travelled to Pierre to try their luck on the 343 homesteads) the hopeful applicants again greatly outnumbered the available claims.

In the fall of 1908, another portion of the Rosebud reservation, 4,000 homesteads in Tripp County, was made available to settlers. The lands ranged in price from $2.50 to $6.00 per acre, with the fees based again on time of filing. To help reduce congestion at the registration points, land office officials established registration centers in six towns—Chamberlain, Dallas, Gregory, and Presho in South Dakota, and O'Neill and Valentine in Nebraska. The winners in the October drawing could not make entry until March 1, 1909, and did not have to establish residence until September. Federal officials hoped that this flexibility would allow settlers enough time to raise the money for their first payments and give farmers the choice of raising a crop at home and then moving to the claim or moving in the spring to begin farming at once. The demand for claims again nearly overwhelmed the system. Applications for the 4,000 claims reached 114,769 before the registration period ended.

Between 1909 and 1915 the land office opened three more tracts in western South Dakota using the registration system. In October 1909, 81,456 people registered for 10,000 claims on the Cheyenne River and Standing Rock reservations in north central South Dakota. In October 1911, a million and a half acres of the Rosebud and Pine Ridge reserves were thrown open. The counties included Mellette, Washabaugh, and Bennett. Proportionately fewer people took part in these lotteries; only 53,728 people applied. In 1915 the land office made 100,000 more acres of the Standing Rock reserve available for general settlement. No registration was held for this tract. Applicants filed on the land at once and a drawing was held only if two or more people chose the same quarter. The government charged a fee for the lands involved in the last three openings, the money ostensibly going into trust funds for use in "civilizing" the Indians. Otherwise the provisions of the Homestead Act applied.[5]

Great public excitement greeted each announcement of a land opening. Registrants came from all occupations. The *New York Times* reported a trainload of five hundred single women teachers from Nebraska and Iowa filing together in Dallas. John A. Dixon, a reporter for *World Today* magazine described his experiences: "School teachers, clerks, lawyers, farmers, physicians, factory workers, mechanics, business men and nearly every manner of citizen were in the throngs who were there anxious to take a chance for reservation land. Many women were among them." Newspapers from the registration towns canvassed the long lines of registrants in search of interesting stories. The Yankton paper reported registrations by sixteen Benedictine nuns. A seventy-eight-year-old woman registered at Aberdeen in October 1909, as did a man from Afghanistan. The Sioux Falls *Argus-Leader* counted 150 black Americans, mostly from Georgia and Kentucky, waiting in the lines in Bonesteel.[6]

The sheer numbers of people who showed up to register created problems of housing, services, and control that overwhelmed local facilities and officials. The 1904 registration in Bonesteel was accompanied by murder and general mayhem. The problems began when Bonesteel grew in a few months from a crossroads store to a tent city of 10,000 souls. Grafters, gamblers, pickpockets, and ne'er-do-wells made the boomtown the center of their operations. The town trustees bargained with a contingent of gamblers, allowing them free rein in exchange for fees as high as $100 per day. The few police were poorly prepared to deal with the chaos. When "Disorder and riot threatened," in the grand frontier tradition the citizens organized, took all the arms from the hardware stores, and conducted a pitched battle against troublemakers in the streets. One gambler was killed and many more were wounded before order was restored. Before the registration closed with 34,064 people filing applications for claims, innumerable fights and robberies occurred and a tornado struck the town. The Bonesteel adventure gave its participants more of the Wild West than they expected and certainly disproved notions that the farmer's frontier was automatically dull. One man, being led away by police after a bloody brawl, was heard to mutter: "If I ever get west of Chicago again you can shoot me for a blanked fool."[7]

No other opening had quite the drama or danger of Bonesteel's, but all were marked by excited crowds desperate for land. Edith Kohl homesteaded in Lyman County before the 1907 Lower Brule opening. After registration began, she later wrote, "We who had grown accustomed to the sight of the empty prairie, to whom the arrival of the stage from Pierre was an event, were overwhelmed by the confusion, the avalanche of people, shouting, pushing, asking questions, moving steadily across the trackless plains toward the reservation." When the second portion of the Rosebud opened in 1908, crowds again appeared. Presho was a registration point, and Kohl reported that five or six trains a day came to the town, bringing 500 to 800 passengers with each trip.[8]

In Dallas and Gregory, towns adjacent to the lands opened in 1908, the influx was equally phenomenal. Lindsay Denison, a writer for the *American Magazine,* reported from Omaha that he saw crowds of landseekers breaking down the gates at the railroad station in their eagerness to board the cars. During the hectic registration days, the railroad line he travelled carried ten times the amount of traffic it was designed to bear. He decided to visit Dallas, the site closest to the

Tripp County lands, where he found thousands of people eager to win a farm.[9]

Although the federal land lotteries drew more attention, the extension of railroad lines through the public domain west of the river also brought people into the state. The Chicago, Milwaukee, St. Paul and Pacific, commonly known as the Milwaukee Road, announced its plans for expansion first. Chamberlain, on the east bank of the Missouri River, had been its terminus since 1880. The company planned to build to Rapid City from that point. The Chicago and North Western line took up the competitive challenge shortly thereafter, announcing its decision to build west from Pierre to Fort Pierre and beyond, with Rapid City its ultimate destination. The routes of both lines passed through the territory ceded by the Lakota in 1889. Because these lands had been available for general settlement for over ten years, the government no longer considered them reservation lands but treated them as nonreservation public domain. Accordingly, homesteaders paid only a fourteen-dollar filing fee and earned the land if they resided on it for five years and improved it as the law required. They could also commute their homesteads after a shorter period if they wished to pay $1.25 per acre for the land. The railroads and townsite boomers along the lines heavily promoted the free lands, and thousands of new settlers poured in.[10]

The advent of the railroad had a striking effect on county populations. Counties not involved with reservation openings but served by the new railroads showed dramatic increases. Stanley County, for example, had 1,341 people in 1900, 2,649 in 1905, as railroad construction began, and an all-time high of 14,975 in 1910. In 1905, Butte County, a huge civil division later split into three large counties, contained only 3,975 people. In 1910, Perkins County, one of the new divisions fashioned from Butte and served by the Milwaukee Road, had 11,348 residents. Lyman County, which benefited from the railroad and from the Lower Brule opening, had only 2,632 people in 1900. In 1905 its population had increased to 4,263, and in 1910, with the railroad in operation and Lower Brule lands occupied, 10,848 people lived in the county.[11]

Settlers came to the west river country of South Dakota at the turn of the century because it was the frontier. Like their ancestors, they were tantalized by the prospect of building a new world for themselves.

Their motivations were complex and somewhat contradictory. They hoped to build a new world that would, in most respects, resemble the world they had left behind. But their world would embody traditional rural, agricultural values and was in some respects a rejection of the new industrial values of the "old" world. These settlers had read of the Great West and had seen pictures that whetted their appetite for wilderness. At the same time, they saw conventional opportunities on the frontier that did not appear to be theirs in settled regions: to own a farm, to run one's own business, to raise a family in an environment that fostered virtue and self-reliance.

Ultimately, of course, each individual's motives were his or her own. Mary Bartels went because "homesteading was the spirit of the times—a big adventure." Elizabeth Henricksen's family took a claim because her five-year-old brother had died and her mother feared that her father would turn to drink to ease his grief in their old home in Iowa. In 1907, Edith Ammons and her sister, Ida Mary, full of happy anticipation at the adventure ahead, left their home in St. Louis to take up a homestead in Lyman County, South Dakota. The young women, aware of their father's financial troubles, had decided to strike out on their own in order to spare him the burden of their support. Although practical economic reasons propelled them west, Edith Ammons explained that their decision was part of the pioneer tradition in their family, whose members were "always among those who pushed back the frontier." Later, when the rushes to reservation lands near her claim began, Ammons believed that the crowds of people "came to see the West while it was still unchanged, drawn for reasons of personal adventure, or because the romantic legends of the West attracted them. People drawn by the intangibles, the touch of the wind on their faces, a return to the simple elements of living." [12]

Perhaps the most convincing testimony about the meaning of the last great frontier comes not from a settler but from the eastern reporter for the *American Magazine* mentioned earlier. Lindsay Denison, who was covering the opening of the Rosebud reservation in 1908, portrayed himself at the beginning of the trip as a bored, disaffected eastern reporter filled with "utter shame for the stinking herd of humanity who were running like greedy cattle to the feeding troughs, for the very remote chance of winning a free farm." After getting better acquainted with the friendly travellers on the train and seeing the clear prairie skies, he began to mellow. Caught up in the excitement of the registration rush in Dallas, South Dakota, Denison developed a new attitude. The rush began to symbolize for him all that was good, all that was real in America. "Here, after all," Denison decided, "was the United States, the heart of them. Here was everything from Lexington and Bunker Hill to El Caney. . . . It would be worth while to live out here on the prairie in heat and in snow, in dust and wet gumbo for fourteen months; to know neighbors who were nearer to you fifty miles away than folks up-one-flight-front in your New York flat." Denison had become personally involved in the homestead epic; he had been propelled from observer to participant. He learned a reassuring lesson on the last frontier. In spite of changes being wrought by the twentieth century, Denison concluded, the people settling the last frontier proved that "the best that was in our fathers . . . is with us yet."[13]

3. FIFTY MILES TO WATER, ONE HUNDRED MILES TO WOOD

An unusual long-exposure photograph of a claim on a cold winter's night. This is the Ed Kopac homestead near Okaton in Lyman County in 1906.

On June 24th we started out in the rain to drive to our "home on the range." As there were no fences or roads—only trails—we lost our way. I shall never forget the utter loneliness which almost overwhelmed me as we drove under dark skies in the rain, over the prairies with no path to follow, as we watched the buggy wheels while on the outer rim they gathered gumbo for eight or ten inches, until it fell off by its own weight. There was no human habitation—only prairie and sky.

Fanny Malone,
Lyman County homesteader

The Lakota's relationship to the plains environment was a model of simplicity and reliability, depending almost entirely on the hunting of buffalo, which roamed the plains in seemingly unlimited numbers and which had few predators other than humans. The miner's frontier was also a simple, temporary economy, relying for success upon the existence of valuable ores and proven mining techniques. The rancher's frontier, too, depended on natural resources, requiring only what the plains produced in greatest abundance: grass. The Lakota, the miners, and the ranchers were three Great Plains groups that asked of their environment only what it gave in abundance. But the homesteader's economy that succeeded them was an eastern transplant that had germinated and thrived under environmental conditions radically different from those present in the west river country. Unlike the hunting, mining, and ranching economies, the homesteader's frontier of small farms depended for success upon a wide array of environmental factors: the type, tilth, and fertility of the soil; the amount, distribution, and regularity of rainfall; the length of the growing season; and the ability of domestic livestock to withstand the climate and predators. Homesteaders, who came with the purpose of permanent agricultural settlement of the entire region, encountered an environment for which their knowledge and their inherited traditions, customs, and folkways would be of little guidance. The common sense that migrated along with the homesteaders was a fertile source of error and miscalculation on the new frontier, but this was not apparent in the early years of settlement.

*Our new home was a story-and-a-half tar paper shack with a "lean-to" at-
tached. Dad, Mother, and all six of us kids tried to squeeze ourselves into
that shack. . . . We were ill-equipped to battle the savage elements. That
flimsy creaking shell that we used as a shelter from the unmerciful elements had only bare two-by-fours in the inside with a single thickness of
blue building paper between us and the outside sheathing. Dad finally
slapped a tar-paper covering haphazardly over the sheathing that was held
in place with laths nailed hit-or-miss fashion. The incessant wind catching
a loose end would create a buzzing noise that was almost deafening during
some of the wildest storms.*

Maude Wright Stearns,
Stanley County homesteader

Homesteaders had to build homes, find water in a semiarid land,
and learn to understand the trials and blessings of the environment
west of the 100th meridian. Although one of the appeals of the last
great frontier was a return to primitive simplicity, settlers found the
problems posed by the prairie to be anything but simple.

Edith Ammons and her sister, Ida Mary, confronted the realities of
the frontier experience as soon as they arrived on their claim. Pleased
because they had purchased a relinquished claim complete with a
house, the sisters had expected a comfortable home in an established
farm neighborhood. Instead their driver unloaded them, she wrote, on
"the sun-baked plains," where there was "nothing but space." The
house that they had looked forward to turned out to be a small shack
that Ammons described as a "none too substantial packing-box tossed
haphazardly on the prairie which crept in at its very door." Their shelter was crudely built of wide boards covered with black tar paper. The
furnishings included a homemade bunk; a small, rusty stove; two
chairs; and a dry-goods box that served as a cupboard. "We were
frightened and homesick," she said. "Whatever we had pictured in our
imaginations, it bore no resemblance to the tar paper shack without
creature comforts; nor had we counted on the desolation of prairie on
which we were marooned. . . . This was not the West as I had dreamed
of it." The young women vowed to return to St. Louis the next day if
they could find someone living nearby who would take them to the
train depot. Soon, however, they found kind neighbors and learned to
understand the country, and their urge to leave subsided.[1]

This was not the West as I had dreamed of it, not the West even of banditry and violent action. It was a desolate, forgotten land, without vegetation save for the dry, crackling grass, without visible tokens of fertility. Drab and gray and empty. Stubborn, resisting land. Heroics wouldn't count for much here. It would take slow, backbreaking labor, and time, and the actions of the seasons to make the prairie bloom.

Edith Ammons Kohl,
Lyman County homesteader

The housing that greeted the Ammons sisters, while shockingly crude to them, was quite respectable by local standards. Frontier housing accommodated faint memories of "civilized" housing to the harsh environment and the settlers' goals and finances. Two structures predominated: the tar-paper shack (which the Ammons sisters found so disconcerting), and the sod house, or soddy. The tar-paper shack was very functional on this frontier, as it had been on other plains frontiers. The lack of a local wood supply and the proliferation of chain lumberyards, which grew up next to the rail lines in small towns, made the tar-paper shack the choice of many. It was inexpensive, easy to construct, and portable. A settler purchased a cheap grade of lumber, a few rolls of tar paper, and some nails, hauled these materials to the claim, and erected a frontier home in a few days. The crudest shanty would satisfy government standards, which required only that a ten-by-twelve-foot structure stand on the claim. Many settlers built larger (but no more elaborate) structures because their families needed more space. "Tar-paper homesteaders" had their choice of red or blue building paper for the interior. Edith Ammons suggested that this "regulation shack lining was a great factor in the West's settlement. We should all have frozen to death without it." The two colors indicated the grade and price. "The red was a thinner, inferior quality and cost about three dollars a roll, while the heavy blue cost six. Blue paper on the walls was as much a sign of class on the frontier as blue blood in Boston."[2]

Tar-paper shacks were flimsy and if not anchored down were likely to

A prairie fire, a common hazard in the grasslands. This one struck near Wakpala on the Standing Rock Reservation in 1909.

Wakpala, S. Dak.
Prairie Fire on the reservation Oct. 25th 09. Fire is about one mile distant
Foto by Frank Fiske   Indians lost cattle and horses

blow away in a high wind. To protect against winter winds, settlers piled sod around the walls or banked them with manure and straw from the barn. In summer the sun heated the black buildings beyond endurance, although the thin walls did allow a breeze to pass through. Because the shacks were small and light, they were easily moved. After the early years of settlement, a lively market in used claim shacks developed. Many who left the country sold their homes to those who stayed. A team of horses could pull the shack to a new location, where it could be used as an addition to a house or as an outbuilding.

Like the tar-paper shack, the soddy was inexpensive, but unlike its competitor, it was a solid structure, built from the prairie itself. A settler with a proper vision of four walls and a roof, a supply of sod from his or her own claim, and a few purchased items like a door and some windows, had all the materials necessary for a substantial dwelling. The soddy's thick walls moderated the extremes of temperature, keeping the structure warmer in winter and cooler in summer than the tar-paper shack. The roof and floor could cause problems, however. The sod roof had a tendency to leak, subjecting its inhabitants to unpredictable showers of dirt or mud. A properly constructed dirt floor would pack to form a hard surface that could be scrubbed in the same manner as a wood floor, but a less carefully constructed floor collected rainwater rather than draining it and was periodically transformed into muck.[3]

Neither the tar-paper shack nor the soddy were attractive buildings. The homesteads of the west river country bore little resemblance to the neat lines of the frame house. The housing was strictly utilitarian; form followed function, as it were, at a great distance. Some newcomers found this aspect of the frontier as visually startling as the prairie itself. Edith Ammons' comment that her shack resembled a "none too substantial packing-box" that looked "as though the first wind would pick it up and send it flying through the air" was representative of the feelings of many. Sound reasoning, however, underlay such houses. For speculators, greater investment would have been inconsistent with their basic strategy. They counted on the efforts of their neighbors, rather than upon the value of any improvements they might make, to drive up the value of their claims. Frequently they returned to more settled areas and borrowed against their claims. For permanent settlers, housing was only one part of their investment,

Winter weather posed special dangers to west river settlers, and the blizzard of March 1913 was one of the most severe. The main street of White River in Mellette County after the storm.

and it had to be balanced against other uses for their capital. Barns, stables, chicken houses, agricultural implements, and livestock were basic farm needs, and they frequently took priority over improved housing. A more substantial house usually indicated that the basic needs of the farm had at last been met or that the owner had more money than most and was willing to spend it on permanent structures. Edith Ammons was impressed with her neighbor's home, which was larger than the usual shacks and had a gable, or low-pitched roof. Huey Dunn had used wood siding as well, which "in the homestead country marked a man's prestige and solidity." She recognized at once that the Dunns were on their claim to stay.

Another basic need not easily met in the west river country was water. East of the Great Plains, water was usually readily available. Although modern water systems were rare, good wells could be found in reasonable proximity to most homes in town and country. The contrast with the plains was dramatic. There, creeks were far fewer in number and much more erratic. In summer they frequently dried up into a series of stagnant pools; in winter they froze solid. Well-digging crews operated from the towns, but their services were expensive and they could not guarantee a good well. Many settlers struggled for years to locate a dependable water supply on their claims, but without success. Those in this predicament tried a variety of arrangements: they might share a dam with neighbors, or share a well, or simply haul water several miles every day from a creek. Edith Ammons' neighbors, the Dunns, hauled water long distances for their own use and also provided water for the Ammons sisters. Mr. Dunn often told the women that he would "have a well if I could stop hauling water long enough to dig one."[4]

The search for water could become a dominating force in a homesteader's life. The Otto Dunlap family, who settled in Lyman County in 1905, were one example. Of their many attempts to sink a well, the deepest went sixty feet, a very dangerous task accomplished by pick, shovel, bucket, and rope. This attempt, too, was fruitless. Dunlap also built a stock dam by scraping away the dirt from a draw that received heavy runoff during rains. Each pass of the scraper yielded six to eight bushels of dirt, which Dunlap hauled to the lower end of the draw. Hundreds of repetitions resulted in a depression, which formed a pool once rainwater accumulated. The excess dirt at the lower end of the depression acted as a dam to contain the precious water. Because a dam of this sort was of necessity located on the lowest part of the claim, it was not convenient to the house. The Dunlaps still had to haul water a half mile using two fifty-gallon barrels mounted on a stone-boat. In winter, this supply could be supplemented by melted snow.

The Dunlaps kept their water barrels outside near the kitchen door; two inverted washtubs protected the water from dirt and stray chickens. Water from the dam contained insects and other debris, so Mrs. Dunlap strained it through a cloth to remove the more substantial impurities, after which the cloth was "well covered with bugs, crawling and hopping." The Dunlaps did not boil their water, because they disliked the flat taste that resulted. They had come from an Iowa farm with a good water supply; the struggle to quench the thirst of a growing family and a farm operation made life in South Dakota very different.

Because water was so precious, its use was carefully monitored. The Dunlaps did not rinse their dishes, nor did they enjoy the luxury of baths in clean water. Two or three family members bathed in each washtubful. After baths the Dunlaps used the same water to wash floors or launder the heavy outdoor overalls. In spite of such caution, Mr. Dunlap had to haul water frequently. In later times, new technology and higher incomes would allow farm families to dig deeper wells and satisfy their water needs more easily. But during the early years only the lucky or wealthy had adequate water.[5]

The frightening, annoying, and novel character of their experiences with weather, soil, plains creatures, and open space led many settlers to make records of them. For most, western South Dakota was considerably different from the lands they had left behind. It was a wild and empty place, and its vast, virtually treeless expanse overwhelmed the senses. Some homesteaders were nearly overpowered, at least temporarily, by the alien environment. Edith Ammons wrote of a "desolate land . . . the endless monotony . . . the forgotten land." To her, the prairie was "drab and gray and empty" and "stubborn and resisting." After one day in her new home, she claimed to understand why sheepherders went insane: they were "swallowed up by that sea of brown, dry grass, by the endless monotony of space."[6] The climate, too, posed unusual problems. The winds, the seasonal extremes of temperature, and the occasional fierce storms threatened people living in crude, makeshift structures.

But not all found the plains threatening. Some were confident of their ability to fill the emptiness with homes, barns, roads, and crops. Homesteaders who gave the country a chance often learned to appreciate what it had to offer. They also actively participated in making it "home." This was an important part of plains frontiering. It took concentrated and sustained effort to make the omnipresent emptiness into a familiar place. But the settlers made marks on the land—built houses, planted fields, and made trails, giving them some sense of control over the land. For Edith and Ida Mary Ammons, adjustment began when their box of possessions arrived from St. Louis. They cleaned the shack and used their rugs and pictures from home to make it familiar. Gradually, their sense of belonging expanded outdoors. "Even against our will," Edith remembered, "the bigness and peace of the open spaces were bound to soak in. . . . We could not but respond to air that was like old wine. . . . Never were moon and stars so bright." After a short time on the claim, their vision "gradually adjusted itself to distance," and the sisters could pick out other shacks on neighboring claims. Other homesteaders heard of their arrival and dropped in to visit. "Almost without being aware of it we ceased to feel that we had left St. Louis," Edith wrote. "It was St. Louis which was receding from us, while we turned more and more toward the new country."[7]

Weather in the west river country posed ongoing difficulties. All seasons of the year were windy. Intense storms buffeted the plains year-round. Tar-paper shacks were particularly vulnerable. Winter winds could penetrate the paper walls or blow the whole structure down. In summer, the black walls soaked up the sun's rays, converting the shack into a solar oven. Outside, few shade trees, or even clouds, moderated the sun's force. On the other hand, violent hail and thunderstorms periodically threatened destruction to house and crops.

Winter was the most difficult season, creating grave physical dangers for the settlers. Homesteaders had to fight the cold and the wind when they travelled or did chores, and they had to fight it inside their flimsy homes as well. On earlier plains frontiers, settlers had developed methods to cope with blinding snow squalls, often stringing

ropes between the house and barn to show the way. The west river pioneers quickly adopted these methods, but until the settlers actually
lived through a plains blizzard, they had little appreciation of its awesome strength and disorienting effects.

On one occasion, as the Ammons sisters returned home late one afternoon from the school where Ida Mary taught, they saw a blizzard
"coming like white smoke" across the plains. Unwilling to trust their
horse's slow pace, they jumped from the buggy and ran the half mile
home. The sisters reached it safely, but within minutes the storm
struck: "We opened the door a crack and looked out. We could not see
our hands before us, and the howling of the wind and the beating of
the snow against the shack made it impossible to hear any other
sound." Although they were safe at home, they could not escape the
fury of the storm. "Cowering in that tiny shack, where thin building
paper took the place of plaster, the wind screaming across the Plains,
hurling the snow against that frail protection, defenseless against the
elemental fury of the storm, was like drifting in a small boat at sea,
tossed and buffeted by waves, each one threatening to engulf you."[8]

Winter required special vigilance. Homesteaders had to lay by a good
supply of fuel for emergency use. As the storms raged, and later when
the deep cold that always followed a storm settled in, they would have
to tend fires all night. To let the fire burn out was to risk frozen food-
stuffs and frozen limbs. Layers of warm clothing were important even
indoors. Severe storms or extended periods of cold could prevent travel
for days or even weeks.

Bess Corey, a Stanley County homesteader who taught at a country
school two miles from her claim, related her winter trials to her mother
in Iowa. "Monday morning," she wrote, "I faced the storm and went
knee deep in snow. Then the wind shifted and I had to face it going
home." In another letter she reported, "Friday it snowed again. When
Mr. Speer came for the children he insisted that I go home with them
again. He said it was no use to start out. I'd never make it in such a
storm. . . . Monday morning was blazing cold. I put a heavy grey wool
skirt on . . . and wrapped as warm as I could. . . . It took me fifteen minutes to start the fire [at the school]." Corey stayed with the
neighbors more and more often as winter progressed. Her coal was
running low at home and the walk to school was exhausting. She
wrote: "Reached school with about enough life to build the fire. I'm at

Speers again." Finally she decided to board there for the duration. "I was over to my place Sunday. I don't expect to go again until spring. They say four horses couldn't get a load of coal over there. Besides I can't wade snow four feet deep four miles a day and sit in school with wet duds."[9]

The arrival of spring, although always a relief from winter, brought its own threats. Violent thunderstorms with hail and high winds wreaked havoc with buildings, crops, and livestock. Lightning killed homesteaders and animals alike. As the season wore on, hot winds and extremely high temperatures sucked the life from tender crops and crushed the hopeful spirit as well. The plains summer, like the winter, saw elements of nature gone beserk. Summer weather was not always bad, of course. There were clear, mild days with skies of a blue not seen in more humid climes. The dry air struck many as a great gift. But summer was an unpredictable season. The fury of the storms that it brought impressed those who suffered through them. Sometimes they blew up suddenly. On other occasions storms built slowly and ominously in the distance; the broad expanse of prairie and sky allowed settlers to watch their progress. "Shortly before noon clouds were observed looming up to the northwest," a local editor reported of one such storm. "Shortly after dinner they had assumed such black dimensions as to portend trouble. . . . At one o'clock the clouds were overhead and the terrific northwest wind was raging in all its fury." Blinding downpours often accompanied such storms, but just as often only a few drops fell. Cyclones were feared, but hail, because it came more often, may have caused more damage in the long run. It battered crops, gardens, and buildings, easily destroying a season's work in a terrifying moment. The Midland newspaper reported of one such storm that "hail the size of eggs and even bigger began to fall, and it was a veritable and merciless bombardment lasting nearly ten minutes and it looked as if everything would be battered to pieces."[10]

After a storm, the sun would resume its place in the sky, while down below settlers surveyed the damage. The effects of storms varied dramatically even within small areas. One farm family could see their efforts destroyed in a flash, while another's fields nearby went untouched. After a storm in 1908, the Midland editor noted, "The hail storm that swept over this part Saturday evening did not do any serious damage to anything, while further out south and east it left desolation in its path." On the plains, luck, as well as hard work, played an important role in the settlers' success.[11]

The wind was omnipresent. A still day was rare and settlers noted it. Marjorie Clark wrote her parents from her claim south of Lemmon: "The wind was too fierce. Really it is something awful and it hardly ever goes down. It actually blows the feathers off the chickens' backs. . . . I can't put up many pictures and things for everytime the door opens they all blow off the wall. . . . It's so funny—we noticed how terrible loud everyone talks out here and now we find ourselves just shouting away at the top of our voices. We discovered it must be the wind and unless you yell you can't be heard at all."[12]

The airy dwellings of many settlers acted as giant whistles. Their inhabitants became rattled by the ceaseless howl and were covered with wind-borne silt. Outside, animals refused to graze, standing miserably, backs hunched. If a windstorm hit on washday it could be disastrous. "Everybody would rush to get the clothes before they blew away," Katherine Taylor recalled. "These strong winds would pick up empty pails, papers, and all lightweight articles loose on the ground. The lighter things that did not catch on the fence would sometimes be blown for miles."[13]

The constant winds helped create another danger—the prairie fire. Fire was a serious threat three seasons of the year. The greatest irony was the link between wet years and prairie fires. If rainfall was plentiful in the spring and summer, crops flourished and so did natural grasses. They grew thick and luxuriant, and when they dried out in the fall they provided a ready fuel. The smallest spark—from a passing train, a careless smoker, or a homesteader's cookstove—could cause a conflagration, and the ceaseless winds drove the flames quickly over tremendous distances. In dry years fires were a problem too. The grasses were not as lush but they were still there and likely to be even more flammable than usual. Any year, then, was a prairie-fire year. Only the snow cover of winter protected homesteaders from danger.

Newcomers only slowly came to understand the threat. One fire in the Mitchell Creek area began when settlers cutting hay built a campfire at lunchtime. The wind caught it and spread it into dry grass. Help arrived from all directions, but two square miles were burned before a light shower and a change in the wind direction put it out. Another fire of unknown origin in the same area the next year burned more than six square miles of grass. Occasionally fires burned on parts of the Lakota reservations or in unsettled areas where no one fought them. Their glow lit the horizon at night, giving observers in settled areas cause for concern. A change in the wind could bring the fire to their doorsteps with little warning. To be the cause of a prairie fire was a great embarrassment, and it also brought legal penalties. A settler convicted of carelessness with fire could receive six months in jail and a thousand-dollar fine.[14]

Plains wildlife also presented novel challenges. Wild animals and snakes, especially coyotes and rattlesnakes, inhabited the prairies. The coyotes were dangerous to stock and poultry rather than people, but their mournful howls through the night added a sense of wildness and isolation that was sometimes appealing but just as often frightening. Coyotes were a symbol of the wildness and freedom of the West. Their poignant call reminded all who heard it that this was an unsettled land where wild animals flourished and people, as yet, did not. As one homesteader commented, "the coyotes remind you that they are still in possession of the plains at night." Their calls accentuated for newcomers the psychological distance between their old homes and the new. On one of their first nights on the claim, the Ammons sisters "were awakened by the eerie, hair-raising cry that travelled so far over the open plains and seemed so near; a wild desolate cry with an uncannily human quality. That mournful sound is as much a part of the prairie as is the wind which blows, unchecked, over the vast stretches, the dreary, unescapable voice of the plains."[15]

The hard-nosed settler saw the coyote as a pest rather than a symbol. Grace Fairchild recalled her efforts to raise poultry her first years on the claim. Without chicken-wire coops to contain them, her hens roamed about the place, easy prey for marauding coyotes. She saw one almost every day crossing the ridge beyond the family home but could do little to protect her investment. The Fairchilds finally acquired two dogs to guard their farmstead. The poultry still had to stay near the house, but the dogs battled coyotes that tried to enter the yard. Fairchild saw coyotes in terms of profit and loss, and nothing more.[16]

No one saw romance in the presence of rattlesnakes. Great numbers of the reptiles lived on the plains, and they did not fear people but slithered into homes and cellars, barns and yards. Reaching for an object in the grass, stepping down from a wagon—any sudden move—

could bring the threatening rattle. Children playing in the yards or fields were the most frequent victims, although adults and livestock also died from rattlesnake bites. Adults and children alike travelled about armed with a stick, a hoe, or another tool to kill any rattlers they encountered.

Snakes in large numbers required more drastic efforts. A den near Bess Corey's claim housed thousands of reptiles. Corey routinely killed a half dozen snakes when walking across her claim, and their presence kept her indoors at night. Some nearby ranchers finally dynamited the den to eliminate the problem. In these actions "they got 300 all together and guessed that 3000 got away."[17]

Edith Ammons' neighborhood suffered from a similar infestation. Hot, dry weather brought snakes out in great numbers. Ammons looked up from her work one day to see a snake's head thrust up through a knothole in her floor. In the same month, a homesteader's little daughter was bitten. Deaths from such bites were not uncommon. Newspapers often included reports like, "Mrs. Freeman Madole, living on Bull Creek near Westover was bitten by a rattlesnake last week and died the next day," and "The fifteen year old son of Geo Shelton living east of Capa was bitten by a rattlesnake. . . . He was beyond help when in the hands of a physician and died in great agony." In Edith Ammons' neighborhood the settlers formed posses to combat the snakes through mass slaughter. Individual caution and group action helped reduce the problem but could not eliminate it.[18]

A final problem homesteaders confronted in the new country was the gumbo soil, the sticky clay that covered much of the west river country. Such soil could be tilled, but farmers first had to understand and adapt to its unique nature. In the early years, gumbo trails impeded travel as well. As Ada Blayney Clark travelled from Chicago to Rapid City to file on her claim, the railroad conductor offered commentary on the country as they passed through the region. "On this side [of the tracks]," he said, "there is some sand in the soil and fairly good crops can be raised when we have rain; but on the east side there is nothing but gumbo, unfit for anything but grazing." She filed on gumbo anyway, because it was on such soil that claims were available. It was sleeting when the party left for their claims in two wagons, with the cows walking behind. The cows were fractious and, Clark recalled, "we took turns walking behind the cows to keep them moving. This was no easy task for by this time the sleet had become rain and the ground was wet. The wet gumbo clung to our shoes and wheels until the accumulated load became so heavy that it fell off, this process continuing without ceasing."[19]

Gumbo, like the other natural elements, had to be endured. The advent of graded roads, and in later years gravel roads, helped the travel problem, but the soil itself could not be changed. "If you stick to this country when it's dry," the settlers said, "it will stick to you when it is wet."[20]

4. THRESHERS CAME RIGHT AFTER DINNER

Four "girl" homesteaders, as they were called, pose outside a small tar-paper shack.

This opportunity of doing exactly as I pleased constituted for me one of the chief charms of the prairie.

Ada Blayney Clark,
Chicago stenographer turned
Fall River County homesteader

Two principal types of homesteaders came to the west river country at the opening of the twentieth century: the absentee homesteader and the bona fide settler. Absentees intended only to prove up and leave the claim. "Absentee" is a general term that denotes speculative homesteaders who had no intention of remaining permanently, but there were varying degrees of actual absenteeism. Some homesteaders resided on their claims continually for the fourteen-month commutation period and then departed for good. Others spent only occasional weekends on their claims and worked or visited elsewhere the remainder of the time. After proving up, some stayed in the west river country in a town or another neighborhood. Others lived at a great distance and maintained no ties. Bona fide settlers, on the other hand, planned to build permanent farm homes.

People who intended only to prove up and leave the country operated differently than those who hoped to build commercial farm operations. In order to win their claims "free," the absentee homesteaders were required by government regulations to demonstrate "actual cultivation" by breaking a few acres of ground, to build a home no smaller than ten by twelve feet, to locate a water source, and to reside on the claim for five years. As mentioned earlier, a homesteader could "commute" the claim by residing on it for fourteen months and paying $1.25 per acre for the title. As a practical necessity, homesteaders also had to provide fodder for their horses, if they had any, and grow or buy enough food and other necessities to insure their survival through the

Friday, August 18, 1910. Quite pleasant. Our little girl arrived today. We
have named her Urilla Luella. Mrs. Duncan and Mrs. Beardsley were here.
Herman and Cecil went to get Mr. Holden to go for the Doctor, but they didn't
get back in time. Threshers came right after dinner. Mrs. Holden and
Mrs. Duncan got supper for them. Miss Bowman came to stay with us for a
time. Our seventeen acres of spr. W. made 10 bu., nine acres of W.W. made
9 bu., the oats made 5 and the speltz made 6.

Rettie Hayes,
Pennington County homesteader

months spent on the claim. These people experienced the adventures
of homestead life, and sometimes suffered from the rigors of it, but because their commitment to the region was weak their experiences resembled an extended vacation (albeit with occasional challenges to for-
titude) rather than the life-and-death struggle that marked the lives of
"real" farmers.

Both male and female absentee homesteaders often had jobs elsewhere that they left temporarily in order to seek their fortunes in western South Dakota.[1] Land had a powerful appeal, and the terms on
which it might be had appeared easy. Residency rules were lenient, so
homesteaders could leave the claim for extended periods to work or
visit elsewhere. As long as they spent occasional nights in their shacks,
they could legally claim residence. Such leniency allowed the absentee
homesteaders to be summer-only residents if they wished. They spent
the long winters working in towns, boarding and teaching in other
school districts, or living at home with family and friends. A train trip
west to the frontier region during the Christmas holidays to spend a
few days on the claim was sufficient to maintain residency until better
weather arrived.

Erikka Hansen, a schoolteacher from eastern South Dakota, developed a homesteading routine typical of many absentees who lived
close enough to their claims to return for the summer or for weekends
during the year. One of her brothers, Ole, homesteaded in Lyman
County and in 1905 urged her to come out and take up land adjoining

his. After a trip to see the land and file on it, Erikka returned to her parents' home in eastern South Dakota to begin preparing for the move. In April 1906 she headed west.

The claim shack Ole provided for her was a one-room, ten-by-twelve, tar-paper structure. Erikka bought shingles to cover the roof because she desired more protection than tar paper alone offered. She also purchased a six-dollar cookstove from Montgomery Ward. The other furnishings were homemade from packing cases and other odds and ends. Life there, she wrote, "was like playing house on a larger scale." A neighbor broke a small garden patch near the house and Ole fenced it for her. Erikka's only farm tool was a hoe, which was used to plant a small garden. She purchased a horse from a departing neighbor and was set for a successful venture.

Maintenance of the claim required little labor. Erikka cooked for herself from the supply of canned goods she had ordered from Montgomery Ward or brought from her mother's pantry.[2] Occasionally she baked bread, rolls, or pies in the small stove. Erikka hauled water from a nearby waterhole. Stray range cattle posed a problem there, but she always brought her saddled horse along to aid her escape when necessary. Care of the horse took some time each day. Erikka kept him in the fenced yard at night but picketed him farther from the house during the day to take advantage of better grass. Her garden was small and required little care. To amuse herself, Erikka sewed, picked wild fruits, and preserved them for winter use.

The first summer on the claim was a bit lonely. Erikka cooked for Ole when he was home, but he was a cowboy and worked away from his claim for long stretches. Erikka had met Mr. and Mrs. Davenport when she had visited the country to choose her land, and they provided much of her social life. Frank Davenport was a deputy sheriff and land locater. His twenty-year-old wife ran a road ranch, essentially a rural hotel, for her husband's land customers. The Davenports lived only a mile and a half away.

Erikka seized every excuse to visit the Davenports. The mail arrived in Van Metre three times a week, and Mrs. Davenport frequently hitched up a buggy or buckboard for the ride in to fetch it. Erikka went along. If she did not make the trip, Mrs. Davenport brought the mail to her door and spent some time visiting. Mr. Davenport's land business kept him very busy, and frequently Mrs. Davenport drove customers about

Homesteaders occasionally built their shacks on the line between claims, allowing companionship and sociability while also meeting residency requirements. These shacks stood in Stanley County in 1907.

or went alone to check the availability of locations. Erikka accompanied her on these trips as well. There were no roads for wagons, only horse trails. The buggy bumped along over the rough ground, occasionally negotiating creek crossings that, while not exactly entertaining, certainly provided some excitement. Mrs. Davenport took it all in stride, carrying baling wire to make needed repairs along the way.

At the end of the pleasant summer, Erikka moved to the Thorne home eight miles from her claim in order to teach school in their district. The Thornes were a ranching family with seven children. A number of homesteaders lived nearby, including Ann Griffin, a musician from Lincoln, Nebraska. She became an especially close friend, and Erikka spent much of her free time at the Griffin shack. On Saturdays Erikka returned to her claim to spend the night, but early on Sunday she returned to the Thornes' ranch to share their dinner. In this way she maintained her legal claim to the homestead. After the weather turned cold and stormy, Erikka did not travel to her claim, but when spring returned she resumed the pattern of weekend visits.

The second summer on the claim followed the pattern of the first but included a wider circle of friends. Other absentee homesteaders from the Thorne neighborhood entertained often for dinner and cards. Erikka knew the owners of the small cafe in Capa and occasionally helped out there. Friends sometimes rode to her claim for meals and overnight visits. Erikka experimented briefly with chicken raising, but coyotes killed her hen and ten chicks. New neighbors moved in, and they intended to remain permanently. Erikka purchased milk, butter, and eggs from them.

When fall arrived, Erikka returned to her parents' home in Montrose, South Dakota. She spent the winter there, except for a brief visit to her west river neighborhood over the Christmas holidays. This visit included one night and two days in her claim shack in the company of a neighbor.

In April 1908, Erikka's brother Chris decided to farm a claim just south of Ole's quarter. He brought cows and a hay mower along and set himself up as a "real farmer." His arrival added some new duties to Erikka's routine. She did not move back to her claim until June, but once there she assumed the task of milking the small herd, churning the butter, and baking for her brother. He, in turn, dug a storage "cave" near her shack to help keep the dairy products cold. Erikka continued her usual summer pattern of visiting, fetching the mail, and berry picking and canning. Because she had little farm work to do, she was able to visit about with agreeable neighbors. Gatherings of other absentees could be stimulating events. Professors, musicians, artists, and others unlikely to remain as permanent residents lived in the area for short periods and socialized with congenial friends.

When fall arrived, Erikka taught at a new school near her claim and lived in her own shack. Chris moved from his claim to Ole's house to be closer to Erikka and the chores. He milked the cows, carried in wood, and saddled Erikka's horse. She cooked breakfast and supper for the two of them and continued to bake for both of them on Saturdays. They continued this pattern until the school term ended in December. Erikka then proved up on her claim and moved back to Montrose the same day. She never saw her claim again. A short time later she traded two of the ponies she had acquired for "a fine piano at a good price." She sold the homestead for five hundred dollars. Years later she evaluated her homesteading venture: "I didn't acquire any fortune," she recalled, "but I did have three pleasant summers, and gained much valuable experience on 'My South Dakota Claim.'"[3]

Erikka Hansen's real work was outside her home. She earned enough teaching school to support herself while providing a necessary service to the community. She believed that she was participating in a fundamental and satisfying activity, and teaching was an occupation in demand everywhere; she would be able to resume that at home if she wished. The homestead shack was a home to her, although she was seldom there. "I always had a flow of satisfaction that this was my own property and home," she remembered.[4] Yet the impulse that prompted her venture was not strong enough to keep her tied to her property. When her parents needed her help, she returned to eastern South Dakota to stay.

Other single women who were absentee homesteaders followed similar patterns. There were job opportunities in the developing country that allowed them to support themselves while proving up. Their participation in actual farm work was minimal, but they earned wages performing traditional "women's jobs" as well as some work that was untraditional. An informal survey of 220 single women homesteaders indicated that 60 percent of them worked for wages while they lived on their claims. Half of those working taught school, but only half of this number had taught before moving west. The remaining women worked as hotel maids, cooks, waitresses, office help, store clerks, hired girls, and mail carriers. Five women edited newspapers, one woman hauled freight, another worked as an osteopath. Those single women who did not work very likely had brought a supply of cash to last them through their months of claim life.

The abundance of teachers in the west river country contrasts with the situation elsewhere, since domestic service was the primary occupation of employed women in the region as a whole. T. A. Larson, for example, analyzed census data from eleven western states from 1870 to 1890 and discovered that domestic service was the most frequently listed occupation for women. Among employed women in 1870, 52 percent were servants, while only 11 percent were teachers. In 1890, 34 percent of employed women were domestics, while 9.6 percent were teachers. His survey, however, took in regions that had been settled for over twenty years and had large urban areas and economies that did not depend solely on agriculture. The west river country was newly settled, and schools proliferated rapidly because South Dakota law did not include a minimum school district size. Any neighborhood that wanted a school could have one if the residents were willing to pay for it. Therefore, the demand for teachers was high. Also, in an area so recently settled, money was short and what money there was went for the costs of building a farm or a town business and a home. Domestic servants may have been an unacceptable expense. While the informal survey of women homesteaders may overstate the number of teachers in the population, since they would have been more likely to live alone and homestead than women hired to do domestic work in someone else's home, census data for the west river country indicate that there were few domestics in the area. In Dewitt Township in Perkins County, for example, with a total population of 666, only three of the forty single women over eighteen were servants, while seven were teachers.[5]

Male absentee homesteaders followed similar patterns of work and sociability, although they had the added diversions of the pool hall and saloon that women did not share. Bachelor men dropped in on married friends or neighbors to get home-cooked meals. Men cooked for each other, played cards, and attended dances.[6] In the summer, local baseball teams took much of their time. According to one local history, each community in Harding County had its own baseball team, "which travelled great distances and often played several days away from home

Washday on a claim near Fort Pierre in Stanley County in 1911.

at a time as there was no necessity of getting home."[7] Like many women, some men took jobs in town and commuted to the claim until they proved up. A wide variety of work was available to them. Those with carpentry or painting skills could work in the new towns, where buildings were going up. Men could also work in livery stables, stores, saloons, pool halls, and on the farms of those who needed extra labor. Their relationships to their claims were equally casual. They, too, could prove up and move away without a backward glance.[8]

In contrast to absentee homesteaders, farm families confronted the enormous task of creating a productive farm from wilderness grassland. It was a job that involved all family members. While some tasks were divided by gender or age, many others, including fieldwork and barnyard chores, were performed by anyone able to do them. In settled areas, where hired help was available and established farmers could afford to pay for it, the niceties of a sexual division of labor could be more easily observed. On the frontier there was not that luxury. Farming required long hours of work both indoors and out, and all hands were pressed into service.

In the west river country, as on earlier agricultural frontiers, it was, quite literally, strong backs and hands that made homes, barns, fences, and fields where none had been before. While agricultural technology was improving rapidly, many of the advances were experimental or too expensive for the average farmer. The Hart-Parr company developed a "gasoline-traction engine" early in the century but few western South Dakotans took advantage of it then.[9] Horse power combined with simple walking implements made up the outfits of many new settlers. The more fortunate had riding implements, such as a sulky plow or a mechanical mower or binder, which saved them from weary miles of walking and stooping. Those families who had not farmed before their move to western South Dakota could not usually afford a large cash outlay for flashy new implements, nor did they wish to incur debt. They bought used equipment or the cheapest, simplest new equipment available. Even those who had been farmers before migrating west often cut back to a bare minimum, selling old machinery to raise cash, for instance, or perhaps to reduce railroad shipping charges. Although farmers recognized that good machinery greatly enhanced their chance for commercial success, demands for housing for families and stock and other critical needs forced them to make do with the least possible. Of course, many believed that they would achieve prosperity quickly and could then purchase the newest and best of everything.[10]

Because farming was not yet highly mechanized, time was a most precious commodity. With so much to do and with the inexorable passage of seasons governing the timing of many tasks, new farmers had to race against the clock and the calendar if they were to succeed. The land could not be broken or plowed until the frost was out in the spring, and optimal conditions for planting lasted only a few weeks. Harvest had similar deadlines, because grain cut too late would bring lower prices on the market. Weather was always a factor. Too much rain at haying time could ruin the coming year's feed, so when farmers sensed changes in the weather, all hands rushed to finish the field-work to protect as much as they could from damage. All work had to be done at the limits of human and animal endurance. The major tasks—plowing, planting, harvesting, and threshing—took place within a framework of daily chores that were equally necessary and time-consuming. Faye Cashatt recalled her father's purposeful rhythm the first years on the claim: "Father always hurried; he never moved deliberately, seeming always to have the routine of his day's activities fixed like a map in his mind, probably sketched there before he went to sleep the night before, so that there was no necessity for wasteful contemplation during working hours."[11]

An important first task for all who farmed was breaking the sod. This was primarily a male task because it required great physical strength and stamina. The new fields had to be plotted carefully, the first furrow run straight and true. Special breaking plows were employed for the task, and obtaining the correct kind of plow was important. The share had to be tough enough to cut through the thickly matted grass roots. Different soil types demanded differently shaped plows. Oscar Micheaux discovered these variations only after hard experience. The "gummy" west river soils, he learned, were best tilled with plows that made a long, slanting cut. His plow made a square cut instead, and this caused roots and grass to gather on the share. Micheaux found he could not keep the plow in the ground, and because he was unaccustomed to driving horses he had added troubles. "I hopped, skipped and jumped across the prairie," he later recalled, "and that plow began hitting and missing, mostly missing. . . . Well, I sat down and gave up to a fit of the blues; for it looked bad, mighty bad for me." After a period of trial and error, he developed a routine. First he learned to plow two or three rods without losing control of the plow. After that distance, however, he had to pull the plow from the sod and remove the compacted grass. Eventually he could, on occasion, travel forty rods between cleanings. In this way he broke ten or twelve acres a week. By the end of the first summer, Micheaux had broken more land—120 acres—than most of his experienced farmer neighbors. He was especially proud of this fact because his position as the only black resident of the region had made him highly visible; he wanted to prove that black men could do as well as white. But he paid a price for his success: "As it had taken a fourteen hundred miles walk to follow the plow in breaking the one hundred and twenty acres, I was about 'all in' physically when it was done." [12]

Other farmers had similar difficulties but were less ambitious. They plowed smaller areas, got them planted, and then continued to plow new land when time and weather allowed. Breaking was not as seasonal as most other farm activities. Farmers could continue to break land well past planting time. The only limit on this activity was snow cover and frozen ground. Some families took up residence on the claim in October and broke a few acres of sod before the snow arrived. Others chose to move in the summer, too late to plant but with plenty of time to break ground in preparation for the following year. [13]

Few other farm activities permitted as much flexibility as breaking sod. The annual cycle of farm labor—plowing, planting, cultivating, and harvesting—shaped a broader family routine. Crop production for the market was the long-term goal, although it took time for a frontier farm to reach a commercial level of production. Men and women, adults and children, worked together to get the process underway. Men tended to be in charge of commercially oriented jobs on the farm, but women and children assisted in vital ways. During the early years on a homestead, money earned by women selling butter and eggs provided a much-needed source of investment capital.

Work patterns on the frontier family farm varied according to family composition, gender, age, and cultural background. The William Miller family was of German origin. Although the mother was born in Chicago and grew up in Iowa, she could not speak English. This greatly restricted her social life. The Millers had an unusually large family—

thirteen children, although only nine survived to adulthood—which limited the mother's outside interests even further. The father was born in Germany but spoke English and apparently got along quite well with his American neighbors. He introduced American ways into the family routine when he found them acceptable. The Miller boys, for example, learned to do the milking—a female chore in German culture—because American men performed that chore. He would not do it himself, however.[14]

William Miller left western Minnesota in 1906, accompanied by his brother-in-law, Charlie Lange. The two travelled to Butte County to establish homesteads on neighboring claims. Each brought a minimum of equipment. They hoped to work together and share what they had. Each man took four horses, four to six cows, tools, a walking plow, and a broadcast seeder. The shared equipment included a hay rake, a mower, a set of sled runners, a drag, and one wagon with a box and another with a hayrack. William's wife, Carrie, and their four children joined him in 1907, bringing the household goods. In the intervening months, William and Charlie Lange built a large sod house on the Miller claim, which they divided in half for use as a barn and a home. They also built a crude dugout on bachelor Lange's claim and broke the required acres of sod on both quarters. They dug a well by hand in the best spot for water, which, unfortunately, was a half mile from the Miller soddy. The men also dug a storm cellar in the Miller yard as a place of refuge from tornadoes, but it was also used as a cool place for storing perishable foods.

After the family arrived in April 1907, farming began in earnest. Carrie Miller arranged the furniture to make the best use of space in the soddy. William Miller had greeted his two older sons with the words, "I have lots of little jobs for you boys," and they began their tasks at once, assisting with the building of a pigpen and shelter, learning how to collect cow chips from the prairie to use as fuel, and driving the stoneboat to the well to get water. A family routine was quickly established. The older boys (Henry and Christoff were seven and eight respectively, Hilda was four, and little Louie was only two) carried in enough wood in the evening to last through the next day, brought in fresh water from the barrel outside, emptied wastewater, and filled kerosene lamps.

After the family had lived on the claim for a few weeks, the boys were given yet another task. Their father had shown them the boundaries of the farm, had taught them to respect rattlesnakes, and now felt that they were ready to assume the important role of cattle herders. Christoff and Henry took the stock to the creek for water and herded them during the day as they grazed. As they herded, they also gathered bones from the prairie that could be sold in Lemmon. Once they had cleared one area of bones they moved on, bringing the stock along, and resumed their collecting in a new area.

As soon as the ground was warm enough, the Miller family turned their attention to spring planting. The ten acres broken in 1906 were ready for seeding. The Millers put oats in that ground, using a broadcast seeder hung on the back of the wagon. The men shovelled grain into it as the wagon moved across the field, and a chain attached to the axle powered a fan that broadcast the oats in a circle behind the wagon. Later the men planted corn by hand in newly broken sod.

Planting the garden was another spring task that had to be done on schedule. The men used the plow to start the garden patch, but Carrie Miller hoed and raked it by hand before she planted the seed. The children helped her with these tasks. The older boys also hoed and weeded the ten acres of corn as it grew, although Henry concluded that "hoeing and weeding were not such jobs as they sound as there were very few weeds in the early years."

During the summer months William Miller cut hay from the prairie grasses using a horse-drawn mower. Then he drove a horse-drawn hay rake over the field to form windrows that cured in the fields for a few days before the Millers raked them into piles called doodles. Finally Miller and his sons pitched the hay by hand onto hayracks. They used the racks to carry the hay in to the barn, where they unloaded it—again, by hand. Later in the summer they and Carrie assisted with the oat harvest. William always ran the mower; Carrie, an experienced field-worker, showed the boys how to follow behind and tie the bundles efficiently. The Millers did not sell their crop but used it to feed the milk cows and hogs in the winter.

While the bulk of the field-related work fell on the males of the family that first year, Carrie Miller was never idle. She managed all the indoor labor—cooking, cleaning, laundry—necessary to keep the farm operation and family moving. Her tasks went beyond the door of the soddy to the garden and the barn, and even the field when she wished. Be-

This west river kitchen was larger than many and had a full-sized stove, rather than the smaller laundry stove commonly used in claim shacks.

55
THRESHERS CAME
RIGHT AFTER DINNER

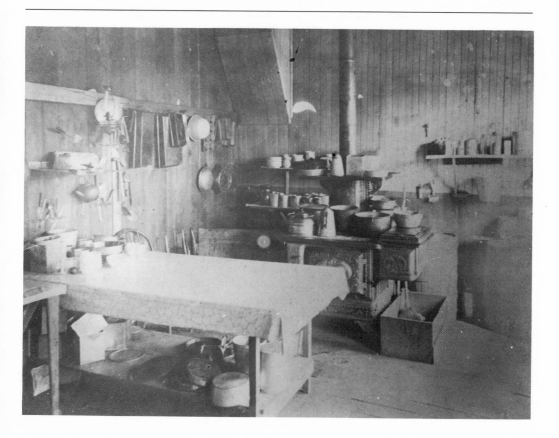

cause she enjoyed fieldwork and the outdoors, she occasionally kept one of the boys in to care for the little children so she could be free to work outside.

A day in Carrie Miller's life that first summer began early, just as it had on the Iowa farm of her girlhood and the Minnesota farm she had first shared with her husband. She left the bedroom she shared with the entire family, built a fire in the cookstove with fuel her oldest sons had brought in the night before, and began breakfast. The Millers initially followed the German custom that assigned dairy work to women. So Carrie went to the barn and milked the three cows first thing every morning. The boys, Christoff and Henry, helped by carrying pails of milk to the cellar and straining it into clean crocks. They then fed the animals and did other chores while Carrie returned to the house to finish the breakfast. After the family of six had eaten and she had cleaned the table and done the dishes, she began her tasks for the day.

Carrie had to integrate major tasks into the daily chores with efficiency so she could accomplish everything. If this was a washday, Carrie would do little other than laundering the clothes, an immense task requiring many gallons of water that someone had to carry in and out. The Millers had no washing machine; Carrie used a washboard and scrubbed the clothes by hand. She made her own soap for this process from bacon grease and store-bought lye.

If it was not a washday, there were many more possibilities. The Millers consumed enormous quantities of bread, all baked by Carrie. Her bachelor brother brought flour or fuel occasionally and she, in return, kept him supplied with bread as well. Baking was not as time-consuming as laundry work. If the bread was started the night before, Carrie could complete the baking fairly early in the morning, leaving the remainder of the day for other chores.

Churning was another possible task for the day. Carrie did not churn every day but waited for the cream to accumulate. After there was enough to make it worthwhile, she filled the two-gallon churn that always stood next to the rocking chair in the kitchen and began the tedious process of butter making. The children helped her work the dasher up and down until the butter had set. This could take from fifteen minutes to two hours, "depending on the age, temperature, and richness of the cream." One of the older boys could be trusted to drain the buttermilk from the crock, but Carrie herself washed the butter.

She also worked the butter, pressing it repeatedly with a wooden paddle. This worked salt in and water out. After it reached the proper consistency and flavor, Carrie packed it into loaf pans and cut it into blocks. She wrapped each block in paper and carried them to the cellar for keeping. She processed and stored butter to be traded in town with special care.

Later that first summer, picking and cooking wild fruits further occupied Carrie Miller's time. Plums and chokecherries grew in abundance along the creek near their claim. Carrie and her children picked the ripe fruit in great quantities and hauled it home. She then cooked it, strained the juices through a cloth, and added sugar. The sweetened juices had to cook until thick. Carrie tested this mixture with a fork; if the juice clung to the tines, it was done. She added a few pieces of greenish fruit to the mixture. They contained natural pectin that helped the thickening process. Once the juice reached the desired consistency, Carrie poured the jelly into jars and sealed them with wax. The family would spread this on their bread and pancakes or, if it failed to jell, would use it for syrup. Plum butter, which used the whole fruit, was also an important staple, and Carrie made that for her family as well. These products added variety to winter meals with little expense beyond sugar.

The sod house had only two rooms, but cleaning it still took time. Keeping it organized probably posed its own set of problems. Although the family had few possessions, six people lived in the small space. Because there were no modern conveniences, the Millers had to include water pails, woodboxes, and other aids to survival in the arrangement. Work clothes and shoes brought in dirt and barnyard soil; there was no groomed yard or cement walk to provide a barrier between outdoors and in. Carrie managed this aspect of her role as best she could, in light of the other demands made on her time. Four-year-old Hilda helped.

Child care was an ongoing responsibility often shared with the older children. The Millers had thirteen children over a twenty-four-year period. The first two were boys born thirteen months apart. The third, a girl, came along two years later, while the fourth, another boy, was born in 1905, three years after the birth of his sister. A fourth boy died at birth in 1906. When the Miller family reached the claim, they had four small children, three boys and a girl. This first summer the two older boys helped with the two younger children when necessary, but changing and feeding the children was Carrie's responsibility, especially when they were infants.[15]

Summertime was also garden time, and gardens required daily work. Carrie and the children hoed, weeded, killed bugs, and harvested the garden crop. The seeds they had brought from Minnesota did not do well in the South Dakota climate, so the harvest was disappointingly small. Daily effort was still necessary, however, to coax whatever would grow from the ground. Meals had to be cooked whether or not bread was baking or jelly simmering. By noon the men had been in the field for five or six hours. They and the horses needed rest and food. Dinner had to be large and punctually served, and Carrie was responsible for this (with the children again providing auxiliary services). After lunch she did the dishes and resumed her job of the day. Suppertime came late. She juggled its preparation with the nightly milking, done again with the help of her sons, who fed the animals and did other chores. After the meal had been cooked and eaten, the dishes washed, and the milking done, the family sat outside and enjoyed the evening and each other's conversation. Often Carrie mended or sewed. Her skill in making over old garments into new ones was important to the family welfare. When the sun went down at the end of the long day, Carrie and her family went to bed. She would rise early again the next day and repeat the routine, always juggling the daily tasks with the seasonal or occasional ones. Henry Miller remembered his mother as "always rushing about." During the first summer on the claim this would have been especially true, but she continued to be busy all the years the Millers spent on the farm.[16]

In the years before 1910, the Miller family made slow but measurable progress. One of their first purchases was a sulky plow. William Miller broke more sod whenever he could find time, and he purchased the sulky plow to replace his walking model. The sulky plow needed four to six horses to pull it, but it moved faster and saved him miles and hours of walking behind the plow. The older boys continued to help in the fields using the old dragging equipment. It was their job to drag down the rough breaking with a one-section drag hitched to "old Fanny." The boys walked behind, but when they tired one or the other sneaked aboard the horse to ride awhile and rest. William never failed to chide them for such selfishness. "She got enough to do without you ride yet!" he said. "You get down and walk."[17] The family's labor paid off in good yields of small grains, which were fed to the livestock, and a small amount of grain hay, which could be sold for cash or traded for necessities. The corn crop remained disappointing.

In 1908 the Millers began construction of a new home. The house, which measured sixteen by thirty-two feet, was a gift to all, a reward for uncomplainingly sharing a sod house with the livestock for a year and a half. Charlie Lange and William dug the cellar by hand. Once the neighbors finished harvesting, they came to help. The bachelors participated eagerly because Carrie invited them in for meals, and this gave them the opportunity to eat a woman's cooking and visit awhile. The children helped whenever they could. Finally, around the beginning of 1909, the Millers moved into their new three-room house.

By 1909 the Millers had accumulated enough cash to hire a well-digging rig. It took a few days for the horse-turned drill to bore deeply enough to strike a good supply of water, following which the well was finished off and a pump installed. For the first time, the Millers could pump their water near the house rather than hauling it a half mile in a barrel.

With hard work and the help of the sulky plow, the Millers cultivated fifty acres that season. The farm was expanding rapidly, although most of the produce still went to support the family or the livestock. The boys took on more tasks, such as hauling rocks out of the field and mending the fences. Carrie and seven-year-old Hilda began raising chickens in the corner of the sod barn, adding chickens and eggs to the dinner table and giving Carrie an added product to trade in town for store-bought items.

In 1910, William Miller and Charlie Lange together purchased a mechanical binder that cut and tied bundles of grain. Four heavy horses pulled the machine through the field and spared its owners much stoop labor. The bundles still had to be put into shocks to await the threshing rig, however, and the older boys learned that skill from their mother and uncle. Carrie knew that the grain had to be shocked carefully to protect the fragile heads from wind and rain. Because threshing rigs travelled around the neighborhood, each farm family had to await its turn. If the rig came late, sloppily shocked grain could be badly damaged, so if her sons' work did not meet Carrie's specifications, they did it again.

In the spring, before planting began, William Miller and Charlie

Lange hauled lumber and built a windmill of their own design. This greatly speeded the watering of stock and provided for household needs. Once his fieldwork was done for the season, Miller, with the help of the neighbors again, built a frame barn for the stock. To please Carrie, he also added a porch to the house and cut a door between the kitchen and the new addition. The year 1910 was a prosperous one for the Miller family. Over the years, selling grain hay, selling or trading calves, and trading Carrie Miller's eggs and butter allowed the family to improve their operation bit by bit. But the weather was turning dry.[18]

5. SOCIABILITY
IS WHAT WE NEED
IN THIS COUNTRY

An outing to the Badlands in Mellette County in January 1914.

The Burroughs and Tom Way families were our nearest neighbors on the west, and often I would look across to see if I could see the lamplight shining through some window through the night. "Social watchfires answering one another through the darkness."

Fanny Malone,
Lyman County homesteader

A s the use of the term "frontier" implies, those who came to the west river country of South Dakota in the first decade of the twentieth century migrated to the geographic and psychological margin of their society. If they stretched the social tether to its limit, they nevertheless remained bound by it. West river pioneers had left behind a full complement of social institutions ranging from the informal friendliness and aid of the neighborhood to a well-defined and highly organized system of churches and schools. The society they planned to build in the new country would not simply duplicate the old, they believed, but would improve upon it.

If the west river homesteaders were confused and frightened by the new terrain, climate, and wildlife, they were perhaps even more deeply affected by the awesome prospect of utter loneliness—a prospect that the landscape seemed designed to assure. More often than not, west river homesteaders were whisked in a matter of days from the environs of the familiar to the nether edge of American civilization. Occasionally they came in extended family groups or with friends, but often they arrived with only their immediate family or alone. If they were to have the comforts of communality, they had to initiate the effort as individuals. Paradoxically but inevitably, the commitment to sociability went hand in hand with a militant commitment to individualism and voluntarism.

Mrs. Cashatt's anxiety in the new country abated when a stranger, working in front of his new claim shack near Dallas, invited her, her husband, and her five children to dinner. In Lemmon, the grocer's wife

To prove up and earn a homestead is a full time job. One must call on every resource and talent he has—many times that isn't enough. There are hardships to struggle with that would make strong men weak and weak men stagger. At times you got so tired you could trip sitting down. . . . It would be so much harder if it weren't for your good neighbors. . . . The only time one would spit in a neighbor's face was if his mustache was on fire.

Edward Boyden,
Mellette County homesteader

fed the William Miller family of six, who had just arrived in the new country after a long rail journey. Edith and Ida Mary Ammons, upon inquiring of their new neighbors about the nearest water source, were treated to a large pail of water that their neighbors had just hauled several miles.[1]

Homesteaders routinely left shacks unlocked so wayfarers could stop to rest and eat. Travellers were welcome to eat any supplies as long as they cleaned up after themselves. The custom was an important one. With distances vast and people few, such ordinary situations as bad weather, illness, or tired horses became life threatening. Erikka Hansen followed the open-door custom faithfully. On one occasion a person passing through left a dime and an apology, another time it was a quarter with a note saying, "Thanks, Pardner." Nothing was stolen from Hansen's shack in the three years she spent on the claim.[2]

Close relations among the homesteaders continued, for good or ill, beyond the get-acquainted phase of the venture. With transportation primitive and distances long, people tended to socialize in their immediate area. The homesteaders established ties with their neighbors, and these friendships provided companionship, entertainment, and news.[3] The neighbors also provided services to the overworked and rituals of comfort and aid in times of trouble.

Bess Corey was a single-woman homesteader in Stanley County. The first neighbors she met were the Stones, a farming couple with four small children. Although Corey had not known them before her move west, they agreed that she should board at their home until her house

Occasionally, neighbors got along like two tomcats, tied by their tails and hung over a fence.

Winifred Reutter,
Mellette County homesteader

was built. Corey paid them for this service because it would be such a long-term imposition. Soon, however, she took over portions of Mrs. Stone's work in the home and paid less board as a result. The two women worked well together. They picked and preserved wild fruits and shared the expense of shipping in apples from Iowa. Mrs. Stone offered Corey extra cucumbers and citrons for her own use. Corey occasionally sewed for the Stone family.

After Corey moved into her own home, her close relationship with the Stones continued, and other neighbors began to offer help and encouragement. On at least one occasion Corey stayed with the Stones and did the baking, cleaning, and other chores to allow Mrs. Stone a much-needed trip away from the claim. The Stones reciprocated with food, often bringing butter, milk, or meat to Corey's shack or to her schoolroom. Other neighbors, the Speers, also contributed food in generous quantities, as well as furniture and a rug for her new home. All of the neighbors indulged in a lively system of borrowing. When Corey made green-tomato pickles, she borrowed vinegar from Grandma Foutts, and when they were done she shared them with her. Another neighbor, identified only as "the Dutchman," borrowed Corey's piece of salt pork to flavor beans he was cooking for company. His dog ate it, however, so she did not get it back. "I try to be neighborly," she concluded, "but sometimes I get disgusted."[4]

On rare occasions Corey rode into town with Mr. Stone to get supplies. More often she left an order with him, or any other neighbor planning a trip, to purchase the items she needed. Anyone going into

A frame house on a Stanley County claim in 1908. The settlers are repairing the telephone line that ran between their home and a neighboring shack.

SOCIABILITY

IS WHAT WE NEED

town picked up the mail for the surrounding settlers and delivered it from home to home. When winter arrived, Corey needed much heavier clothing than she owned. Mr. Speer was delegated to shop for her on one of his trips. He returned with "heavy union suits, some woolen stockings, and heavy brown outing flannel for bloomers."[5]

The winter season frequently made the long walk between claim and school too difficult. On those occasions Corey stayed with the Speer family. In January 1910 she ran low on coal and moved in with the Speers until spring. Again, because it was a planned, long-term imposition, she paid them board.

When her outhouse was blown over, Mr. Stone set it aright. When her stove smoked violently, driving her out into the cold, neighbors took her in until they could solve the problem. The Speers entertained her for the holidays, and she helped them by making candy and doing other cooking.

In such a small world, everyone knew everyone else's business. Bess Corey quickly learned the disadvantages of this when the many single men who homesteaded in her community began to show an interest in her. The attention pleased her but also set the neighbors buzzing. At a box social all eyes watched to see who would be high bidder for "Miss Corey's" box lunch.[6]

In this highly localized world, the people on the next claim *were* the news. This was not necessarily a bad thing. The all-seeing eyes of the neighbors evidenced interest and concern for the individual. What a person did, no matter how ordinary or trivial, took on special significance. A funny line or an embarrassing incident made the rounds of the neighborhood. Such thoroughgoing integration of one's daily life into the collective community conversation gave new settlers a sense of belonging, but it was inevitable that occasionally conversation became malicious gossip and rumormongering. The rural correspondents of the local newspapers reported who was doing what kind of work with what kind of equipment. One fall, when an early snowstorm caught many homesteaders with their corn crops still in the field, the rural correspondents teased the unlucky ones for weeks. Had they been better workers during the long Indian summer, one correspondent implied, they would have had their crops safely indoors. The same correspondent teased Jud Pepper, a local homesteader, for the clothing he wore in the fields and speculated about the costume's meaning: "But what do you think of a man driving 6, 8, or 10 . . . horses on a disc . . . preparing the land for seeding with a pair of low oxford shoes on with sox to match, a pair of ice cream pants, claw hammer coat, an automobile cap, clean shaved, and smoking a cigarette. . . . Now Jud must be getting reckless and very extravagant or else he had just come home from—well you know. Jud, speak up, how about it?"[7] Another correspondent, writing from the Weta community, reported that one friend had "ordered a tailor-made suit at Ed Freemole's store the other day. That puts people guessing," he concluded. Another homesteader received a hazing for falling asleep at the Literary, another for falling in the mud at a party.[8]

The eyes of the neighborhood saw more than the humorous, however. They often caught people in threatening behavior or wrongdoing and advertised it to the community. Thus papers included announcements from Busy Creek that reported: "The party that was seen taking some lumber from the Busy Creek school house last week had better return same and avoid further trouble." The guilty party may not have been seen but could he be sure? Knowing the community's propensity for careful observation and gossip, he might be made uneasy enough by such an announcement that he would return the lumber, probably after dark. The Weta correspondent tried to head off trouble there by reporting a local problem: "This carrying concealed weapons may not be what it is cracked up to be if some of you do not take a hint and trade them for plows."[9]

Neighborhood parties and dances provided direct and organized sociability. Surprise parties, for example, were in vogue. As many as thirty or forty neighbors travelled together to the home of the victim, refreshments in hand. Because the open prairies provided no shelter for their movements, parties waited for the cover of darkness before paying their call. The intended hosts were delighted (or pretended to be) at the compliment they were being paid. Dancing, cards, and conversation filled the night. The hostess and her female visitors prepared a late lunch before all departed for home.

Dances were held to celebrate any kind of occasion, and often for no occasion at all. Homesteaders with the largest houses tended to serve as hosts. They set a date and spread the word. All were welcome to attend; the customs of the country required that no one be excluded. Alcohol was discouraged, however, and potential troublemakers were told to watch their behavior.[10]

Entire families attended these functions. Small children watched the dancing until they fell asleep on the beds or piles of coats. Practical jokers occasionally switched tiny babies as they slept out of the main paths of traffic, and neighbors maintained such tales as part of their lore for years after the event. Dances generally lasted until dawn. The trackless prairie posed a challenge to travel on a moonless night. Tales of those lost trying to get home before dawn also enriched local lore. The hostess served a large supper at midnight, aided by the contributions of the other women attending. Wash boilers full of coffee simmered on the stove until serving time. The dancers ate their fill of sandwiches, cake, and scalding coffee and, thus fortified, returned to the dance floor.[11] Homesteaders writing about their lives years later generally described these dances as important highlights of their social lives. The details were lovingly recalled, the humorous events savored and retold again and again.

In a new country without hospitals for medical care or churches for comfort, friends and neighbors stepped in to perform rituals of aid and comfort in time of crisis. Birth, illness, accident, or death mobilized the community. Birth was not treated casually, but neither was it surrounded with medical magic. If an expectant couple lived close enough to reach a doctor, if they could afford the fees the doctor charged, and if they had the time to contact one when labor began, the birth would be attended by a physician. If a couple could not afford help or reach it in time, the birth occurred with the aid of neighbor women or the husband alone. Homesteaders certainly recognized the threat to life and health that difficult births posed. But the harsh realities of frontier life often prevented medical care. Even when doctors attended births, the aid of neighbor women was important. Doctors were only individuals with little black bags of medicines and forceps.[12] Friends and neighbors comforted the mother, washed and dressed the newborn, and assisted the doctor in a number of ways. They also helped care for older children, cook the meals, and do the housework until the family developed its own system for handling such tasks.

When Mrs. Langenfelder, for example, one member of a large extended family from Missouri that had settled on a claim near the Cashatt family in Tripp County, went into labor with the first of her many children, she never considered calling a doctor. Instead she sent a child to fetch Mrs. Cashatt, whose knowledge of midwifery was limited, her daughter recalled, to "her own personal experiences in childbirth and what father could tell her about deliveries of farm animals." Although Mrs. Cashatt was frightened, "there was no refusing such necessity." The baby was healthy, as were all the later arrivals, each one ushered into the world by Mrs. Cashatt.[13]

The Dunlap family in Lyman County also called on their neighbors at confinement time. When Gladys was born on Christmas Eve in 1910, two neighbor women managed the delivery while Mr. Dunlap put the other four children to bed. A doctor attended later births because Mrs. Dunlap's health was poor, probably due to her repeated childbearing. Neighbor women continued to assist at delivery time, however. During later pregnancies, hired girls came to live and work with the family while the mother was incapacitated. This continued until the oldest Dunlap daughter was able to take charge of the family when necessary. This daughter, Ione, missed a year of school at one point because she was helping her mother at home. When labor began in this case, Ione ran a mile and a half for help, returning with the faithful neighbor, who delivered the baby.[14]

Grace Fairchild, who lived near the town of Philip, bore nine children, the last seven at home on the claim. When the first was born, a blizzard prevented the midwife's arrival, and a neighbor woman came over and delivered the baby by the light of a single coal-oil lamp. Another neighbor woman came the next day to help, and by the third day Fairchild was up and doing the work for her family herself. The family followed the same pattern for the next two babies, but by the time a fourth was due a doctor had moved to a claim nearby and he came to oversee the birth. When her labor began for the fifth child to be born on the claim, Fairchild used the newly installed barbed-wire telephone to ask a neighbor to go for the doctor. When the weather turned nasty, she called again to keep the neighbor from risking his life in the storm. Then she sent another neighbor, a bachelor homesteader, to get the nearest woman to come and help. These people struggled through a blizzard to her aid, arriving only an hour before the child's birth.[15]

Other homesteaders demonstrated their commitment to the community by contributing money and aid when illness, injury, or disaster struck. Many settlers could easily see themselves in the place of the sufferers, and that thought prompted them to open their pocketbooks to help. Fires and accidents with guns and horses were frequent causes of distress. The community responded with "subscriptions," the passing of the hat to raise funds. Volunteer labor helped rebuild in the case of destruction by a fire or storm.[16]

While the mostly young and always optimistic settlers were prone to bolstering themselves with remarks like "People in this country don't die easy," deaths of people of all ages occurred regularly.[17] Babies and young children were especially susceptible to disease or snakebite, and settlers of all ages risked fatal accidents and illnesses. Quite often in the earliest years of settlement there were no cemeteries, no undertakers, and no ministers to fulfill the rites of death. Friends had to step in to serve the grief stricken. They provided comfort and practical assistance. Neighbors made the casket, washed and dressed the body, and organized the small ceremonies.

Death in the new land had a peculiar power, transforming the homesteaders' confidence in the westward march of progress into bone-deep loneliness. Possibilities looked fewer and distances from home longer. The first funeral that Mrs. Elizabeth Graham attended on the South Dakota frontier was for a baby. A family friend "made a little casket and gilded it on the outside. . . . The funeral was held in the home. Somehow everyone felt sad and as if they were a long way from civilization." The funeral for a young boy who died in Lyman County was held in the family's home. Flowers "gathered by kind neighbors from the prairie" decorated the home.[18]

As soon as settlers could gather in a group, they began planning to build formal institutions to supplement their informal social world. Schools, churches, Sunday schools, and literary societies all played important roles in rural life. These institutions were relatively easy to organize but difficult to maintain in the face of population fluctuations. Committed individuals concerned about community welfare helped spur institutional development, but forces beyond their control often hindered their efforts.

Churches and Sunday schools were among the first institutions founded after the settlers' arrival. They began as loosely organized, voluntary gatherings but quickly developed an institutional structure. Most common was the organization of a Sunday school by a self-

Perkins County homesteaders enjoying their first Christmas dinner on the homestead, 1907.

appointed committee that would spread the word of a meeting, and all who were able and interested came. Such groups often formalized their organization through the election of officers and the appointment of teachers, who handled either adult classes or youth classes. Other Sunday schools did not divide the members by age. Instead, adults and children met together and sang hymns and heard scripture read much as they would have in a formal church. Sunday schools allowed people to gather without a minister at the head of the meeting. Because ministers were few and usually served a large area, individual clergy often could not attend a local gathering each week, so lay people conducted services at Sunday school meetings. The Sunday school could always suspend its usual program in favor of a more formal church service whenever a minister was available.[19]

Churches also began because denominations, as part of their missionary activity, sent men into the western South Dakota mission field to organize scattered congregations. The Catholic diocese of Lead, established in 1902, assigned priests to parish churches, usually in towns, and also gave them the responsibility for small mission churches across a wide area. The priests said mass in private rural homes until churches could be built in nearby towns. Catholics then began worshipping in the towns, although on an irregular basis. Because priests were spread thinly, Catholics might enjoy services only once a month, and that on a weeknight. Some communities had to wait until the 1920s for a full-time priest. Under such circumstances rural children might have catechism class only once in six months, or for confirmation they might travel long distances to another town better served by the church.[20]

German and Scandinavian Lutheran denominations also sent preachers to serve their primarily rural congregations. German homesteaders founded St. Peter's Evangelical Lutheran Church ten miles from Midland with the help of missionary ministers. Their formal organization began when, according to a local historian, a minister living east of the river "received word that there were some Lutherans near Stamford and came by train to investigate. He held the first worship service at the homestead of Mrs. Christina Rothenberger." In a very short time the minister organized the church, and the congregation built their own church building. It was dedicated as St. Peter's Evangelical Lutheran Church in 1907. The congregation there was lucky, because the missionary minister appointed in 1908 chose to homestead near their church.[21]

St. Paul's Lutheran Church, located seventeen miles northwest of Draper, was organized in 1909 after two years of occasional informal meetings in homesteaders' shacks. It was part of the same circuit as St. Peter's, but there were thirty to thirty-five "hearers" in the area whose distance from other churches in the mission field hindered their formal organization. Eventually the denomination office assigned an exceptionally energetic missionary to the field, and he organized the congregation and the construction of a church. Three years later he had the church moved a considerable distance to land he had homesteaded about ten miles north of the town of Draper, where it remained. The church never had a resident minister. Instead one travelled a hundred-mile weekend circuit to bring the word to St. Paul's.[22]

The Methodists also tried to serve rural congregations from their home churches in town. In Draper the Methodist church began with the visits of two ministers who conducted Protestant interdenominational work and organized a Sunday school. Shortly after this, the Methodists in the area built their own church in Draper and were served by a resident minister. They shared him with three rural congregations. The Rousch, North Star, and Vera schools served as church centers for these rural Methodists. When the minister was absent, local residents held Sunday school meetings. The Murdo Methodist minister also served rural areas around Murdo, travelling to the Harrington and Highland schools as well as the school in the hamlet of Okaton to preach the Methodist word.[23]

Like the church and the Sunday school, the ladies aid fostered religion and sociability; in fact, they often acted as organizing mechanisms for churches. For example, in 1907 a group of Lyman County women gathered under the name "Helping Hand Society." They planned "to help the Sunday School and any worthy cause in the neighborhood." A short time later the society decided to hire a minister at two dollars per service to hold church regularly. They found two men willing to share the responsibility, and regular services commenced. A continuing influx of Scandinavians into the region helped the society to prosper, but in the fall of 1908 the Norwegian women separated from the original group and formed their own United Lutheran Ladies Aid. Their goal was to "help pay the minister, parochial school teachers, and in time build a church." The aid met monthly in various homes. The hostess served a dinner at midday and dessert during the afternoon. After the congregation obtained a regular minister who could hold services once a month, the ladies aid began to serve a dinner to those who attended both the Norwegian service in the morning and the English one in the afternoon. The congregation alternated between the east and west schoolhouses in the district so that all could attend. The ladies aid also held bazaars to raise funds for church work.[24]

The Deep Creek Ladies Aid, also Norwegian Lutheran, provided similar services to the congregation and the community. They organized in July 1908 and began working to raise funds. After several years of steady effort, the women were able to contribute $900 toward building a church. After it was completed (members of the congregation built it themselves), the ladies aid continued to help with its support. As time went on they bought pews, the pulpit, the altar ring, the baptismal font, window glass, paint, and other items necessary for maintenance, as well as paying for parochial school teaching and books. They also constituted the nucleus of worshippers. Without the ladies aid, there would have been no church.[25]

Sophia Marrington wrote that the Deep Creek Ladies Aid was "an important part of my whole life." Her participation began when, as a child, she accompanied her parents to the first meetings. The group met once a month except during the winter. "In the forenoon," she recalled, "the families would arrive. Many of the young bachelors came on horseback. When everyone had arrived, the ladies called their meeting to order." Grandma Nesheim led the singing and devotions for the group and occasionally gave a small sermon. After the meeting was over, dinner was served. "The men folks and the children were served out of doors, and the older girls were called upon to pass the lunch around until everyone had eaten as much as they could." Getting ready for the meeting was no small task. "All the bread and cakes had to be baked at home, and it took a considerable amount of food to satisfy the appetites of all the people who came such a long, slow distance."[26]

Members of a ladies aid often went to great trouble to attend the meetings. A member of the Hilland Ladies Aid in old Stanley County remembered one couple travelling three miles by wagon in twenty-below-zero temperatures. A mother and daughter walked a mile that same day. On other occasions, the president of the aid walked three miles carrying a suitcase loaded with aid work. Another member walked six miles to attend. People lingered after dinner was finished: "Because the homes were so far apart, and people got together so seldom, everyone was reluctant to go home until choretime. The rest of the day was spent in visiting while the children played outdoors."[27]

As they did with religion, settlers quickly invested in formal educational institutions. Like churches, schools were as important for their opportunities for community socializing as for their stated mission of educating the young. School buildings were strategically located in the neighborhood, and the activities of school children provided a focal point for social gatherings. Settlers formed school districts as soon as there were enough children to justify the action.

The state government provided a variety of alternatives for homesteaders planning schools. Although an 1883 law mandated township districts, a provision of that law allowed county commissioners to ignore township lines if local school patrons wanted smaller districts. Often they did, or, if they had begun as a larger district, they might later choose to break up into smaller ones when squabbles broke out over the location of the school or the teacher's pay. The members of each proposed district called a school meeting to establish boundaries and elect their school board members. The board had great power over school affairs, establishing the length of the term, hiring the teacher, and choosing the curriculum beyond that set by state law. To support the local district, the board levied a tax on all eligible property within the district. It could also choose to issue bonds for new buildings, although voters had to approve such a step. The state made available a small amount of aid for school maintenance from a permanent school fund, which was supported by funds earned through the sale or lease of sections sixteen and thirty-six in each township, but the schools relied heavily on local taxes. As a result, population fluctuations upset planning and on occasion necessitated the closing or moving of schools.[28]

The tremendous rush into western South Dakota after 1905 resulted in the rapid proliferation of school districts and school buildings. The Stanley County superintendent reported that twenty-nine new schools had been built in her county in 1908. In the four years ending in 1908, settlers in Stanley County had formed sixty-three new school districts and built 132 new schoolhouses.[29]

Schools were one element in life over which adults felt they maintained control. Parents jealously guarded their role, and schools easily became the focal points for community tension. In the Lakeside neighborhood, the issue became centralized schools, which meant the elimination of the small neighborhood schools in favor of one central school per township. Some parents petitioned the board to centralize District 27, and the author of the Lakeside Ripples column ardently supported their cause. "Oh, how we would like to see Stanley county adopt the centralized school system in every township. She would be the banner of the state," the correspondent concluded. The district called a special vote on the issue, but it lost—"twenty votes for and twenty-five against, there being six too many Russians."[30] (The Lakeside correspondent attributed the defeat to the ethnic cohesiveness of the German-Russians, who wished to maintain their local prerogatives.)

In the Plum Creek district in Stanley County a factional fight resulted in chaos. The Plum Creek board bought a building for a school and moved the furniture into it. Then, a Midland newspaper reported, "a special meeting of the residents of the school district was held, the fixtures moved into another building, and a committee appointed to see to the erection of a new schoolhouse." One member of the board, infuriated at the actions taken at the special meeting, headed to Fort Pierre to persuade the state's attorney to swear out warrants for the arrest of those who moved the school fixtures from the building designated by the board.[31]

Most of the time, however, the schools provided students with the rudiments of an education without trouble and filled their important social role as a community center quite well.

Bess Corey, who lacked a high school education, began teaching in the fall of 1909. Her school, in Stanley County, consisted of nine pupils, although she expected more to begin once they had finished their fall farm work. Although she was busy studying for the teacher's examinations in November, she planned an entertainment for her school children and their families on October 30. The children performed a variety of speeches and tableaus, all chosen or written by their teacher. Corey prepared amusements and, she recalled, "read the

A country school in the Brave Bull District, Stanley County, 1908. Many districts used sod houses, tar-paper shacks, or log cabins to house their schools.

program, drew the curtains, and did all the dressing room work." The evening included an auction of box lunches that the women had prepared. The community attended the event and enjoyed it fully. The box lunches netted $15.35 for the school fund. This "was considered fine," Corey boasted to her mother, because "they had two socials last year and only took in about $12.00 between the two of them."[32]

On other occasions Corey prepared holiday programs for the children, who performed pieces and received Christmas gifts under the approving eyes of family and friends. One program included a contest with the pupils of two other schools. Corey drilled her scholars in recitations for days before the meeting, and they won the contest easily. That event was followed by a social at Miss Whelan's school and all who could attended. When Christmas came near again, Corey created another program, complete with a taffy pull, Christmas pie, and gifts for all. Parents and friends attended.[33]

In Tripp County, an inspired teacher marshalled the resources of a poor and struggling community to recreate a traditional Christmas. One parent donated a wild plum tree from his land, another parent had a bucket of dirt that had once held geraniums and could serve as a stand. The women donated odds and ends of carefully hoarded wrapping paper to make decorations. One family contributed an apple for each student; another made little decorated baskets for each pupil and heaped them with popcorn and added to each the one small piece of homemade candy that they could afford to give. The community celebrated Christmas together in the crowded schoolhouse, singing carols, listening to pieces, and enjoying the Santa Claus who came to help distribute the gifts under the tree.[34]

School gatherings had a practical side as well. The $15.35 that Bess Corey's first social netted her school financed amenities that she could not have purchased otherwise. The Franklin Creek school, also in Stanley County, held a social one January night to finance lath and plaster for the school building and help pay off the barn the school board had built behind the school. The affair attracted 125 people, including 35 from the nearby town of Kadoka. A band, two quartets, and a group of "lady minstrels," besides the usual recitations, provided the entertainment. The auction of the box lunches, each trimmed with a bandana, capped the evening. Thirty-five adults and eighteen children purchased boxes, and the school district netted $58.60 from their sale.[35]

Another concomitant of increasing settlement in the west river country, however, was social conflict. Difficulties developed in some communities when feuds started between neighbors and each side in the dispute developed a following. Boundary lines, the use of "free" range, and stray stock were common causes of argument. Such disputes caused rifts that lasted for years and sometimes resulted in violence. In one case, two farmers fought for a year over the rights to a piece of hay land. A shooting resulted when one homesteader arrived at the quarter in question and found his neighbor busily cutting the hay. They had words over it and the homesteader, Hugh Wiley, believed it had been resolved in his favor. When he came with a group of helpers the next day, however, there was the neighbor, C. H. Nolting, cutting hay again. They had words again, and Nolting shot Wiley with a single-shot gun. Before he could reload, Wiley was back on his feet, pitchfork in hand. Wiley stabbed Nolting with it and then left to swear out a warrant against him. When the court heard the case it dismissed the charges and let Nolting go.[36]

Circuit court reports relate similar tales of neighborly terrorism. In 1909 the October term of court held in Fort Pierre heard five cases relating to neighborhood quarrels. In one case, P. H. Peterson, who lived near Cottonwood, was fined fifty dollars and sentenced to thirty days in jail for shooting his neighbor in the back. In another case, S. Adams, "who wanted to take a shot at his neighbor, Wm. Nordlander, but couldn't because his revolver caught in the lining of his clothing and spilt all the shells out of his gun," pleaded not guilty to charges against him.[37]

Disputes over wandering stock occasionally led to mayhem. Antagonism was particularly strong if the offending neighbor happened to be a large rancher who could not adjust to the new homesteading order. F. E. Olney and his cowboys caused a number of incidents. In one case, two brothers were arrested and charged with malicious mischief for shooting into the Olney herd, which roamed freely across parts of Stanley County. The grazing livestock threatened the brothers' crops.[38] In another case, an Olney "would be if he could be" cowboy threatened a homesteader with a gun because he had objected to the Olney cattle eating his haystacks.[39]

In some cases, neighbors worked out problems on their own. Grace Fairchild gladly paid damages to her neighbors when the Fairchild calves trampled their new orchard. She knew that the family had little food and less cash, so she paid them the first time and on the second time took the mother of the family to a nearby store and bought her a load of groceries.[40] In another case, Erikka Hansen accompanied a friend to the home of a neighboring rancher whose cattle had trampled her garden. He paid ten dollars in damages with no complaints, although Hansen did not think this made up for the good vegetables destroyed. Fresh food was too hard to come by.[41]

6. THE BEST AND MOST PROGRESSIVE TOWN

The town of Midland in Stanley County, looking south toward the Bad River.

Don't sit down in the meadow and wait for the cow to back up to be milked. Get up and go after the cow.

Kadoka *Press*
January 1, 1909, explaining the Kommercial Klub creed

Homesteaders were not the only settlers of the west river country. Town-builders also played a vital role in the region's development. With boundless faith and unbridled optimism, they raised up villages on the empty flatness of the west river prairie. The town-builders were often forthrightly materialistic, but they also acknowledged less-obvious motives. They were proud of their new communities, and they liked being in on the ground floor of political and institutional development. Townspeople had their own image of success—modelled generally on the small urban centers they came from or knew of. In the west river country, they too faced the reality of a new and different world. Although the town-builders were infected with a strong conviction that they could build a world to their liking, a variety of factors, which were often beyond their control, shaped their endeavors. The railroad, for example, played the most significant role in the success or failure of a town. Railroads had become a crucial factor in frontier settlement during the last half of the nineteenth century. Before this time, rivers had dictated the flow of commerce and the success or failure of new settlements. Canals added some flexibility, but even then water transportation could not match the power of the railroads in making or breaking towns. The railroads had made large-scale settlement on the Great Plains feasible in the last decades of the nineteenth century. West river boosters worked hard to attract a line and exhibited a great willingness to accommodate the demands of a railroad corporation.[1]

The standardization and specialization of economic life in the na-

They keep on building at Murdo. They cannot wait for the lot sale. The en-
thusiasm and faith in the future of the town is so "catching" that structures
spring up in any old place at any hour of the day. None seem to be immune
from the feverish haste to "get in on the ground floor." "There is a tide in the
affairs of men which, taken at the flood leads on to fortune," is proclaimed
from the house-tops, and "now is the accepted time, now is the duty of sal-
vation" is believed as fully as that it sometimes rains in South Dakota.

Highland *Herald,*
quoted in Murdo *Coyote*, July 13, 1906

Are you boosting or knocking Midland?

Midland *Western Star,*
November 30, 1906

tion as a whole also affected the development of towns west of the river.
The dominance of the railroad led to what cultural geographer John
Hudson has concluded was a remarkable uniformity of the central facilities in Great Plains towns. Within each town, a variety of businesses sprang up, including both old-fashioned general stores and
modern chain merchandisers and specialty stores. Although each town
had a variety of businesses, there was little diversity in business houses
from town to town. Goods and services rarely varied in type, although
larger towns had greater selection. Businessmen showed little loyalty
to a particular calling. If clothing was not selling well, a clothier might
become a grocer. The buildings erected by merchants also changed
function with comparable ease. Change in the business community
was a constant during the early years of settlement.[2]

Factors unknown to plains towns in 1880—such as the automobile,
the mail-order house, and the replacement of labor by capital in agriculture—ultimately had the greatest effect on the future of the town.
These factors were directly involved in the development of west river
towns. The first automobiles reached the area about 1908, tractors
and other heavy machinery became available at the same time, and
mail-order catalogues (known among local businessmen as "town-
killers") arrived regularly, much to the dismay of newspaper editors.
While the long-term effects of the auto and heavily mechanized agriculture were unclear, local businessmen understood the threat posed
by Montgomery Ward and Sears Roebuck immediately.[3]

Town-builders also busied themselves with internal political and institutional developments that were more susceptible to local control than were railroads and economic changes. Many towns hoped to become county seats. Civic improvements and business promotion were two methods by which each town competed against its neighbors for the business of the countryside. Amenities for farm families and advertisements for goods and services attracted trade, the lifeblood of the town. Town-dwellers often disagreed about the direction of these developments in their communities, and factionalism was the result. Those unwilling to conform to majority opinion could find themselves ostracized as "knockers," the ultimate insult in the age of the "booster."

The coming of a railroad radically changed the pattern of life in a town. For the population of the area, towns with railroads were links to the outside world. Railroads speeded travel and communication and allowed more goods to reach more stores more quickly. Once railroad service reached Midland, for example, the two-day stage trip to Fort Pierre, the county seat, was cut to a matter of hours. In prerailroad days, the Midland newspaper went to press Saturday morning after the stage had arrived with the "ready-prints," the pages of state and national news printed in cities like Sioux Falls. The paper had to be published and ready to send within three hours, because the stage departed with the passengers and the mail after a brief layover and did not return until Tuesday. After the Chicago and North Western began service to the town (and after some struggle to improve mail service) mail arrived daily, and the newspaper was free to publish on its own timetable. J. C. Russell's General Store, a fixture in Midland since 1890, received its goods overland before the railroad arrived. Dan Bastion, a teamster, spent most of his days on the trail between Fort Pierre and Midland hauling goods for the store. Many issues of the *Western Star* recorded his comings and goings. Drummers (salesmen of wholesale goods to retailers) travelled the area in wagons or on the stage, but their numbers were few. After the railroad arrived, Dan Bastion left the freight business and built a hotel. J. C. Russell had all the merchandise his store building could hold and plenty of competition as well. Drummers visited the town more frequently, bringing their catalogues and order forms. Midland, which had been a true cowtown, became a different place when the train came.[4]

When rumors spread in 1904 that the Milwaukee Road and the Chicago and North Western would build west from the Missouri River, population boomed in the west river region. Both railroads platted towns along the proposed line using the standard "team-haul" principle, which charted the intervals between towns based on the distance farmers could travel to town by team and still return home in one day.[5] Further, the towns built by the railroad companies had a distinctive pattern that was not present in river towns or other centers that preceded rail development. Railroad town plats are called "T towns" because the rail line and the main street typically met to form a T-shaped intersection. The towns of the west river country for which plats are available follow this design. The lumberyards and grain elevators (if any) were located on one side of the tracks, and the depot and residential and business districts lay on the other. This design minimized traffic over the tracks and kept heavy wagons out of the residential district. Main street ran perpendicular to the railroad tracks, with the depot at one end and a public building at the other. This thoroughfare was typically lined with business buildings, with banks occupying prime corner locations, and residences widely scattered throughout other areas of town.[6] Plats of Herrick in Gregory County and Kadoka in old Stanley County and photographs of many other west river towns show this kind of arrangement.[7] The scattering of residences during the early years gave towns a haphazard appearance. In Kadoka this dispersion was the result of settlers leapfrogging the Milwaukee Road's residential plat and buying one-acre lots from local real estate agents. The result was a community with a compact, carefully designed center based on the depot and main street but without any real residential neighborhood.[8]

Towns that had been established before the railroad arrived took the necessary steps to conform to railroad plats. When the railroad plat for Midland was made public, it was discovered that J. C. Russell's store stood in the middle of a proposed street. He quickly announced plans to build an impressive new building that conformed to the plat. The newer businesses opened their doors while perched on blocks, waiting for the lot sale to be held and permanent locations established. Later the paper announced that the railroad would hold no public auction of lots (probably due to the lateness of the season), but that business people could buy at the list price if they wished. Most did so, in order to establish themselves as quickly as possible. The railroad arrived on December 10, 1906, and passenger service began the week of December 21, bringing a flood of settlers to the town. By late January, merchants had moved their buildings to their lots facing Main Street. Twelve business houses lined the north side of Main, and ten lined the south, with two more under construction. When editor Gueffroy surveyed the scene at 6:30 A.M. on Monday, March 18, 1907, he counted thirty-seven "substantial business houses." For fifteen years before the railroad arrived, the trade center of Midland had had only two businesses—a hotel and Russell's General Store. After three months as an official railroad town, it had attracted thirty-five more and, despite its age, it had the look of the standard railroad town.[9]

Counties without rail service or with inadequate service recognized the importance of the railroad to business development and the power of the road to make or break a community. Perkins County, for example, had inadequate rail service for its size and population. The Milwaukee Road main line bisected the extreme northeast corner, serving the town of Lemmon, which quickly became one of the largest communities west of the river. A branch line of the Milwaukee Road reached Faith, in the extreme northeast corner of Meade County in 1911, providing rail service to the southeast sections of Perkins County. The remaining trade centers in Perkins County were inland towns (towns without railroads), and inland towns were sometimes willing to go to great lengths to become railroad towns.

Daviston, one such town, began in the land rush of 1908. At first it consisted of a post office, a grocery store, a lumber business, a newspaper, a restaurant and hotel, and a blacksmith's shop. Many of the businesses started when homesteaders in the area decided to take advantage of the influx of settlers and become business people as well. In 1910 the Milwaukee Road surveyed a route through the county. The Lemmon Land Company, gambling that the railroad would follow through and build the line, purchased land on it and platted a town. The Daviston business people then decided to move the community south to that new location. A moving gang with many teams of horses hauled the buildings and established them on their new lots.

The hope of a railroad also appealed to others, who established businesses in New Daviston and gave it the appearance of a boomtown. Before long the village contained two banks, two hotels, two hardware stores, two lumberyards, two pool halls, a butcher shop, two drugstores, a grocery, a general mercantile store, a print shop, a black-

Lakota people dance on the main street of Kadoka in 1910. Photo courtesy of the Kadoka *Press.*

smith's shop, and a Presbyterian church where thirty youngsters attended school. The women of the town quickly organized a ladies aid, while the girls of the community formed a female baseball club. The men also had a baseball team. New Daviston was a lively place that served a growing farm community while it waited for the rail line. But the railroad never came. The drought years of 1910 and 1911 decimated the local population, and New Daviston began to lose its trade area. The Milwaukee Road decided that a branch line through Perkins County would never pay off and none was built. The town survived until 1919, when Ella Baxter and her husband "moved all the buildings to the farm, pulled up the sidewalk, and that was the last of Daviston."[10]

Not all inland towns suffered the same fate. Harding, Perkins, and northern Butte counties were never adequately served, yet some trade centers in these areas survived because people needed the goods and services they offered, and until the automobile became common (after 1915 or so in the west river country) the difficulty of travel kept people nearer home. Population density was important, however. When the west river population dropped in 1911, an inevitable pruning of trade centers took place.

Even before this, however, inland towns had suffered from commercial disadvantages that diminished their trade. High freight rates added to the cost of goods and prices were consequently higher, while the variety of goods offered for sale was less. Homesteaders travelled considerable distances to railhead towns to take advantage of lower prices and greater selection and patronized inland towns only for their immediate needs. Though this was generally not enough to support such centers in the long run, some substantial farming areas remained so isolated that their inland towns did survive.[11]

The residents of such isolated areas were not content with their inland status, however, and worked ceaselessly to attract a railroad. The "last big rumor" of a railroad swept the Harding County town of Buffalo in 1916. When nothing came of it, the local citizens tried to build one of their own, but the effort failed. Then in 1921 the citizens proposed to build a short line from Lemmon in Perkins County through three inland towns in that county to Buffalo and then south to the line in Belle Fourche. That plan failed as well, but by then civic leaders had turned their attention to highways. As early as 1915 they had held meetings to promote better roads. By 1917 work had begun to improve the trail between Buffalo and the railhead at Bowman, North Dakota. Overall, however, the failure of the railroads to build in the area during the settlement rush—coupled with semiarid conditions, especially in Harding County—retarded the development of the northwest corner of the state.[12]

West river towns, like plains towns before them, reflected national developments in specialization and standardization that came to the towns along with the founders. Architectural standardization within towns allowed buildings to make the transition from general store to meat market to post office to farm building at the whim of each owner. West river towns, like the plains towns described by John C. Hudson, experienced rapid business turnovers, with merchants "often engaged in a sequence of sometimes quite unrelated businesses." Hudson found that such fluidity generally lasted for ten years before they attained a measure of stability. "By that time," he concluded, "nearly all plains towns were marked for either growth or stagnation, whether by circumstances of geography or by the entrepreneurial skills of their business people."[13]

The new towns had the advantage of all the innovations developed in the nineteenth century. They had a standard currency, a marketing system, and, after the arrival of the railroad, a reasonably efficient transportation system. Merchants specialized in the sale of certain items, although some general stores remained. Grocery stores, drugstores, hardware stores, confectionaries, and other specialized businesses moved into new towns immediately upon their founding. Within weeks of the establishment of Murdo as a railroad townsite, for example, forty businesses and two or three residences had been built. The list of businesses, which included only two general stores, featured one hardware store, three drugstores, a furniture store, a feed store, two meat markets, and a branch of the Fullerton lumber chain.[14] Other towns demonstrated similar variety. The list of businesses in Newell included three general stores, three lumberyards, two hardware and implement stores, a drugstore, a meat market, and three livery and feed barns.[15]

All of the businesses advertised national name brands. Confectionary stores made their own ice cream—at least until a system of refrigeration allowed standard brands to be transported—but few other products were manufactured locally. Chains like Fullerton, Jas. Smith, and Peter Mineter supplied lumber, though a few locally owned yards struggled briefly before selling out to them. The newspapers gathered news locally, but half of each issue consisted of "ready-print." Neighboring papers thus could be identical in half their content if the publishers subscribed to the same ready-print service. Drugstores sold current magazines and city newspapers, which helped tie the new towns into the media culture of the nation.[16] Thus, although the town-builders may have thought of themselves as pioneers in the wilderness, they were strongly tethered to the national economy and mentality.

The boomtown atmosphere of west river towns has already been noted. What may have been surprising to area residents and still confounds present-day historians is the sustained nature of change in the business community of the towns. Only doctors and lawyers appear to have had any attachments to the idea of profession. Business people changed professions easily and often. For instance, Harry Haulman, who had managed the Kadoka Butcher Company in 1908, managed a furniture store in 1910, moved to Iowa for a short time, returned, opened a meat market with a partner in October 1911, sold out in January 1912, and bought a mortuary business in March of that year. In 1911, after returning from Iowa, he also ran the Kadoka Farmer's Institute, which promoted scientific agriculture and taught modern techniques.[17]

Some business people traded their stores and stock for claims. R. G. Skrove traded his furniture store to a Mr. Rasmussen for a two-hundred-acre farm in July 1910. He did not plan to live on it long, however. After harvest, he announced, he would move to western Canada to pioneer again. The new owner of the furniture store traded it the next week for some horses. The third owner, George V. Jones, traded it to Scott Wellman in December for his farm. In another case, F. E. Reidinger, a real estate agent and entrepreneur par excellence traded in his pool hall for Albert Gardner's farm. Gardner also received some of Reidinger's town lots and cash besides. In later years Reidinger owned a garage and auto livery (to serve people who earlier would have rented a buggy) and a clothing store.[18]

In contrast to the instability of this business climate, towns battled with each other to become county seats because of the stability and economic progress that such a designation insured. West river towns engaged in county seat fights in ways that had become traditional for

Election day on the main street of Meadow in Perkins County in 1910.

**THE BEST AND
MOST PROGRESSIVE
TOWN**

ELECTION DAY,
MEADOW S.D. Nov. 8TH 1910.

the plains by the time the towns were founded. The underpopulated stretches of the west river country had been organized into huge counties that encompassed the Indian reservation lands, which had no county government. After the homesteading rush began, however, new settlers demanded county governments and the convenience of nearby, centrally located county seats in which to transact their business. Towns so located hoped to be chosen for the honor, and towns not so fortunate agitated for new county boundaries that would put them at an advantage. In old Stanley County, for example, the founders of Philip very early began to suggest a division into two counties, the lines of one of them, of course, favoring Philip as the logical county seat. The backers of this plan hoped to derail the plans of Midland and Kadoka, as well as smaller towns, to win the honor.[19] Other towns, unable to use their location as a selling point, instead promoted the progressive character of their merchants and the variety of services they offered. Camp Crook, in far western Harding County, certainly could not argue the virtues of its location, perched as it was four miles from the Montana border. But it did have the advantage of development, having been a trade center since the open-range days of the 1880s, and had developed into a creditable little town. Voters in Harding County, however, chose to go with Buffalo, a "sheep wagon," not a town, according to Camp Crook residents. It had to be built from the ground up but had the advantage of central location.[20] Perkins County residents did the same, choosing the inland town of Bison near the center of the county rather than Lemmon, a railroad town of some size and importance. The battle was bitter, and Lemmon lost by only fourteen votes. At the time of the election, Bison consisted of four sod houses and a combination store and post office. The newly elected county officials, most of whom already lived in Lemmon, refused to make the move. A judge forced the commissioners to meet in the new town, and eventually the bitter feelings subsided. In May 1909, four months after the vote, ox teams moved the official records and paraphernalia to Bison, which remains the seat of government of Perkins County today.[21]

Entrepreneurial wile also played an important role in county-seat battles. The Jackson brothers, two sons of Iowa governor Frank Darr Jackson, had played a key role in attracting the Chicago and North Western to Dallas in Gregory County and now demonstrated their

The main street of White River in Mellette County in 1912.

WHITE RIVER S.D.

prowess in Tripp County. The county was organized in March 1909, and the contest for a temporary county seat began immediately. The original two contestants were Lamro, population 750, and Colome, with 450 residents. Neither was a railroad town, because the Chicago and North Western had not yet extended its lines from Dallas in Gregory County, but both argued that they would become railroad towns soon and both used central location as their argument, although Colome had to alter the usual stance by proclaiming itself the center of population in the county. Lamro advocates pointed out that the center of population would change with advancing settlement, so their advantage of central geographic location was thus more important. Lamro won the election handily.[22]

The Jackson brothers and their Western Townsite Company quickly altered the destiny of Lamro. When the railroad began its survey (which ultimately bypassed both Lamro and Colome), the Jacksons purchased 800 acres of land north of Lamro, paying the unheard of sum of fifty-nine dollars an acre. The Jacksons urged the now-edgy citizens of Lamro to move lock, stock, and barrel to the new site, but the Lamro leaders stiffened, smug in their conviction that the railroad could not afford to miss their town. The Jacksons, in the meantime, had used their connections with Chicago and North Western president Marvin Hewitt to assure the triumph of their site. They then offered the Lamro merchants town lots for half price if they would make the move, again to no avail. The Jacksons went about their business, confidently naming the new town Winner. The Lamroites responded with hoots of derision and began civic improvements of their own. When the lots in Winner went on sale, the Jacksons took in $84,000, but little of it was from Lamro.

Having failed to lure the Lamroites with good deals, the Jacksons settled upon a strategy of selective wooing of key Lamro merchants in the plush offices of the Western Townsite Company. Their first break came when the owner of the Lamro hotel sold his building and corner lot in Lamro to the company for $7,500. The Jacksons closed the hotel, "the largest and best building in Lamro" and moved it to Winner, leaving "the dark cellar over which it stood gaping like an open grave." The fierce loyalty of Lamro merchants, once broken, faded into memory as they scrambled to get in on the ground floor in Winner.[23] A residue of bitterness remained, however, and most Lamro merchants built on the south side of town, while the original Winner merchants built on the north. The move had been a wise one, however, because Winner became the county seat in the November 1910 election, thus assuring its success as a town. The few remaining holdouts in Lamro were left with nothing.[24]

Towns also competed by means of civic improvements and business promotion. The newspaper columns reflect these concerns and describe the actions residents took. Water supply, fire protection, and law-and-order issues were frequently discussed. A good newspaper editor willing to promote such public issues was vital to a town's success. Kadoka had such men in Edward Nellor and William Durkee. Their Kadoka *Press* was closely allied with the Kadoka Kommercial Klub, the leading booster club and business organization. In its first month of operation, the *Press* discussed the Klub's well-digging plans, demanded fire protection on two occasions, urged residents to beautify their lots with trees, shrubs, and flowers, suggested that the town develop a park, and tried to derail a proposed meeting to form a homesteaders' political party on the grounds that it would divide citizens who were really of common interest. In the next issue, the editors urged action on the part of residents to remove "sources of trouble" and "breeders of disease" from their backyards and alleys, chided petty thieves in the area for stealing railroad property, asked citizen support for political candidates from the west end of the county, called for a good blacksmith to locate in town, and published the first city ordinances as they were acted upon by the new town council. These articles were intermingled with a variety of notes welcoming new residents, promoting agriculture in Stanley County, and boosting the county generally.[25]

The *Press* also provided detailed accounts of Kadoka Kommercial Klub activities. Most businessmen in Kadoka appear to have been members of the Klub, although no membership list was ever published. Attendance ranged between thirty and thirty-five in the early days. (Fifty-two men voted in the town incorporation election held in May 1908.) The town's milliners, seamstress, postmistress, and telephone company manager, all women, apparently did not belong to the Klub—it was a man's organization. Frequent reports on the progress of the town well, financed by the Klub, appeared in the *Press*. The well was completed in August 1908 and was described as a donation to the public from the group. The Klub hoped that the well would attract farmers to town to trade in the stores. At their July meeting, members considered the merits of establishing a fair association, building a road south of town, and planning railroad crossings within the town. In October it met to discuss a waterworks for the town. In November the group appointed a committee to investigate all possible water systems and estimated the cost at $5,000 or more. Issues discussed during the winter of 1909 included the purchase of a chemical fire engine, the organization of a fire department, and the need for a town hall. At a later meeting the group voted to buy the fire engine and to investigate the possibility of stocking the railroad reservoir with fish. The *Press* also reported much enthusiastic discussion of a proposition to build a bridge over the White River because the river discouraged trade from the region south of town. Another large project occupied the Klub later in the spring, when it agreed to help the Pine Ridge reservation officials build a road from the reservation into town. Kadoka's share of the cost was to be $150, and a committee of two set about raising the funds. (Fund-raising was ceaseless. Subscriptions supported the town band, the baseball club, and many improvements. When a regional commercial club was founded to help promote the reservation then opening to the south, Kommercial Klub members donated more money to that enterprise.)[26]

The Kadoka Kommercial Klub also performed an important community function in advertising the town's businesses through unique promotional schemes. Besides urging that all members advertise, the members took over the Market Day promotion organized in January 1909 by George Inman and the editors of the *Press*. Under the auspices of the Klub, a sale extravaganza was held one Saturday each month. Farm families trekked into Kadoka to auction off their stock and produce. Each business offered prizes to customers. The Klub raised premiums to be given to participants. These included five dollars to the person spending the most money in town on Market Day, three dollars to the largest family in town, a dollar and a half for the person marketing the most butter, and so forth. The *Press* reported a crowd of between eight hundred and a thousand at the February sale and similar success at others. The technique worked so well that other towns requested advice from Klub members on how to establish their own Market Day program.[27]

Small-town residents in the west river country did not always work together successfully or harmoniously, however. Although the Kadoka paper tried hard to obscure any signs of dissension, occasional glimpses of factionalism and pettiness appear. For instance, when George Inman and the *Press* editors developed the idea of Market Day, some accused them of being grafters. To mollify their critics, they lowered the charge for advertising for the event from forty to twenty-five dollars and turned control of Market Day over to the Kommercial Klub.[28]

Some factionalism also developed at the time of town elections each year. Two businessmen published poems in the 1909 postelection issue of the *Press* about people who refused to work along with the majority. The problem may have been related to liquor. In every election, the voters decided whether to grant liquor licenses. Kadoka voted for liquor every time, so temperance probably was not much of an issue. (The yes votes totaled 38 in 1908, the no votes 11. In 1909, 39 men voted yes, 12 voted no.) The question of who was to receive the licenses, however, may have caused the problem. A state law passed in 1907 allowed only one saloon for every 300 people. Kadoka had seven saloons in 1906, although the departure of the railroad construction crews soon lowered the demand. By the time the town incorporated in 1908, the new law was in place and the town board had to vote on saloon keepers' applications. Kadoka was allowed only two licenses. Because the business was so profitable, those who were not awarded licenses quickly became bitter and blamed graft and corruption for their defeat. The *Press* referred to "some strife" over the issue in December 1908 when the Black Pipe Saloon closed its doors, allowing the council to choose a new licensee.[29]

In the Tripp County town of Winner, the liquor license issue became one focal point for the residual bitterness left from the Lamro versus Winner battles of 1909 and 1910. The Winner council consisted of six members. Three represented the former Lamro business people in the south part of town, three others represented the original Winner faction. In 1913 the town council had one liquor license available. Neither faction had a majority, and the mayor refused to break the tie. After several fruitless meetings with no progress on the issue, the mayor voted with the Winner faction, which caused, one historian has noted, "considerable comment to say the least."[30]

People who were out of step with the prevailing faction were subject to exclusion. In Kadoka that rejection was reflected in the statements of E. L. Senn, the owner of the rival paper, the *Reporter,* and his local editor. Bitter about their failure to receive any job work from the Fair Association, they accused the town leaders of "running the affairs of this town as a private snap." "If our enthusiasm fails at times," they went on, "and we do not appear to be doing as much as the other paper to boost the enterprise, remember that they are getting a good size roll of the long green and we are getting   ." The *Press* editors responded with their own salvo: "The Reporter never has boosted for any public enterprise for Kadoka, but has always had their little hammer out to knock . . . BOOST! DON'T KNOCK! If you can't say a good word for a fellow or a town, forget it."[31]

Individuals, too, felt the pressure to conform. The town of Kadoka engaged in a lengthy battle with a man named Al Stahl over the direction of Stahl's life. He did have trouble with the law on occasion (he "roped, dragged, and pounded" a neighbor and stole a claim shack, for example), but he blamed his fall on the closed circle in Kadoka, which refused him admission and allegedly ruined his life. The *Press* editors, for their part, gleefully published meticulous accounts of Stahl's misadventures. Apparently an abrasive man with high aspirations but little talent for success, Stahl targeted Kadoka businessmen as the real culprits in his life of petty crime. In an interview granted to the Mitchell *Gazette,* he named the "Dirty Dozen," a Kadoka clique, as the conspirators responsible for his endless string of court appearances. The "Dozen," he claimed, had been "pegging at me for the past year, because I refuse to make investments in the town and knocked several propositions for the Kadoka Commercial club. I have been opposed to Kadoka misrepresenting their town to eastern investors and speculators and for this reason they are down on me." The *Press* responded calmly: "Stahl is, and always has been the laughing stock of Kadoka, because of his bull-headedness, and extravagant habit of using the King's English, and not being able to make good."[32]

Town-dwellers had the same sense of building a new country as the homesteaders. They wanted economic progress for the town, personal profit for themselves, and a good community life, although they often disagreed about what that meant. Town building always began with high hopes but often ended in failure or stagnation. It was punctuated with conflicts, disasters, and militant boosterism. The town-builder's last frontier was a haphazard mixture of individual action and national economic trends over which town residents had little control. Railroad corporations, merchandising systems that emphasized name brands that were sold across the nation, and the increasing specialization of the economy all affected west river town development. Even on a regional level, chain merchandising of lumber, the prevalence of newspaper ready-print, and the presence of large-scale real estate entrepreneurs limited the individual's ability to shape the direction of development. On another level, however, opportunities still existed for town-dwellers to build the kind of world they wanted. They were able to maintain some control over the political and institutional development of their communities, and they exercised that right with vigor. Although corporate America impinged at every turn, the individualist frontier ethos did remain viable in the west river country.

7. HAPPY HOMES, FINE RESIDENCES, AND GOOD SCHOOLS AND CHURCHES

The town of Kadoka in Stanley County sometime before 1910. Photo courtesy of the Kadoka *Press.*

The ladies of the Presbyterian church will serve a Harvest supper at the church on Saturday afternoon from 5 to 8 o'clock. All are invited to attend. The proceeds go toward the expense of painting and finishing the church. Come out and help the ladies in this good work.

Kadoka *Press,*
July 31, 1908

A very pleasant time is reported.
Standard conclusion to
Kadoka *Press* social notes

Three factors shaped the patterns of social relations that town-dwellers developed. The first, already described in some detail, was the optimism of the frontier. The second factor was the small size of west river towns. The togetherness that Lewis Atherton described in his towns on the Middle Border was an important part of west river town life. That this quality often led to gossip and conformity was an accepted part of the bargain.[1]

Furthermore, a small population insured a close working relationship between farm and town. Harlan Douglass, in his classic work *The Little Town*, decried the urban orientation of small-town residents. Their sense of superiority, he believed, was an important factor in the hostility between farmer and town-dweller in settled areas. But Douglass also believed that towns with fewer than 500 people were less likely to suffer from pretentiousness. West river towns usually had fewer than 600 people, and relations between town and country people tended to be cordial. Townspeople travelled to country schools for literary society meetings, dances, and fund-raisers, and country women brought their fund-raising projects to town, serving dinners or ice cream to the larger market there. Farm people attended town churches if they lived close enough.[2]

Finally, the historical context in which these communities were founded shaped their social patterns. Lewis Atherton has described the pre-1890 community as one of informal organization. Most people lived their lives in a rhythm of seasonal community celebrations in which all participated without needing an invitation. For individuals, the turning points in their lives—birth, marriage, and death—attracted local attention. Few occasions were private. But in the twentieth century, Atherton suggests, the rise of social cliques based on exclusive memberships limited full community participation. Atherton describes this change as the "loss of togetherness" and attributes it to the arrival of city values on Main Street. West river towns were transitional entities with elements of both the eras that Atherton describes. There were clubs of all descriptions in each town, and with each passing year more developed. But it is easy to exaggerate the degree of hierarchy present in small towns, despite the rise of clubbiness. In west river towns, at least, membership in organizations was not exclusive. And the easy informality of social relations is reflected in the social notes of the local papers, where the latest victims of practical jokes were revealed, illnesses chronicled, weddings, births, and anniversaries celebrated, and deaths mourned.[3]

Kadoka was founded in 1906, although the railroad did not arrive until early in 1907. The Kadoka *Press* began publication in May 1908. The *Press* worked hard to be a "newsy sheet," the small-town paper's highest goal, and provided excellent coverage of social developments. It began publication the week the town voted to incorporate as a municipality under state law, an important symbolic step in the life of a new town. In early July 1908 the Presbyterians dedicated their church building, the first in Kadoka. Late in July local voters decided to establish an independent school district for the town. Over the next two years churches proliferated, along with lodges, clubs, and other organizations.[4]

According to the 1910 federal census, 222 people made Kadoka their home.[5] The town was three years old when William Schwictenberg, the local watchmaker and town marshal, made the count. The first boom had passed and the town was more stable than in earlier years, although families continued to move in and out and people changed their employment with surprising frequency. Forty-six married couples lived there; thirty-seven of them had children. A divorced woman with one daughter also lived in Kadoka and taught at the school. Among them, the families had fifty-eight children under the age of eighteen. Fifty-five percent of the children were under age five. Ten people in the community were over sixty, including three widows and two widowers.

More single men than single women lived in Kadoka. Forty-two of the men of the town were single or widowed. Thirty women were in the single, widowed, or divorced category. While no divorced men lived in the town, four divorced women, including the schoolteacher, did. Most single women worked to support themselves. Only six did not, and all these lived with some family member. Those who worked filled traditional female jobs. Four were teachers, one of whom was the principal as well. Three women were dressmakers; one was a milliner. Ten of the women, including three young women between the ages of fourteen and seventeen, worked as waitresses, maids, or cooks. The remaining single women were employed as salesclerks in the stores, except for one, who was a nurse. Only one single woman, a thirty-nine-year-old dressmaker, lived alone. The others either boarded at the hotel where they worked or, in the case of the principal, lived at the hotel rather than maintaining a residence alone, or they lived with a sister or another relative or boarded with a private family. Women workers ranged in age from fourteen to forty-five; seventeen were thirty or younger. Seven were thirty-one or older.

The single men of the town, on the other hand, had more diversity in employment and lived alone more frequently. Of the forty-two unattached men in Kadoka, thirteen owned businesses, five worked for others in positions of responsibility (e.g., town marshal, priest), twenty-three were clerks or laborers, and one had an independent income. Five of the thirteen business owners were under twenty-five, as were eleven of the twenty-three clerks and laborers. Seventeen single men lived alone, while seven boarded in hotels or private homes. The remainder lived with relatives.

Only three of the forty-six married women in Kadoka worked for wages, namely the manager of the telephone company, the postmistress, and the only stenographer in town. The first two had been working widows until they remarried in Kadoka. The manager of the phone company had just remarried before the census was taken. The postmistress had remarried two years before and had appointed her new husband assistant postmaster. The telephone company manager employed her twenty-one-year-old daughter as a "hello girl"; the postmistress had a seven-year-old son at home. Both performed their jobs within the home. The stenographer had no children and worked at a real estate office. Another married woman had owned the town millinery shop until the fall of 1909. She gave birth to a daughter in the late winter of 1909 but maintained her shop in a building downtown for six months after. She sold out to a young single woman, who then moved into town with her sister and took over the business.

The married men of the town worked in a wide variety of occupations. Twenty-four of the forty-six owned their own businesses, eight managed the businesses of others (as a railroad agent, bank cashier, or grain elevator manager), six were laborers, and one was a minister. Six town-dwellers listed themselves as farmers on the census reports. Almost half of the owners were under thirty-five (eleven of twenty-four). Four of the married laborers were under thirty-five, as were three of the six farmers. The remaining owners were fairly evenly distributed in the age groups ranging from thirty-six to fifty. Only five of the twenty-four owners were over fifty, and only one laborer fit into that category.

The community overall was, in fact, quite young. Ninety-eight of the 222 residents were between 18 and 35 years of age, and there were fifty-eight children under eighteen. Thus nearly three quarters of the population (70.7 percent) was under thirty-five.[6]

Kadoka's appearance was different from that of the settled communities of the Midwest. No trees or real lawns as yet decorated the town, and people did not live in neat little cottages side by side. Almost half the people (45 percent) had jumped beyond the railroad plat and lived on unnamed streets beyond. These people built their homes in a scattered fashion on one-acre lots. The remaining 55 percent lived in the platted town, but 39 percent of those (forty-seven people) lived on Main Street either in the hotels or in their business buildings. The remaining seventy-four people lived in unpretentious houses sprinkled here and there on named streets. D Street, for example, contained only two houses. First and Second avenues had three each. B Street had one "residence" that appears to have been the livery stable, where the owner and his employee lived as well as worked. Except on Main Street, where buildings rubbed shoulders, people certainly would not have felt hemmed in by their neighbors.[7]

Amenities were few. There was no water system in 1910; Kadoka residents patronized the water wagon or drew water from a town well on Main Street. There was also no electricity. Families used kerosene lamps and cooked on wood, kerosene, or coal stoves, which were also the sole sources of winter heating. Many residents kept cows and pigs in town. Town lots contained outhouses, and they also had small out-buildings to shelter the animals and store coal and other items. The smell was frequently bad, and the manure piles and carcasses of dead animals posed an obvious threat to health. The town doctor made up the Board of Health, and he inspected lots and alleys and urged people to clean up. The *Press* reported such actions and repeatedly mentioned the sanitation problems the town suffered from. Women followed the usual pattern of spring cleaning and, while the *Press* editors complained about the inconvenience of the women's annual ritual, they applauded when such efforts included the residents' yards. Enough people gardened that the *Press* could report in April that gardening was "the rage" in Kadoka.[8]

The men of the town worked long days. Merchants opened their stores early in the morning and closed them late in the evening. At one point a group of seven businessmen placed an advertisement in the *Press* announcing their decision to close at eight every night except Saturday, when they planned to remain open as long as customers appeared. Kadoka businesses apparently closed on Sunday (not all towns followed this pattern), although the post office was open then and businesses like the meat market, which sold a fresh product to homes without refrigeration, may have opened briefly to supply the Sunday dinner table. Men ate three meals a day at home but spent most of their time downtown.[9]

Most married women worked hard in their homes, cooking, maintaining the home, and caring for the children. Only three women in Kadoka had hired help, although most housework had to be done without the aid of technology. Four women took in boarders, and only one of these women had hired help to assist her. Two of the four had teenage or older daughters at home, who may have helped with the load. Eight other women had adult relatives living with them, and seven of the relatives worked in town. It is not clear whether they contributed to the household budget. Certainly they made more work for the unsalaried women at home.[10]

The function of the school in town life differed somewhat from that of the country schoolhouse. Because there were so many other social outlets, the school did not serve as the central place for entertainment as it did in the country. Instead it stood as a symbol of progress and town pride at the end of Main Street. In July 1908 an election created

The interior of a hotel in Belvidere in Stanley County.

the independent Kadoka school district, and two weeks later the district elected its first school board. The members included the railroad agent, the owner of the confectionary store, three farmer entrepreneurs (men who had claims on the edge of town but who also had business interests in town), a bank cashier and federal land commissioner, and one of the editors of the Kadoka *Press*, who served as the clerk. The men ranged in age from thirty-three to forty-three and all were active in the commercial interests and social life of the town. Their first order of business was the proposal of the bond issue necessary to build a schoolhouse and the rental of a temporary schoolroom until the new building was completed. School opened in September with thirty-five pupils in attendance and, the *Press* noted, "prospects for double that." The bond issue passed unanimously, all thirty-two voters supporting the $2,800 indebtedness. A variety of problems slowed completion of the project, but on January 3, 1910, the new two-story, four-room building was dedicated. In 1910 the board included owners of a hardware store and a clothing store. The treasurer's seat remained in a banker's hands; the original treasurer had "removed" from the town, as the saying went, and his replacement at the bank became his replacement on the board. The board demonstrated its concern for good education through its hiring of well-qualified (often college-educated) and experienced personnel. In April 1909 the board published a statement announcing strict standards for students who wanted to pass from one grade to another or to enter the ninth grade. To equal the standards of east river high schools was a matter of pride, although the Kadoka school only offered ten grades.[11]

The church was another important institution in Kadoka. The Presbyterians were the first to organize a congregation, but the Catholics were not far behind.[12] The Methodists established the third church in the community. There was some concern that Kadoka could not support two Protestant churches, but the Methodists sent a permanent minister anyway.[13] The need for churches was generally accepted. Just as homesteaders who may not have been especially religious at home supported church organization in the country, so too did townspeople in their communities. People of all faiths contributed to build the Catholic church in Kadoka, for example, and the entire community patronized the fund-raisers held regularly by all three churches. The

Press helped with church promotion in August 1908, promising to give fifty cents to the building fund of either Kadoka church for each new subscription (the Methodists had not yet arrived). The offer was a generous one; the *Press* cost only a dollar a year.[14]

Town-dwellers were more likely than homesteaders to have a formally organized church. The Home Mission boards of the various Protestant denominations tried to provide preachers to all, but practicality dictated that towns would be better served. Travelling ministers had a difficult time reaching the scattered schoolhouses where homesteaders met to worship, but towns, especially railroad towns of some size, could usually depend on regular Sunday worship and might even have a resident minister. The Reverend D. S. Brown arrived in Kadoka in 1906 and preached to Presbyterians and other Protestants in the Johnson store building, the Harry Hammond home, the Dacotah Hotel, and elsewhere. The group began raising funds for their own church building soon after their formal organization in June 1907, and their building was dedicated in June 1908 with a $365 debt remaining, although $160 of that had been pledged. During this time Reverend Brown served other towns on the rail line as well. The Presbyterian Board of Home Missions provided most of his support. In February 1909 the *Press* reported that the central organization had thus far provided $3,000 in financial aid to Brown's field, but local contributions also aided the effort, of course. Because of the Presbyterian commitment, Kadoka area residents had weekly preaching at regular hours, a Thursday-night prayer service, and a minister on call to serve their needs.[15]

The Catholic church was also on the Kadoka scene early. Although the *Press* did not recount its early history in the area, it did cover the laying of the cornerstone for the new building in August 1908. A large number of people from the east river town of Tyndall had settled on farms nearby and in Kadoka itself. They tended to be Bohemian or Irish Catholics, and they quickly established a church to serve their needs. The priest, Father McNaboe, actively promoted his religion in the town, writing a column for the *Press* on the Catholic faith. He castigated the "faithless" who had separated from the true church at the time of the Reformation. Such a statement surely rankled the Protestants, and the column did not have a long run. Simple time constraints may have been another explanation for the column's disappearance, however, for Father McNaboe served a number of mission parishes in the area besides the Kadoka church.[16]

The Catholic church appears to have had fewer activities than either of the Protestant churches, but when Catholic events were covered, they were handled enthusiastically and in great detail. The *Press* also gave detailed coverage to the activities of individual Catholics in the area and appeared to work well with them.[17] Perhaps the more-closed society of Catholicism led to fewer such communitywide activities. Other than for the annual bazaar in the fall, Catholics did not extend open invitations for all to attend their services or related activities; their Altar Society and Holy Name Society were more religious and less social in nature. Although their church operated in greater isolation, however, individual Catholics worked hard for the community in secular endeavors.[18]

The Methodists organized a congregation in June 1909. Reverend Royce, the district superintendent of the Black Hills area, came to town and perfected the organization. It began with a dozen members. Repeating the assurances first given in February, when a "scout" for the church had assessed the need for a Methodist congregation, Reverend Royce stated that his intention was not to hurt the Presbyterians but only to "hold the field."[19] He promised that services would not conflict with scheduled Presbyterian meetings. In September 1909 a permanent minister from Indiana arrived and began preaching in the schoolhouse. Within six months, the two Protestant churches were holding worship at the same time on Sunday mornings and evenings, but relations appeared to be cordial. The Methodist minister spoke at a Presbyterian gathering and one Easter the Presbyterians held an afternoon service only and joined the Methodists at night. Both Protestant groups opened their doors to the community and depended on the public to finance many of their good works.[20]

For both Protestant churches, the ladies aids played a vital role in the support of the church and its work. Presbyterian and Methodist women of the ladies aids dedicated themselves to an endless string of dinners, socials, mission teas, bazaars, and sales, and they cooperated on scheduling so that they never competed for the community's attention. Notices for such meetings often included an invitation for all women to attend. Some women without official church affiliation must have responded, because the Methodist ladies reported an attendance of sixteen and more at their sewing meetings.[21]

The town ladies aids differed from those in the country in a number of ways. First, their meetings were exclusively for women. Second, while country ladies aids held box socials in the school to raise funds for church projects, town women had a far wider range of fund-raising possibilities. The Presbyterian women held theme socials (one a poverty social, where all were to dress in rags, another an "experience social," where the members had to raise a dollar and explain how they did it) and dinners at which generous meals were served for twenty-five cents. They also held ten-cent mission teas, served dinner to the public on circus day and election day, and made goods for Christmas and sold them in conjunction with a chicken-pie dinner. The Methodists tried to find other appealing activities that would lure the public without duplicating Presbyterian efforts. They, too, held theme socials, served public dinners, and began a sewing program to help raise funds. The Methodist women gathered every two weeks and worked on orders for sewing placed by families who paid for the service. They advertised unbeatable quality and prices. There is no indication of how the three dressmakers in town felt about the competition. The Methodist ladies aid also instituted a Saturday baked-goods sale that rotated from store to store. They advertised its location in the *Press* each week and urged the other women in town to come in and buy and in that way avoid cooking on Sunday.[22]

The ladies aids made a surprising amount of money through their activities. The Presbyterian Christmas bazaar in 1909 netted them seventy-nine dollars—fifty dollars from the sale of goods made at home by the members and donated to the cause and twenty-nine dollars from the proceeds of the chicken-pie dinner. Another dinner with a "fish pond," in which people fished for prizes from a pool, made thirty-five dollars for the group. The bandana social given by the Methodist ladies aid on a stormy March night put twenty-five dollars into their treasury, "in spite of bad roads keeping people at home." The Presbyterian women's funds built a belfry, painted the church, and supplied it with necessary equipment.[23]

Kadoka also had a wide variety of nonreligious formal institutions and social groups, which tended to be divided by gender, although some groups were mixed. There appears to have been little exclusivity beyond gender, however. The great variety of organizations in Kadoka provided almost constant opportunities for sociability. During some seasons it would have been possible for the average Kadoka male to be absent from home every evening. The average married woman would be more likely to spend an afternoon or two and at least one evening away from home per week.[24] Men and women met in same-sex groups, although there were many more groups available to men, including three lodges, a fire company, formal and informal baseball teams, a tennis club, a band and a junior band, political clubs (especially in election years), a short-lived boxing club, and an ad hoc group that planned the Old Settlers and Cowboys Reunion. When the activities of the Kadoka Kommercial Klub are included in the list, it becomes obvious that men, especially, led complex and busy lives.

A survey of male associations demonstrates the flexibility of membership in the small town as well as the interrelationship of groups. Two of the men's lodges were active at the time the *Press* began publication. The Masons had fifteen members, and the officers included the town photographer and early editor of the *Reporter*, a real estate man with farm interests, a bank president who ran a hotel and a ranch, the druggist; the Presbyterian minister, a farmer, and a housepainter. The list of new officers elected in December 1908 included the assistant postmaster, the owner of the harness shop, the manager of one of the chain lumberyards, an elderly farmer, a blacksmith, and the owner of the confectionary store. The Masons met the first and third Mondays of each month but were not particularly active as a group in the community. The list of the Masons' officers included men who also served as school board members, town officials, and directors of the Stanley County Fair Association.[25]

The Modern Woodmen of America (MWA) were more visible, sponsoring box socials and other entertainments to raise funds for their lodge. A few of the officers of the MWA also held offices in the Masons, but the Woodmen appear to have had a broader appeal and a more diverse membership. The town doctor belonged, as did one editor of the *Press*, a farmer who ran the water wagon in town during the winter, a store clerk, two real estate men, and the railway agent. New members inducted at one meeting included the manager of the grain elevator, two butchers, and a clothing store owner. The membership included active Catholics as well as active Protestants. Woodmen officers also

A pioneer family's Christmas tree in their home in Presho in Lyman County in 1909.

The children first Tree at Home

served their community in other positions: some were school board members, town officials, or officers of the Stanley County Fair Association and the Kadoka Kommercial Klub. The lodge met on the first and third Tuesdays of each month.[26]

The third lodge was not organized until May 1910. The Knights of Pythias lodge was organized in May 1910 with twenty members, some of whose names appear on the lists of both the Masons and the MWA. Store owners, a banker, and the Methodist minister mingled with the pool hall manager, the barbers, and a number of farmers. The officers of this lodge, too, included men who also served on the school board, the town government, and the Stanley County Fair Association.[27]

The story is the same for the other formally organized male groups. Few appear to have been exclusive. The small population ensured that almost everyone who wished could belong to at least one group. Men who had been recognized as leaders in one area tended to take leadership roles in other areas, and they tended to be young, indicating the relationship between business careers and club memberships.

The tennis club, whose presence in a raw new town seems incongruous, boasted twenty-five members. They built their own courts south of the depot. The members competed with each other and also participated in an annual regional tournament that included Murdo and Midland players. The men involved in the club included both *Press* editors, a restaurateur turned homesteader, the railroad agent, the Presbyterian minister, a Catholic merchant, and one of the town's real estate agents. All of these names but one also appear as officers or active participants in church or town affairs.[28]

Some men in the community did not belong to any groups and therefore did not appear to participate actively in town affairs. They were all Catholic and did contribute to the church, as their names were included on committee lists for a Catholic fund-raising fair. Frank Simek, who was the owner of one of the saloons, the Rohan brothers, early Kadoka businessmen who ran a livery stable and blacksmith shop, and two men of the Solon family, both railroad workers, fail to appear on lists of officers or participants. Nor did these people participate in the short-lived gold-mining expedition that thirty-two members of the community undertook in May 1909.[29]

These Catholic men were not ostracized, however, and their activities did make the news. When Frank Simek married in Scotland,

South Dakota, the *Press* carried news of his departure for the ceremony and, after the event, copied the description of the wedding from the Scotland paper. The Rohan brothers received a glowing front-page tribute that lauded their pioneering business efforts after they announced their plans to sell out and move to homesteads to farm. J. J. Solon, the head of the large Solon family, was the first Kadoka resident to purchase an automobile, and the *Press* described it in some detail. One Solon son appeared regularly in the paper because he played baseball for the town team. The other, however, was not included on any list of members or officers.[30] The coverage of social news unconnected with clubs indicates the importance that the "informal" community continued to have. Although some men were not joiners and held no memberships, they were still considered part of the community and their activities made the news.

Women's organizations tended to have less-elaborate organizational structures than male groups; the lists of officers include far fewer names and make women's social relationships harder to identify. Active women from the organized churches led their respective ladies aids. The two groups in town that were not church affiliated were the Excelsior Club and the WCTU. The Excelsior Club was organized in September 1908 after a visit from the state representative of the Federation of Women's Clubs. Eight attended the first meeting. The woman elected president was Grace Stuart, the wife of the bank cashier and an active member of the Presbyterian church. Maria Crawford, the wife of the town baker, was chosen vice-president. The doctor's wife, Martha Newcomer, was elected secretary-treasurer. Stuart and Newcomer were young women with no children. Crawford was in her sixties with only one daughter living at home, thirty-year-old Ella, a dressmaker. The group frequently met at the Stevenson home. Libby Stevenson kept house for her merchant husband and cared for their young son, born sometime in 1908. The club advertised that membership was open to anyone upon application to the president. Other names associated with the club over the years included a woman who worked for the Indian service on the reservation, school teachers, the school principal, the druggist's wife, and America Serr, wife of a bank cashier, who became an important figure in the club after her family moved to Kadoka in 1909. At least one Catholic woman belonged to the club. Few of the women listed had children at home, and those who did had few. Mrs. Dorn, the druggist's wife, had no children after nine years of marriage. The members of the Excelsior Club, then, tended to be educated professionals, such as teachers, or wives with few encumbrances.[31]

The members met regularly for entertainment and edification. They adopted the Bay View Reading Course, a prepared study packet for women's clubs, for study. They also provided opportunities for genteel socializing for their members. The accounts of the gatherings include mention of "dainty" two-course and three-course luncheons, fancy-work, and other amusements. They also met to honor members who married or were leaving town. On one occasion the Excelsior Club sponsored a music recital in the opera house that featured a performer from a neighboring town accompanied by Grace Stuart on the piano and the Excelsior Club Quartette. The women were also active in reform activities, managing the Equal Suffrage campaign in town and working to provide a park for the community. They convinced the Milwaukee Road to donate land and furnished the remaining items themselves.[32]

The local branch of the Women's Christian Temperance Union (WCTU) was formed in 1910 after a representative from Chicago spoke at the Presbyterian church. The wife of the Presbyterian minister hosted the first meeting, and all ladies, whether or not they were members, were invited to attend. They began to plan fund-raisers, with coffee, sandwiches, and table games as the main feature of each. They also served coffee and sandwiches on election day. The membership of the WCTU and the Excelsior Club apparently overlapped to some extent, because they held at least one joint gathering to honor a newly married member.[33]

The Eastern Star lodge was also organized in 1910. It was primarily a women's organization that served as the Masons' auxiliary, but it included males in its governing hierarchy. In most cases, married couples held the offices. This group did not receive much attention from the *Press*. Perhaps, like the Masons, they preferred to operate out of the public eye.[34]

Another town group that included both men and women was the Kadoka Dramatic Club. Organized in the winter of 1910, this club at first performed popular comedies to benefit the Modern Woodmen lodge. Their first effort at the opera house drew a standing-room-only crowd and netted the Woodmen $46.45. The success of the home talent entertainment prompted the formation of a more permanent group that began to prepare other plays for the town. The Dramatic Club travelled to the Willard neighborhood and performed under the auspices of the ladies aid there. Members also entertained themselves with group picnics and gatherings. The women involved in an April 1910 presentation included two salesclerks, a hotel cashier, and the local milliner. One of the grocers' wives played the piano. The men included the printer at the *Press* office, a barber, a real estate man, a hardware store owner, and a farmer.[35]

Not all community activity depended on formal organization. The "informal" community survived as town residents gathered for impromptu entertainments that were open to everyone. In August 1909 the men of the town played a series of baseball games, choosing teams on the basis of marital status—single men versus "the benedicts," those who were married.[36] On another occasion, the young single men of the town planned a "Big Blow-Out," as they termed it, a dance for all to attend at the opera house.[37] The *Press* carried frequent notices for dances that seemed to have no specific sponsor but ladies were encouraged to bring baskets. Some Kadoka residents organized a dance band in January 1911. The musicians included the printer at the *Press* office on the drums and the saleswoman at a local grocery store on the piano. Both were members of the Kadoka Dramatic Club as well.[38]

On one occasion a trainload of Omaha boosters stopped in Kadoka to visit the businessmen and urge them to do their wholesale trading in Omaha. The entire town prepared for the visit, the band played, and cowboys from nearby ranches galloped down Main Street and put on a show. A number of country people were in town to observe the festivities. After the Omaha men left, a large crowd from town and country milled about, not quite ready to go home. Some men chose sides for pick-up ball games, while others watched the cowboys put on a bucking bronco show behind the livery barn. A careless smoker started a fire, and the fire company with its chemical engine added to the amusements. The day's excitement, planned and impromptu, satisfied everyone.[39]

Because Kadoka was located on the rail line, travelling shows from faraway places could reach the town easily. Comedy companies, drama companies, lecturers, and moving-picture shows frequently enter-

tained at the Kadoka Opera House. The town people could easily distinguish a good show from a poor production. Most shows were greeted
enthusiastically, although legitimate shows that differed too much
from popular tastes received mild criticism. Such was the case when
the great classical violinist, Ole Theobaldi, performed at the opera
house. A full house heard him play, but the *Press* remarked in its next
issue that the violinist, while interesting, would have made a greater
hit had he played a more popular grade of music.[40]

Kadoka was a busy place in the early years of settlement. Just as
businessmen enjoyed being in on the ground floor of economic developments, so too did town-dwellers relish their opportunities to shape
the developing social life of the community. It seemed to them that all
things were possible if people were only willing to work hard for the
future. In Kadoka, men and women, Catholics and Protestants, merchants and laborers, all participated in the many projects designed to
do just that. For many it was satisfying work. Because the town was
small and relations among residents personal, individuals could see
the results of their efforts and knew that their participation mattered.
They had arrived on the last great frontier as strangers pursuing individual dreams. From that chaotic beginning, Kadoka residents built a
workable and enriching social world—a community. In the years before the drought, their faith in their ability to maintain and improve
their town was boundless.

8. WE'VE REACHED THE LAND OF DROUTH AND HEAT

Admiring distant claims in Tripp County near Colome in 1910.

Many were the disappointments and heartaches and ever battle with the elements of nature and insecurity. Grain seeded in the spring didn't sprout until September when there was light rain. . . . Many people became disheartened and moved away. Others grit their teeth and remained—surely they thought, next year would be better, which is the eternal hope of those who suffer. This is Home, they said. Here our children have been born— some have died and lie buried in the soil that has had no rain. Surely the Lord is still merciful—the rains will come and the land and the graves will be green and the soil will produce and yield and increase our wealth and health and honor.

Clara Bentley Teter,
Stanley County homesteader

The Indian and ranching societies that preceded the homesteaders' agricultural society had simple economies in that they relied upon what the west river country produced in greatest abundance: grass. Grass dominated the region because it was perfectly suited to the conditions of precipitation, sunshine, and temperature that prevailed on the high plains. The agricultural economy that the twentieth-century homesteaders imposed on the plains was more complex. It had relatively little tolerance for variation in environmental factors, the most critical of which were the amount and timing of precipitation. But the fragility of their world was not apparent to the homesteaders, who buried whatever doubts they may have had beneath the frontier ideology of optimism and hard work. Doubt was the natural predator of the pioneer spirit, and settlers hunted doubters as ruthlessly as they hunted coyotes and rattlesnakes. Doubts and fears and failure did not fit the settlers' image of themselves and the empire they intended to build. For the first few years of the migration, abnormally high rains had lulled even the doubters, but with statistical inevitability the plains environment corrected its course in the years 1910 and 1911. The drought of those years desiccated the once-thriving immigration and drastically altered the meaning of the homesteading experience for those who participated as well as for those who observed it from afar. The farms, the towns, and the social world the settlers had so optimistically built and so carefully nurtured were threatened with total ruin. As the drought deepened year by year, the region's greatest promoters, the editors, strove to explain the causes of the settlers' defeat

Where would you go? Back to the place where you were dissatisfied with
when you came out here? What assurances have you that it is going to
better your condition this year? . . . Say, are you not afraid that the ghosts
of the old-time homesteader who went through the privations of real hard-
ships in taming what is now old settled high priced land will haunt you
and make you feel like a 29 cent quitter?

Davenport *News*,
reprinted by the Kadoka *Press*
June 30, 1911

and to devise solutions. Many homesteaders abandoned their claims, while those who stayed were forced to struggle for mere survival. Some tried to organize relief efforts for immediate aid, but no centralized and effective program ever developed, so most settlers were on their own. Although the drought lessened somewhat in 1912, the optimism and energy of the boom years vanished. The remaining settlers recognized that the country would not yield easily to their efforts. They had not conquered nature; it had conquered them.

The years immediately preceding the drought had been good ones. In five short years, the region had been transformed from open range into intensively cultivated, geometrically subdivided farmland. In the spring of 1909, the atmosphere of the west river country was charged with energy and hope. Local newspaper editors delighted in the new pastoral scene.[1] They issued glowing notes on crop prospects as each season progressed. The Midland *Western Star* reported the happy news in June 1909 that "Never was there a more luxurious growth of everything in our part of the country than now." In July the editor announced that "crops of all kinds in Stanley county promise an abundant yield," and rhapsodized, "A trip out in the country these days reveals a picture of beauty and prosperity such as gladdens the heart of every resident of this end of the state. Driving across the unfenced country the fields of living green stretch away on either side to the horizon, as fair a land as lies outdoors."[2]

The rural correspondents frequently included crop notes in their neighborhood news columns. They, too, charted the progress of growing crops and area farmers. The Pleasant Hill correspondent reported the corn there to be good, "just as good as can be raised anywhere." The writer from Lakeside had termed the 1908 season a success: "We all have our threshing done and are well pleased with what this gumbo can produce." Great pride in the homesteaders' accomplishments marked these reports. While empire building was difficult, the rewards seemed to be substantial.[3]

Not everyone shared in the progress and self-congratulation, however. Life was hard on the claims, resources were often scarce, and failures inevitably occurred. Windstorms and hail devastated small sections here and there, taking crops and gardens and leaving some families in dire straits. Prairie fires occasionally burned out families, and sickness or accident claimed livestock. But during the good years settlers conceptualized the problem of failure in a way that harmonized with their ideology of optimism and hard work. Basically, they recognized two types of failure—the temporary and the personal. Fire, tornado, wind, and other disasters of short duration tested the mettle of their victims, but the true pioneers rose to the challenge. The most exquisite personal tragedy was subsumed in the pioneer mythology of heroism. On the other side of the equation were the untalented, the witless, the ne'er-do-wells, the whiners, and the malingerers, whose character defects, the settlers believed, explained their lasting failure on the last great frontier. Their lack of success was not the fault of the country. Local observers suggested that malcontents should return to their former homes.

During the late summer of 1909, however, a warning of the struggle that lay ahead visited the claims of the west river country. Dry weather and hot winds burned crops and frayed tempers. Anxious notes appeared in the rural correspondents' columns. Lakeside, in Stanley County, reported "awful dry" weather and yellowing corn leaves in the August 8, 1909, issue of the Midland *Western Star*. Indian Creek, also in Stanley County, worried about the corn and related the difficulties of finding water for stock in that neighborhood. A shower fell before the next issue appeared, and all the rural correspondents mentioned it, the writer from Driggers revealing much with the line, "It gave the farmers new hope." By August 20 the rural writers worried in print about the hot, dry winds and evaluated the effects of the earlier rainfall on the corn. Could it be saved or was it too late? The editor of the paper, trying to put the best face on things, reported, "Returns from the threshing now in general progress here indicates a much better average and quality than was anticipated." Finally, late in the fall, the rains and snows came, ending the dry period. The settlers heaved a collective sigh of relief and turned their attention to the next season. The correspondent from Mitchell Creek summed up the experience: "The best news in this valley is that the water drouth is ended; prairie fires are impossible, so are dirt blizzards and the dust blankets are discarded, and the white blanket of promise for the coming year has cheered the pluckiest settlers and ranchmen that ever deserved these blessings of the beautiful. The valley never had more stayers, and these stayers never had more confidence in their near prosperity . . . so 'all is well that ends well.'"[4]

Although settlers generally seemed confident that all had ended well, the dry period in 1909 apparently revived discussion about the value of the country for agriculture. Old doubts surfaced and nagging fears were discussed over the winter. Such hesitation did not sit well with the editor of the Midland paper. In January 1910 he attacked those who questioned or worried: "The present fall of snow is worth many thousands of dollars to the Stanley county farmer and only the one that plowed his land deep last fall will reap the benefits this year in a bountiful crop while the ones that came to town seven times a week 'after the mail' and sit around telling how worthless the country is, will be in the same boat this year." When planting time arrived, the editor reported on the confidence local farmers had in their soil and their future. "Most all of them are putting up fences, building dams and enlarging their houses and out buildings," he noted. The tone was meant to be reassuring, and certainly some saw the touch of drought as an aberration. Land values continued to rise, at least according to the Midland *Western Star* editor, and the rural correspondent from the Pheba neighborhood reported the sale of an unimproved quarter section of land for $2,500, or $15.65 an acre, in March 1910.[5]

The problem, however, was that the dry weather did not end. When drought again stalked the land during the summer of 1910, people worried and talked. Crops had been short in 1909; another year of diminished yields, they knew, would be damaging, even dangerous. Some editors leaped to the defense of the country and blamed the farmers rather than the climate. Fred Mix, editor of the Ft. Pierre *Fair-*

play, published reports of farmers who had good crops, and he praised their methods. Mix reported a "glorious stalk of alfalfa" sent to him by S. Oliver, an area homesteader: "That doesn't sound as though Stanley county had gone entirely to the bow wows, does it? But Mr. Oliver is a farmer who farms." The next issue of the *Fairplay* contained a similar item. C. H. Leggett, a homesteader on Antelope Creek, reported to the paper that "his crops have never looked better." He went on to say that his neighbors "who have gone about it right" also had excellent crops. Editor Mix concluded this story with an opinion of his own. "It is the same old story. . . . The man who farms gets a crop, whether the season is wet or dry, while the man who tills the soil while sitting on a box at the corner grocery, never raises anything, and then cusses the country and the weather." Other editors maintained their silence, perhaps afraid to publicize the drought by condemning its victims. The editors had to walk a fine line. Their papers were important instruments of promotion for the region, but the editors also had to live with the settlers. When they saw real hardships caused by the weather rather than individual failure, they might elect to remain silent.[6]

Rural correspondents were not as closemouthed. The author of the Lincoln Township notes that appeared in the Murdo *Coyote* remarked that harvesters and threshing machines in that neighborhood "would take a rest this season." The Eastern School notes reported farmers taking their stock to the White River for water or hauling water from that source. And "A. Jay Soddy," an anonymous contributor, described his disenchantment in a poem entitled "The Soddy's Lament." "Oh, but I'm weary of case hardened skies, scorching south winds and land agents lies," he began, and he went on to denounce the weeds, the snakes, the heat, and the farming methods advocated by the editors. "I am tired of 'dry farming' with its plowing so deep, and I'm weary of sowing where no one can reap." After an imagined revel with "cold lager beer" that bolstered his courage, "Soddy" turned on the land to tell it to "go to the Devil" but feared that he might learn a terrible truth—that he was already in hell with no escape, "for of hell around here there is more than a trace." The soddy poet concluded with a complaint growing more and more common among the homesteaders: "In the meantime I'm hungry and thirsty and hot, and I'm sick of the country and sick of my lot." The poem appeared on the front page of

Fred Mix's *Fairplay* three weeks after his series on successful farmers who knew how to work.[7]

Farmers who kept records evaluated the 1910 season according to their location. The Miller family in Perkins County had a fairly prosperous year. Rettie Hayes, whose family lived in Meade County, recorded yields of ten bushels per acre of spring wheat, nine per acre of winter wheat, five per acre of oats, and six per acre of speltz. They had few acres under cultivation, but they did get a small crop. John Johnson, farming in eastern Pennington County, had forty acres in crops by 1910 but raised only "ten bushel of poor corn." Because he had twelve cattle, three horses, three pigs, and fifty hens to feed, besides his family, such a crop failure was disastrous.[8]

The homesteaders' ability to survive crop failure varied. Some had come with enough extra cash to get by, others had nothing. The men of some families took stock to water and pasture in Nebraska and other places where crops and grass had been more successful. Reports of destitution were rare in 1910, although a statewide syndicated news service reported that a family of four had been found in bed, near starvation, on their claim in the Camp Crook vicinity. They had little coal and only a bit of rice on hand. One child, the report said, "was literally nothing but skin and bone." He was taken to town for medical care. "The county will look after the needs of the family until spring," the report noted.[9]

The second summer of drought prompted thoughtful people to consider its causes and potential cures. Some continued to maintain that failure due to dry conditions was a personal problem that could be licked with greater attention to duty. Others raised pseudoscientific themes as old as agricultural settlement on the plains. One rural correspondent, after happily reporting several showers that had started the grass growing again and aided prospects for a corn crop, concluded that "There is too much prairie in this country and when the ground is broken up there will be no more hot winds. . . . The question of wells will be settled when the country is broken up and the moisture is retained instead of running off into the draws and creeks."[10]

A contributor to the Philip *Weekly Review*, E. L. Keith, the local lumberman, responded to the growing confusion and discontent with "A Sermon for the Discouraged" that many other papers reprinted. In his lengthy analysis of conditions and prospects, Keith replied to "the knocker . . . abroad in the land." While his piece was a spirited defense of the country and a holy injunction to stay and do the farmer's hard duty, it also admitted that conditions were different in western South Dakota and always would be. Keith called for the use of scientific farming methods and adaptation to the land. "Our problems here are very different from what most of us have encountered before coming here," he wrote, but "we will learn to know our land and its problems in time; and when nature once comes to have a familiar look to us, we will go forward to grapple with the problems of agriculture joyously and with confidence in our strength. We will not only learn much about conservation of moisture, but we will learn much about the crops and their adaptation to the conditions that we find here." He rated "knockers" with the "adverse conditions that characterize this new country" and consigned them to "the beaten track . . . some little eastern town," because "they are not the stuff of which nation builders are made." Keith concluded his exhortation with an appeal to pride and duty. "The real empire builder will stay right here. They will grapple with the difficulties of pioneer life joyously, like 'the strong man who goes forth to run a race.' Undaunted by obstacles in their path and never for one moment discouraged at seeming defeats, they will go on with the work yet hardly commenced."[11]

E. L. Keith's message may have inspired some of the homesteaders, but others were too discouraged or too desperate to listen. While there are no reliable figures on the number who left the country or began to discuss the proposition in late 1910, remarks made in the newspaper columns indicate a growing problem. The correspondent from the Maximilian neighborhood observed that the residents there were putting up ice during a January cold snap and concluded, "This means they will be here for summer at least." In the same issue the editor commented on a resolution before the legislature to repeal the herd law during the winter months and reinstate it for the growing season: "The measure has some merit and certainly at the present time when so few people are here it would seem to be fair and favorable."[12]

The papers also reveal the desperation, confusion, and disappointment of those remaining. Some settlers indicated their willingness to try any new methods that might help their cause. News of a dry-farming congress to be held in Pierre prompted one rural writer to remark that "Our entire valley will turn out for the 'Dry Farming meeting' at Pierre if the organization will furnish transportation." Others lashed out at scapegoats. The editor of the Midland *Western Star*, obviously bitter about the events of the past year, wrote a glowing account of the arrival of an Iowa farmer with all his machinery and household goods. He weighed this man's experience and potential against the quality of other settlers and found the others lacking. "Mr. James," he noted, "is not a retired soda expert, or broken down bartender, neither is he a dissatisfied loan shark or a stock broker seeking diversion. We have had plenty of such farmers. Mr. James is a farmer with years of experience and has come to farm his place." [13]

In this climate of disillusionment, doubt, and confusion, the spring of 1911 arrived early and was unusually warm and much too dry. It was the beginning of a growing season that would exceed all others for drought, heat, and wind. This was the season that shattered any remaining illusions about easy prosperity or empire building overnight. The most seasoned veterans of plains farming quailed in the face of this disaster, and the strong joined the weak in a rush for the border. Those who stayed perhaps did so in the spirit of an old plains folk song first sung two generations before but revived in Stanley County in 1911: "We do not live, we only stay. We are too poor to get away." [14]

In the six years he had farmed in Gregory and Tripp counties, Oscar Micheaux had plowed and planted industriously. By 1911 he had 410 acres planted and was renting out another 110 to another farmer. He assessed his crop yields as having been fair to good every year, although 1910 had been dry. Land values were rising in his area and he felt reasonably successful. The first inkling of trouble came in May when a field of spelt, so green and fresh earlier, began to look "peculiar." When Micheaux examined the plants, the soil seemed very dry, although it had rained ten days before. The wind came from the south but brought no rain. In mid-June a heavy downpour soaked Gregory County, but Micheaux's flax crop in Tripp County received no rain. The next day hot winds began to blow fiercely from the south, continuing for seven weeks without interruption. As Micheaux later wrote, "I had never before, during the seven years, suffered to any extent from the heat, but during that time I could not find a cool place. The wind never ceased during the night, but sounded its mournful tune without a pause. Then came a day when the small grain in T[r]ipp county was beyond redemption, and rattled as leaves in November. The atmosphere became stifling, and the scent of burning plants sickening."[15] Micheaux's flax failed and his Gregory County wheat furnished only a partial crop. His prospects were bleak. He had borrowed money to put in the crop but harvested too little to pay back the loan. Others around him fared worse and faced actual starvation. They loaded their goods and moved out. On a trip to visit friends who lived seventeen miles from his home, Micheaux passed forty-seven houses. "Only one had an occupant," he wrote.[16]

The Miller family in Perkins County faced similar disaster. For them 1911 was a year of individual as well as communal tragedy. They proved up on their claim in the early spring, but that same day the new barn burned, taking with it much of the Millers' stock, harness, seed grain, and hay. They confronted the growing season in a condition that would have made success unlikely in the best of years. The drought compounded their difficulties. Mrs. Miller and the children planted the garden as usual that spring, but the seeds blew away. The boys herded cattle, ranging farther and farther from home searching for good grass. The corn planted in 1911 never sprouted. Hot winds killed the small-grain crop that came up, and there were no grasses to cut for winter hay. The Millers, however, were determined. They did not want to sell livestock because that would be a further setback, and they doubted they would find a buyer anyway. In July, Mr. Miller decided to travel to North Dakota to some good hay land he had heard about and cut a supply there. He was gone until October.

In his absence Mrs. Miller and the children took full responsibility for the farm. Little water remained in the well, so the boys herded the stock to Grand River to drink until the river there went dry. The family worked together doing the daily chores that continued in spite of drought. By fall they were out of fuel and the children wandered across the prairie searching for combustibles. Their work continued after their father returned, since he was occupied hauling hay daily from Lemmon, the nearest railhead, fifteen miles away. The hay had to reach the farm by snowfall or there would still be nothing for the stock.

The Millers survived the dreadful year, but few others in their neighborhood remained. The first indication of depletion came on the Fourth of July. By custom, neighbors tried to be the first to wake the community with shotgun fire commemorating the holiday. In 1911 "the silences in some directions" marked empty farms. The arrival of fall brought further evidence. "So many families had moved away that there weren't enough children to keep a school open," son Henry remembered. Area parents converted an empty claim shack into a school, but it was four miles from the Miller home. The final and most painful loss came early in 1912 when beloved Uncle Charlie, a neighbor and partner in the venture from the beginning, announced his departure because, as he said, "This country is too much for me." The Millers bought him out, improving their own chances of long-term success.[17]

Homesteaders' memoirs of this period speak a litany of suffering. For months, one family ate only rabbits and cornmeal mush; another recorded a special treat served by a beloved neighbor woman known for her ability to bring cheer. She had made the usual main (and only) dish, a "pudding, wheat ground in a coffee mill, cooked for hours." But, amazingly, greens accompanied the meal. The ingenious woman had cut Russian thistles that had sprouted after a light shower and cooked them for dinner. A fresh cow provided cream for the pudding, which added to the festivities.[18] Other people reported digging up and eating the seed potatoes planted so hopefully in the spring. It became steadily more difficult to find water. The Bad River dried up until only potholes of dirty water remained. Homesteaders boiled it and stored it in jars. The Wasta *Gazette* reported that Mrs. C. J. Harris had come home to live with her folks because she could find no drinking water near her claim in northern Butte County. Farmers drove their stock long distances for water and forage.[19]

In the face of such trials, many people quit the pioneering enterprise. The correspondent from the neighborhood around the post office called Jack Daly recorded the news in a terse line: "More people leaving the country all the time." Homesteaders living near major trails saw constant reminders of the exodus. Press Seymour in Lyman County recalled that "during that summer it was seldom that you couldn't see someone from the west pass our place." The Pascoe family, who had homesteaded in eastern Pennington County, was among the migrants. They prepared food for the long journey, "locked the door, loaded the four children into the rigs and started out. . . . We drove day after day through the dust and heat without seeing any living things except an occasional band of wild horses." If they travelled alone it was because other homesteaders had beaten them out of the country. But at Fort

Pierre, she noted, "so many wagons were ahead of us that we had to wait two or three days for our turn at the ferry."[20]

The exodus was so great that entire rural communities were depopulated. Fred H. Root and his family had started a small store in 1907 and had also run the Inavale post office. They had served sixty patrons before 1911, but only four remained. The family closed the store and post office and ate the remaining grocery stock. The next available census figures, a state tally done in 1915, give some indication of the depopulation, although by 1915 some who had fled in the drought years had returned. Old Stanley County had 14,975 residents in 1910. Its citizens voted for county division in 1914, and the three counties that resulted had only 7,881 people in 1915. Perkins County, with 11,348 settlers in 1910, contained only 7,641 residents in 1915. Even Gregory County, the richest and wettest land west of the river, lost 1,142 people, 10 percent of its population, during the five-year interval between federal and state censuses.[21]

Settlers who wanted to stay were forced to find alternative sources of income. Around Midland, people gathered bones from the prairie for sale to a local firm. The men in some families opted for work in the harvest fields of richer regions. They took teams if they were strong enough and equipment if they had any, but they sometimes brought only strong backs and willing hands. In July the Wasta *Gazette* contained notes of departures, men in search of wage labor elsewhere. Mrs. Galland, who lived in Perkins County, remembered many men leaving to pick corn in states farther east to "replenish the shrinking pocket books." In October 1911 the Eureka correspondent noted only two men still home in the district—otherwise, just "old maids" and "grass widows" remained. The Dupree paper carried a story in January 1912 about a man unable to find enough work in town to support his family and with "no means to get away other than to walk." He walked the 108 miles to Mobridge in search of a job. The temperature never climbed above zero during the four-day hike, and at one point it plummeted to thirty-five degrees below zero.[22]

Other settlers took advantage of their neighbors' departure to aid their own chances for survival. Henry Miller of Perkins County recalled that once word was out that a settler had gone, neighbors went to the homesite and divided the goods left behind. The claim shack might go to the one with the biggest family—"In many cases that doubled the

size of the house." Other buildings served as stock sheds on someone else's claim. "Anything usable was taken by someone," he wrote, and that often included "books, furniture, curtains, windows and doors." The Millers and their neighbors also used the land that others had abandoned to graze their livestock. Grace Fairchild and other families in her part of Stanley County did the same thing. "We cut hay on the low land and harvested anything we could find," she later wrote. "In the years after 1911, we got enough crops from these abandoned claims to pay up the back taxes and get clear titles to the land."[23]

The Olseth family in Harding County divided their efforts to insure their survival. Mr. Olseth walked fifty miles to the railhead in Bowman, North Dakota, to get work on the railroad section. He left his wife and six small children on the claim twenty miles from a doctor and two miles from the nearest neighbor. They scoured the prairie for usable items. The boys gathered cow chips for fuel and sheared any dead sheep they found for the wool. Mrs. Olseth then cleaned it and converted it to warm clothing for the children. A neighbor bought groceries for them to supplement their diet of mush, and friends back in eastern South Dakota sent a box of clothes their children had outgrown. The pockets of each garment contained a nickel or a dime. This combination of hard work and charity pulled them through the crisis.[24]

The magnitude of the drought in 1911 was too great for it to be dismissed as an aberration. No longer did accusations of poor farming techniques provide a comforting rationalization of the disaster. The newspaper editors realized that the problem went beyond anything they had seen before, and they responded with a new argument calculated to quell the panic and halt the exodus. Many papers began to report the wide extent of the drought. The Belvidere *Times* informed its readers of the short crops predominant in Iowa and Illinois and urged them to "thank your lucky stars you are not paying five or six per acre cash rent for the use of your land" like the people in those states. The Faith *Gazette*, in an article titled "Drouth is General," appealed to its readers to observe the weather reports for the entire Northwest, noting, "This is not the only place where moisture is needed." The Davenport *News* discussed reports from "all over the country" of a "shortage of rainfall and prevalence of hot winds." Harry Lovald of the *Cheyenne Valley News* urged his neighbors to get information from back east before returning to the "wife's folks," because "It may be that your father-in-law has just about all he can take care of now, without assuming the extra burden." He reported burned crops in western Iowa and equally poor conditions in Minnesota.[25]

The same editors appealed to the homesteaders' pride, comparing them with earlier generations of pioneers, who had experienced harder times than these. The Kadoka *Press* reprinted an article published east of the river recalling the 1870s and the grasshopper plagues in that region. These pioneers, the article stated, "were of a class who knew how to face pioneer conditions and meet adversity with stout hearts and unflinching purpose and they faced conditions unknown before or since." An east river paper, the Yankton *Press and Dakotaian,* urged people west of the river and all over the state to remember their history. Eastern South Dakota had experienced hard times in the early days, and so had Iowa. "History," the editor observed, "has repeated itself in this regard in every section of our country in its early years, from the starving time of the Pilgrims in Massachusetts . . . down to the homesteaders in Stanley and Perkins counties, South Dakota. Why draw sweeping conclusions in this last case?" The Davenport *News* asked pointedly, "Say, are you not afraid that the ghosts of the old time homesteader who went through the privations of real hardships in taming what is now old settled high priced land will haunt you and make you feel like a 29 cent quitter?"[26]

Another common argument appealed to the settlers' common sense. Where are you going to go? the papers asked. Will it be better anywhere else? Harry Lovald asked his readers to consider the costs of moving and compared their situation to the transplanted alfalfa plants just becoming popular in the region. Those plants suffered root damage when moved and, because it took time for new roots to grow, their development was delayed. "The trouble with most of us," he concluded, "is a restless spirit. Instead of making opportunity come to us we are chasing our legs off running after it. Sit down and think it over before you make a move. Opportunity is coming our way. Don't be a quitter." The Pierre *Journal* mentioned the story of a Cottonwood-area homesteader who first loaded his goods for shipment to Miller, South Dakota, but he received reports of drought there so he reloaded for shipment to Pierce, Nebraska, only to receive similar reports from that region. He decided to stay on his claim.[27]

A final tactic used by the editors was the appeal to the settlers' pocketbooks. Most settlers had come to South Dakota with high expectations. They hoped to make substantial profits in a short time. Those hopes were now dashed. The editors, however, realized the potency of the dreams and tried to revive them, albeit in a modified form. They asked their readers to look back at long-settled regions. The rich families there, they claimed, were those who had withstood the adversities of early settlement. These people had sacrificed much initially but through perseverance had won out. The Pierre *Journal* commented, "The pioneers of the east who staid through the discouragements are the ones who are now wealthy and living in homes of comfort, while those who pulled out through discouragements are many of them wishing they had stayed." Harry Lovald said virtually the same thing: "Remember that the fellow who stuck in former days while the country was new in what is now old settlements was the chap who made good." The Yankton *Press and Dakotaian* reminded all that "rich rewards" had come to the "strong and steadfast" on other frontiers; the same would happen west of the river and "much quicker," too. Another east river editor applauded his west river brethren for their efforts to keep homesteaders on the claim and added, "The same thing [drought] has happened right here in Hanson county at one time and the men who have the money now are the ones that stuck it out. It means hardship and the depriving of the families of some of the good things of life, but eventually the men that stay and stick it out are the ones that will be worth the money in after years."[28]

E. L. Keith, a perennial contributor to the Philip *Review*, was frankest in his economic appeals. He addressed the issue of land values directly: "If we choose to sit down and cry, or even allow ourselves to think what could possibly happen to us now [that] the outlook is pretty bad, we are in a position where we can depreciate the value of every dollar's worth of property we have in Stanley county to less than ten cents and do it quick." Quarter sections that had sold at high prices the previous year would not find a buyer at any price unless the settlers worked to stop the panic. He urged "the heroes and heroines of the county" to "prove to the world that every dollar that has ever been invested here is worth one hundred cents."[29]

The editors also worked with innovative settlers to promote alternatives to traditional farming in the region. The suggestions ranged from the promotion of dry-farming techniques to trials of new and exotic crops, irrigation, and diversified farming with an emphasis on dairying. The Kadoka *Press*, always a leader in the promotion of scientific agriculture, filled its front page with articles detailing dry-farming techniques from a variety of sources. Alfalfa received considerable publicity. Professor Hansen of the state college at Brookings spent much of his time perfecting varieties of the forage crop, and his expertise was quoted frequently. Harry Lovald of the *Cheyenne Valley News* suggested the cultivation of hamus, a field pea, and published a lengthy description of cultivation techniques. E. L. Keith promoted the cow as the salvation of every new county. Stanley County had the grass to provide excellent beef, but settlers interested in milk production, he argued, could help nature along by planting alfalfa to feed their dairy cows. He provided information on soil preparation for the crop and urged his readers to go out and "Do it now! It will keep you from getting the blues . . . and in the spring you can get a crop started that will raise your mortgage, feed the goose that lays the golden eggs and establish an empire in Stanley county."[30]

The editors' suggestions for long-term solutions to the region's problems were certainly useful, but settlers needed immediate relief. Winter was approaching and many were short of food, hay, and coal. They had raised no seed for the following year's crop and could not afford to purchase any. None of the homesteaders had imagined that a disaster of such magnitude could befall them; failure and suffering had not been part of their plan. But in the fall of 1911 they faced a harsh reality. The settlers were proud people who had never asked for relief before. Now they had to turn to government and to the railroads for help.

It was the homesteaders and the editors who initiated efforts to obtain relief. The need was especially acute on the Cheyenne River and Standing Rock reservations, which had just been opened for homesteading in the spring, and the appeals for aid began there. Settlers on the northern reservations suffered from two problems. First, they owed money on their lands because reservation homesteads were sold at prices set according to the time of entry of the land. Some owed as much as $6.50 per acre and had to make regular installment payments to maintain ownership. They had raised no crops, however, and had been forced to purchase feed for their livestock as well as groceries for themselves. The money for the payments simply was not available. The second problem stemmed from the date of their settlement. Farmers arriving in the spring of 1911 had no reserves to fall back upon. They had not made hay the year before, so there was no leftover hay to feed to their cattle in the emergency. Also, they did not know the country well and so were less able to use what natural resources were available to them. Any extra cash left to them after the move to the claim was quickly spent on necessities. The potential for real suffering and deprivation was great.

The reservation newspapers responded to the crisis with spirited calls for assistance and urged their readers to organize for relief. The Dupree *Leader* printed a statement by the state immigration officer in which he suggested that town and county governments issue bonds to provide money for public works. Such a relief program, he believed, would give jobs to needy homesteaders while building up the country. The editor of the Dupree paper added that it might be wise for the Ziebach County commissioners to invest in road improvements throughout the county. "Many homesteaders," he wrote, "would doubtless remain in Ziebach county this winter instead of going back to their former homes if they had work that would bring them in a small amount of money. Furthermore, Ziebach county would look more attractive to investors, who are sure to flock here next year, if the roads are in good condition." In the same issue, the editor printed reassuring comments from papers east of the river supporting relief efforts aimed at reducing or delaying the land payments homesteaders owed. The Aberdeen *News* concluded, "This is an appeal simply for a square deal. The settlers went upon these lands in good faith. . . . They are not to blame for their failure."[31]

The reservation settlers in turn organized to aid themselves. They appealed to the railroad for help and requested that their county commissioners take action. In the Isabel area, the Commercial Club called a meeting of "all homesteaders" to "arrange cooperative purchasing and transport of hay, feed, and coal." In Dupree the homesteaders met at the courthouse to discuss ways of "procuring hay, grain, and coal for the coming winter, and potatoes and grain for next spring's seed." The settlers also hoped for direct relief from the railroad. Freight rates were too high in the best of times, they believed. In the crisis of 1911 they feared that no one would be able to pay for necessities. Homesteaders' groups and commercial clubs took this argument directly to the railroad management. They pleaded for free freight on relief goods, including hay and other livestock feeds, as well as seed grains and coal.

The reservation counties also struggled with federal regulations governing the payments on their land. The newspapers spearheaded letter-writing campaigns in support of deferred payments and flexible residency requirements on homestead lands. In August 1911 local delegates presented their case to their representatives in Washington and won support for a bill to defer payment on homestead lands for one year provided a 5 percent interest charge was added to the cost. South Dakota congressmen and senators promised to press the settlers' case.[32]

The railroad responded most quickly and effectively to the homesteaders' appeals, although its efforts proved to be short-lived. In August the statewide syndicated news service reported that the Milwaukee Road was firing its Italian laborers in order to hire drought-plagued homesteaders in need of work. The news service reported that a number of homesteaders took advantage of this opportunity in spite of the low wages of $1.50 per day because it allowed them to stay in the region rather than go elsewhere for work.

When the homesteaders demanded free freight, the railroad complied, at least initially, although it demanded some kind of control over the enterprise. Only agents appointed by the county commissioners, for example, could authorize free or reduced-rate shipments for individual farmers. By February 1912, however, the Milwaukee Road had reached the limits of its largesse (the Isabel paper estimated that the line had sacrificed more than $100,000 in freight rebates). It refused to allow seed grain to be shipped free of charge unless counties had issued bonds under Chapter 225 of the Code of 1911. That law allowed a county with fifty or more freeholders to issue bonds to buy seed and sell it to local farmers on time payment. The reservation counties had no freeholders, because their residents were homesteaders without patents to their claims, meaning they did not yet own their land. Thus, these counties could not issue bonds, and the railroad granted no free freight. The railroads defended their decision with the claim that counties east of the river that were well able to care for themselves had repeatedly taken advantage of their largesse.

The county governments' response to settler appeals hinged directly on the railroad's willingness to give aid. In August 1911 the Ziebach

County commissioners appointed five men, one for each town, to take charge of the receipt of relief goods if and when they began to arrive. They did nothing, however, about procuring free seed. Corson County also did nothing about seed. Dewey County, on the other hand, tried to find a way to get seed into the hands of its settlers and offered to aid those of Ziebach and Corson counties as well. When the railroad refused to grant free freight unless the counties issued bonds, however, the Dewey County board dropped its plans for relief and never developed any new ones. Each farmer in the three-county reservation area, then, was on his or her own.[33]

The state government also failed to provide more than moral support for the settlers on the reservations. Governor Vessey, accompanied by the commissioner of immigration and other state officials, toured the drought-stricken reservations in August 1911. They brought a "message of good cheer" to the region, encouraging homesteaders to stay on their claims and "pledging every reasonable assistance within the power of the state administration" to help them survive the winter. Those hearing the speeches came away reassured, the Dupree *Leader* asserted, that "the state of South Dakota will not permit any of its citizens to suffer personal want." Some branch of government, they were told, would provide work programs "for those actually in need." The counties, however, maintained the responsibility for relief and public works, and the state undertook no centralized effort.[34]

Reservation settlers were more successful when they approached the federal government for help with their land payments. Congressman Eben W. Martin was immediately sympathetic and argued for special treatment for west river residents in light of their difficult circumstances. Congressman Charles H. Burke and Senator John R. Gamble sponsored legislation during the next session of Congress, and in April 1912 the bill passed and became effective at once. It contained fairly generous provisions, allowing settlers without money but with the required residency time to prove up and pay later. These provisions were intended to encourage people to stay on their claims and improve them rather than to move elsewhere to earn cash for payments or give up the venture entirely. Proponents of the plan believed that most homesteaders would be able to profit from their claims in normal years and would eventually have the money to pay the debt they owed.[35]

In areas with established farms and towns (a relative status, because most people had been in the region fewer than ten years), the issues were similar but public concern over them was not as visible. Some settlers appealed to township and county governments for aid, but relief efforts were not as well organized and lacked the urgency expressed on the reservations. One man, Albert Sellars, who addressed his letter "to whom it may concern," urged Stanley County residents to put pressure on the county board to bond for relief. "It is not a case of charity," he argued, "but necessity. . . . I feel that the rest of you, like myself, came to this country with a little money. We have spent it, but want to stay and try to develop the country. If we do not get help we cannot stay." Sellars' letter pointed out an important fact. A survey of the county that he had taken revealed that two-thirds of the land had been proved up, and "the most of this is non-resident." He argued that it was only right for those who had homesteaded and then left to help pay the taxes that would allow the true developers to stay. Sellars urged the commissioners to assess taxes that would fall on nonresidents as heavily as on residents. His argument would reappear with greater frequency in the years to come.[36]

Other solutions to the relief problem also arose. Township or county bond proposals received publicity in the newspapers. The Wasta *Gazette* reported good attendance at a joint meeting of five townships held to discuss selling bonds to raise money for public improvements. The ideas of the commissioner of immigration that towns and counties undertake public works was reviewed favorably in the Kadoka and Murdo papers. Congressman Martin urged local commercial clubs to organize relief efforts and survey county lands for road building as an effective solution to the work problem. Martin also suggested that the federal government provide aid through the office of the secretary of the interior. He noted that the Black Hills National Forest needed roads, and that a public works program there could employ victims of the drought. New federal buildings being constructed in Lead and Rapid City also might employ the west river homesteaders, he believed. No action appears to have been taken on his proposals, however.[37]

The townships and counties in longer-settled areas were able to take action denied the reservation counties because they had a body of landowners who could approve bond issues. Marietta Township in Stanley County joined with another township to sell $10,000 in bonds for relief to be "worked out" on the roads. In addition, the Stanley County commissioners, after receiving the necessary petitions, voted in January 1912 to provide seed grain to the farmers in their county under the provisions of chapter 225 of the Code of 1911. In a four-day meeting in February they decided which applications to honor and which to reject.[38]

Local efforts to grant aid met with criticism for their lack of generosity and fairness. Shiloh and Grace Fairchild, for example, lived in Marietta Township, which had sold bonds. The Fairchilds had been on the claim since 1902 and by 1911 had accumulated a sizable herd of cattle and horses, but after the drought struck they had nothing for taxes or food. Shiloh Fairchild took the stock to better pasture in Nebraska, while the family stayed behind. The township board refused aid to the Fairchilds initially, apparently because they believed the family to be too prosperous to need it. Grace Fairchild, however, was strong-willed and cantankerous. "I told the town board," she later wrote, "that I wanted the $50 since I would have to help pay back the bonds when they came due, and that I wanted my part of the road work done right near our place. I would see that the work was done right."[39]

In Stanley County, the commissioners received criticism for their failure to grant enough aid or to provide it to the right people. The Fort Pierre *News* complained about the commissioners' transfer of extra monies to the general fund with no provision for seed-grain relief. The paper was "heartily in favor" of using the money to buy seed grain for farmers who could not afford to purchase their own and concluded that "The present law, which provides that the seed grain furnished a settler shall be a tax on his land is unsatisfactory. There is no reason why the non-resident should not help share the burden of those who are sticking and helping to develop the country." The editor of the Kadoka *Press* took offense at the county board's decision to reject some applicants for seed grain because of their level of indebtedness. The paper declared that a "common sense application of the matter would be to let all the farmers have the grain who desire it, and not simply because they happened to owe a little more than the commissioners thought they should, be refused the help." Men who could pay on their own or get credit with little trouble did not need the aid, but the board had granted it while excluding the true victim, the editor complained.[40]

Throughout the crisis of the drought years, no centralized relief effort was ever instituted. County governments were the most visible and active agencies in the west river country, but their primary role was taxation and the construction of roads and bridges. There was no guiding philosophy to govern relief efforts. Therefore counties functioned in hit-or-miss fashion on the aid question. Some settlers received relief, such as it was, while others received nothing. Many observers, including state and federal government officials, suggested plans for relief, but little was done.

The drought that peaked in 1911 marked the end of the first phase of the settlement process in the homesteading country of western South Dakota. Their numbers decimated, their hopes dashed, the settlers faced an uncertain future. The newspapers tried to reassure them and looked to the future with confidence. The editor of the *Western Star* observed that "The late fall rains, with the absence of frost, have brought out the pastures in fine shape and placed the ground in better condition for cultivation than it has been for a number of years, and the settlers have begun to take heart and fall work is being pushed with a vim. The change from the dry weather of the early summer has made everyone feel good and the prospects are good for a rousing crop next year."[41]

But no matter how they might try, newspaper editors and other boosters could not erase the recent disaster. Settlers would have to rebuild their lives on new assumptions, recognizing that economic insecurity and social disorganization might be chronic problems tied to the environment rather than temporary accompaniments of life in a new country. With the drought years of 1910 and 1911, the west river frontier made the transition to "next year country"—a world where this year was always hard but next year would be better.

9. LET THE GOOD WORK GO ON

Farm scene on the Missouri River in Stanley County in the early twentieth century.

Now, God never made Stanley county in vain, and with land in Iowa soaring skyward, people are not going to give up Stanley without making a desperate effort to subdue and bring it under the plow and make what God intended it to be; a lovely place to live in; a land with big barns and lovely homes, school houses and churches and railroads, and all that goes to make a beautiful country.

George H. Dunn, letter to the Midland *Mail*, February 22, 1912

Drought, deprivation, and depopulation continued to shape life in the west river country after 1911. The weather remained dry until 1915. People did without amenities and often without necessities. They continued to dream of success and prosperity but recognized that attaining them was uncertain. Many settlers abandoned their claims or their businesses and moved to kinder regions. Some counties lost half their populations, others lost a quarter or a third.

The settlers who remained in the west river country following the great drought faced a harsh reality. It was obvious that they had not lived up to the standards of success established by earlier frontiers, but they had failed to live up to their own expectations as well. The pioneers had moved to the last great frontier with plans to build an empire. Now they were impoverished and the society they had built was disorganized and struggling. Agriculture as they had known it appeared to be impossible. But those who stayed could not blame the country for their disaster. If they did, such blame would stand as an admission that their decision to stay was foolish. The settlers grudgingly admitted that their new home was different from the old, but they assumed full responsibility for its initial mismanagement. They assumed full responsibility as well for finding ways to make the plains "blossom as the rose."

"Eb and Kate" were a fictional farm couple from Stanley County whose musings and debates appeared in the Midland *Mail*. Kate always urged patience and hard work, while Eb vacillated between optimism and despair. By April 1912, Eb had been convinced, at least tem-

Let us all keep pulling together and the day will soon be here when the man of the East will look more favorably toward our great "West River Country."

Midland *Mail*,
January 15, 1914

porarily, of the wisdom of their decision to remain in Stanley County. He declared his newfound faith that "things are sure going to come our way this season" and went on to express his gratitude: "I am glad we are here and thank the Lord for help to do our part in making this one of the garden spots of the world." Eb's utopian vision included "a fine two-story home on each section, all painted white and trimmed in green and purple with a basement and furnace underneath . . . and a big red barn with white stripes on its side, . . . a high galvanized tower with a wheel on top, driven by the wind, pumping a cooling stream of water, . . . [a] hog house with concrete floor and cement walks from house to barn." Eb went on to describe his dream of tall trees, flowers and vines growing in the yard, and lush orchards blooming nearby, while "out on the green pasture graze the cattle on a thousand hills or basking in Nature's sunshine all content and satisfied with their lot and all doing their best to please their master, the man who stuck."[1]

Kate replied with her own rosy vision: "I have always told you there would be no shadow were there no sun," she began. "I have been thinkin' a great deal about what the future of this country is goin' to be myself. I have decided that what folks stayed here are the best, they are the salt of the earth. They are to be depended upon and I think, worth tying to." "We are in Western South Dakota now," she reminded Eb, "the land of sunshine and clear skies, the land that flows with milk and alkali water, the land of the cactus and the mosquito, the land of opportunity and hard work where the promise still holds good for those to come who have a good strong back and are willing and wanting to build for their future happiness, welfare and posterity. And it seems to me Eb, that of all times this is the time for them to come."[2]

While Eb and Kate talked of their hopes for the future, real people had to face the issues of drought, deprivation, and depopulation head-on. The settlers knew that they had not been successful pioneers by earlier standards. Why had they failed? Who was at fault? What would it take, in both method and spirit, to succeed? Could other kinds of success compensate for the lack of material success? These were the questions of the postdrought years as the settlers discussed the issues and worked to redefine their ambitions and group identity.

The newspaper editors were important figures in the debate. They recognized that long-term prospects for the west river country depended on development and implementation of dry-farming techniques, but they also realized that inducing the remaining pioneers to stay and fight for the land was critical in the short run. The editors encouraged settlers to remain on the land by assessing blame for their failure, offering reassurance of their intelligence and worth, and redefining success in terms of brave hearts and the ability to endure hard knocks, qualities that the "stickers" had already demonstrated.

In March 1912, Harry Lovald, editor of the Midland *Mail*, devoted his editorial column to words of praise. His first note described the neighborhood gatherings held in the Sansarc-Davenport region of Stanley County. Each month the neighbors gathered to share a meal and discuss their plans for the future. Lovald endorsed such meetings and urged his readers to attend one or start one: "When you begin to get a feeling that there are no people left in your community," he noted, "it will brace you up considerable to attend." He praised the homesteaders for their "enthusiasm and stick-to-it-ive-ness" and reminded his readers that those who had stayed in the country were the true pioneers.[3]

Later in March, as the growing season approached, Lovald quoted four farmers on the work going forward in the Hayes area and concluded, "They are all satisfied that normal conditions have arrived again." He also cited the arrival of seven cars of new pioneers: "Reaction has set in. We felt it in our bones all winter that we had the right view of affairs and that what is happening now would take place." Lovald reassured his readers that they had made the right decision in wintering on their claims: "You would be surprised to see all the letters that are written by people who moved away and are sorry they went. They claim they have spent more money than would have kept them here nicely like the rest of us, and they would have been ready for spring's work."[4]

In a similar vein, Lovald resorted to attacks on those who had departed, castigating quitters in increasingly harsh language as time went on. In March 1912, for example, he was still speaking kindly of those who had departed, while reassuring those who remained. "The weeding out process that the dry year of 1911 perpetrated on us," he wrote, "was not all for the bad. A new country, that is indiscriminately opened for settlement has no choice in the selection of her citizens. People from every walk of life, see the lure for a free homestead, and with the prospect in view of bettering their conditions, or at least acquiring 160 acres of land, rush in. The inevitable result is that some find themselves unfitted to cope with the strenuous task of subduing the land. With all due respect for those who have left us, and ever mindful of the fact that circumstances over which there was no control, had a great deal to do with their going, nevertheless the fact remains, that the ones best fitted to build up a new country are still here. It is another case of the survival of the fittest."[5] A few months later, however, Lovald dismissed the out-migrants as "crooners," whose brief stay in the new country had always been "to the detriment of real live empire-building homesteaders who are staying and, as Henry Jeffries of Sansarc says: 'Getting the "Indian" out of the ground.'"[6]

By October 1914, Lovald was no longer content with moralizing and began pouring vitriol upon the departed: "After the elimination—that is when the school ma'ams, preachers, lawyers, drummers, clerks, street car and railroad employees, carpenters, bricklayers, and old maids had about all commuted and moved back to their former haunts . . . it was found that the work of opening up and tameing a new, wild country had been attempted by an exceedingly large percentage of misfits." A new sense of betrayal, and an implicit admission that those who departed had taken some of the prospects of the new country with them, crept into Lovald's commentary. "While nearly all who proved up and went away, very cheerfully lied to us when they bid us goodbye, and said they would be back in the spring," he opined, "we realize that it was done with the best intentions, namely of showing up those of us who remained."[7]

Another approach to the problem of image and attitude was the use of the success story to illustrate to doubters locally and those long gone that people could succeed using a new agricultural program. In 1912, Harry Lovald began a series of accounts of successful farmers and their approach to the problems of life west of the river. He began on August 1 with a report on Otto Bork, a homesteader of seven years' residence near Stamford. He described Bork as a "real, live, progressive farmer, who farms with his head as well as his hands." Bork owned two farms, one his homestead and the other purchased "with money made since he came here." In 1912 he had planted eighty acres of corn and thirty-two acres of winter wheat and was growing potatoes, flax, and alfalfa besides raising stock. He milked thirteen cows and expected twenty-two more to become fresh before the end of summer. "The cream checks come in pretty regularly," Lovald noted. "The cow plays an important part and helps wonderfully toward that enthusiasm that makes farming a pleasure."[8]

By 1913 editor Lovald was emphasizing dairy cattle and forage crops as the salvation of the country. His vignettes of pioneer success all featured farmers who milked cows. Chris Larsen, who lived seven miles north of Midland, had lived in the county for twenty years, first as an open-range stockman and later as a dairy farmer with a small acreage of well-tended fodder corn. "He plows deep," Lovald commented, "keeps his fields clean and does not work more ground than he can handle right." Mr. E. E. Teaney and family on Burnt Creek were also featured under the headline "Stanley County-ites Who 'Make Good'." The Teaneys raised horses, mules, and milk cows. "Last year was the first we took to milking cows," Teaney told Lovald, "but when a can of cream will bring you from eight to ten dollars in the summer time, it comes in pretty handy." A second farmer featured under the same headline, James Nelson, also had recently turned to milking cows. Lovald noted that "Jim says it is rather hard work to milk when you are not used to it but thinks that practice will overcome that. During the month of May his cream checks were over seventy dollars, and June promises an increase over that."[9]

Other papers also used the individual success story format to encourage the old settlers and attract the new. The Kadoka *Press*, under the headline, "Homesteader Makes Good, D. F. Klotz of Kadoka, Starts with Nothing and Is on Way to Wealth Today," told in great detail the accomplishments of bachelor farmer Klotz, who in ten years had gone from hired hand to owner of a farm with assets of $6,120. The editor used the story to illustrate his belief that "Jackson county is not the barren desert which some people may think it is, but offers golden opportunities to the person who is a real red blooded man, and who is not afraid to work."[10]

The *Press* also reprinted two items from other papers about men who had wrongly concluded that they had been failures and had therefore sold out and returned east. In one case reprinted from the Philip *Review*, a man came to Stanley County in October 1907, and "his entire worldly possessions did not aggregate more than three hundred dollars. He struggled and struggled with the pioneer conditions of this new country until it seemed that he could struggle no longer; so a short time ago he gave it up." The homesteader held a sale and paid off his mortgage and his bills. "Then this failure counted over $3260.00, put it in his pocket with the patent to his homestead and went back East to begin life anew." The second story came from the Pierre *Capitol-Journal*, which had learned about a Stanley County man from the register of deeds. This settler, too, had arrived there with only $200 and had lived on his claim for six years. "Sometime later," the story went, "he got possession of a couple of cows and an old mare. Last summer his cream checks amounted to seventy-eight dollars a month, and he is expecting sixteen more fresh cows within the next six weeks to supply him and his customers during the winter. He decided, however, that this was not success, and that life here was a failure." The settler sold his claim, his cattle, and other possessions. "He said that he had netted at least six thousand three hundred dollars but he went back to Iowa, where he wouldn't be a 'failure' and where he could live in a more prosperous way." The *Capitol-Journal* concluded that the lucky buyers of the farm, people who recognized opportunity when they saw it, would "probably make better citizens of western South Dakota than the first holder."[11]

The "stickers" had to contend with the demoralization occasioned whenever defeated neighbors departed, and the announcements appeared frequently. The Mitchell Creek correspondent reported on the departure of the Brown family from that neighborhood: "The farmstead here has been traded for a good home in Minnesota. In discussing the moisture proposition, Mr. Brown was told that it might rain on him next year but he promptly answered 'Not here.'" In the Kadoka *Press*, the Willard-area correspondent mentioned that a family who had moved away had written to friends in Stanley County: "H. P. Clarke writes, that he would come back to old Stanley county if he thought he could make it go. All the encouragement we will give, is to say, we are living here, and will welcome him back." Another Mitchell Creek note discussed the imminent departure of a neighbor and concluded "Mr. Fennefos prefers farming to plastering but so far has failed to turn out from $6 to $10 per day in Stanley county, so those of us who have no other profession than farming will just keep pegging away and take what we can get." One former resident wrote to the Midland *Mail* to say that, while he wished his best to the "stickers," talk about better conditions and free freight on seed were not enough to entice him back. But, he added, "if you can find anyone that will GUARANTEE that crop will grow this year and next, I will come two days after I receive the guarantee." Learning to live without guarantees was the most difficult proposition for those who stayed.[12]

A related problem that west river residents contended with was the low opinion that outsiders held of their region and, by association, of them. They resented the implication that their region was a drag on the state. That such talk circulated is indicated by an article from the Sioux Falls *Argus-Leader* reprinted in the *Mail*. The editors of the *Argus-Leader* had received a letter from H. W. Fields, the manager of the Roswell Farmer's Company of Roswell, South Dakota. In the letter Fields advocated the division of the state on the Missouri River. "I have presented the idea to many citizens of eastern South Dakota," he wrote, "and the idea meets with their hearty approval; in fact I have found no one to whom it was presented that was not only in favor but anxious that a move be made in that direction." The *Argus-Leader* presented Fields' reasons for such a division: "The eastern part of the state is a crop producing section while the western portion will be devoted largely to stockraising . . . and mining in the Black Hills. Mr. Fields argues that the farmers and business men of the eastern half could borrow money under more favorable terms, that it would be easier to accomplish results in good roads work, and generally that the situation would be better for the eastern half of the state." The *Argus-Leader* opposed a division of the state, however, and urged patience.

"When another generation has gone by," the editor concluded, "the western part of the state will be a sure winner."[13]

While some west river residents worried about morale and image problems, others debated the merits of livestock and dairy production versus traditional grain farming. The editors promoted stock raising because it promised a cash return that drought could not destroy. Many farmers invested in milk cows; others ran beef cattle on abandoned quarter sections. The trend toward stock raising worried those who feared that the recommended changes in farming practices might diminish the way of life and the institutions they had struggled to build as a farming people, and possibly even return the land to open range. Because they believed farming to be the true work of the world and therefore much more virtuous than mere herding, they occasionally fought proposals to encourage dairying or livestock production. The debate centered on the real meaning of work—were people who ran stock deadbeats, or were they the wave of the future?

The fence problem was an important related issue because around it crystallized the hopes and fears of those who still lived on the land. The herd law provided penalties for those whose stock ran free and destroyed the crops and gardens of others, but in the grim aftermath of 1911 some settlers flaunted the law and allowed their cattle and horses to range freely on abandoned claims without regard for the consequences. Many farmers who opposed a transition to dairying or stock raising saw this irresponsibility by a few as a portent of things to come if stock advocates got their way. There would be no room for the "legitimate" farmer, they feared, and the social world such farmers had built would be destroyed. Farmers who recognized the need for dairying or stock raising argued that the more traditional farmers should take some responsibility for their livelihood and fence their land. They did not advocate irresponsible herding but recognized that neighborhood harmony would be better maintained if farmers took some defensive measures. Those in favor of stock raising in conjunction with farming did not believe that a changed economic base would necessarily destroy the farmers' social world.

The debate began in the pages of the Midland *Mail* in February 1912. Rasmus Kjar, a farmer in northern Stanley County, wrote a letter to the editor discussing a local case of horse impoundment in which fifteen horses had been captured and the owners forced to pay a fine to reclaim them. Kjar did not excuse irresponsibility on the part of the horses' owners but he did express some sympathy for them. He also gently chided those who did not protect themselves from loss. "It occurs to me," he said, "that those of us who came out here with the intention of building up a 'happy home' ought not to neglect to build a good fence around our gardens and other things that we wish to keep the old cow out of. I am aware that it is not compulsory but it seems to me that it is a matter that we owe ourselves and our neighbors."[14]

The next issue of the *Mail* carried a response to Kjar's letter. Written by two farmers in the Grandfield area, it presented "the other side of the fence question." The authors explained that "in the first place a good many of us that came here to build a happy home had very little money to start with, and with the dry weather and other backsets we have had to contend with, most of us have a good deal less now and it costs money to build fence." The farmers went on to argue that the land was no longer government-owned range but privately held land upon which taxes had to be paid. Stock raisers, they believed, should not expect to use this land for their own benefit without assuming responsibility for fencing and other care. Why should the bona fide home builders be expected to fence their land "in order that some one who has stock may turn them loose and not be bothered with them?" The farmers concluded their letter with a warning to the true builders of the country. "We also have men here with stock that do not intend to build a home. In fact some have traded their homestead for stock to graze over other peoples land without as much as saying by your leave. If the homebuilder is asked to fence against this class of citizen he sure has an uphill road to travel, for the more homebuilders that leave the better it suits him."[15]

But Kjar remained firm in his conviction that stock raising was the key to the future success of farming in the west river country. "We ought to have at least two milch cows and four horses," he insisted. "Still better if you have 20 cows and eight horses."[16] Kjar's insistence on stock, especially milk cows, duplicated the program urged by the editors of the Midland and Kadoka papers. More and more farmers took the advice, as cream sales reports from the two communities indicate, but not all grain farmers were willing to abdicate so quickly. They feared an economy based on grazing because it might lead to

even greater depopulation of the region as grazing displaced the more
labor-intensive use of the land for growing grains. A letter to the Midland *Mail* from a departed homesteader suggested that the irrigation
of small plots of land might be a more successful approach. "It seems
too bad," the homesteader concluded, "after the homesteaders have
spent so much money there, to let it go back to the free range where it
would only benefit a few men."[17]

The correspondent from the Davenport neighborhood struck a
middle ground that best illustrates the vision held by Rasmus Kjar and
other advocates of dairy farming and adapted crops. The "Echoes from
Davenport" author noted the arrival of two trainloads of stock in the
Midland area: "This, we think, is a move in the right direction. Stanley
county did make a good living for a bunch of stockmen—say about
100 of them. Now, if Stanley county could be made to make a living for
a bunch of good farmers—say about 1000 of them—it would be the
same as making ten spears of grass grow where only one grew before."
The Davenport correspondent did not feel threatened by the advent of
a farming and grazing economy but instead saw its potential, conclud-
ing that "the next step in the development of this country would be a
farmer on each section with nice buildings and 45 or 50 good milch
cows around him, and it is no dream either. Good many of us expect to
live long enough to see it come true."[18]

The hard questions of failure and adjustment occupied the minds of
the remaining settlers after the drought of 1910 and 1911. They had
not accomplished their goals, had not built the successful society that
they had envisioned when they moved to the last great frontier. Their
image of themselves as valiant pioneers completing the American saga
had not been realized. The settlers were forced to create a new image
that better suited the realities of their situation. They did this by
adopting independence, self-reliance, and the ability to withstand
hardship and live with deprivation as the badges of successful character. Settlers who left the region, in this view, were weak and not the
stuff of which pioneers were made. The questions they had asked in
the period immediately after the drought—Why had they failed? Who
was at fault? What would it take to succeed? Are there other kinds
of success beyond the material?—had answers at mid-decade. The
settlers had failed because they "had commenced wrong at the start."[19]
They only had themselves to blame, although the people who had

struggled too briefly and then left for more comfortable climes shared the responsibility for the depth of the crisis. To succeed, it would take a willingness to experiment, to sacrifice, and to do the hard duty, but success *would* come for those who were faithful. In the meantime, the joy of the struggle, of knowing that they were doing good work and that they were of tougher character than those who lived easier lives, was compensation for the lack of money and comforts. In the twenties and thirties, when low prices and drought again ravaged the land and the triumph of urban values in the larger society overwhelmed the accomplishments and culture their persistence had so painfully built, cynicism found a comfortable home in the west river country. But in the years before World War I, pride, independence, and self-reliance, combined with disdain for those who wanted more than the country could give, became the hallmarks of west river character.

10. TO OVERCOME THE DRAWBACKS AND FAILURE

Main street, Belvidere, Stanley County.

All of us have learned our lesson—we know about what to do and there is none who can say, but that Jackson county is the place for a man who will mix in a few cows and the brood mare with his farming operations. By doing this he can prosper.

Kadoka *Press*,
April 30, 1915

While the redefinition of success and the molding of a new image and identity for the region were important developments of the postdrought years, the settlers also confronted a series of practical economic and social problems that had to be solved if they were to survive. The critical area of concern was agriculture. Settlers had to learn new techniques and try different crop varieties if they were to build a successful agricultural economy. Some of them organized agricultural societies to spread information and provide moral support in this difficult endeavor. A second practical problem concerned the social institutions the settlers had built in the period of optimism before the drought. West river residents recognized their need for sociability and culture, but depopulation and poverty limited the base of support for many institutions. Schools in rural districts were especially hard hit and often managed only bare survival. Organizations that demanded less money to maintain were somewhat more successful. But with fewer people to participate, each remaining member had to work that much harder to keep his or her group alive. The struggle for solutions to the practical problems posed by drought, deprivation, and depopulation dominated west river life after 1911.

Editors, rural correspondents, and other interested participants recognized the necessity of change and adaptation in farming practices. The editors of both the Midland *Mail* and the Kadoka *Press* urged their readers to adopt scientific agricultural techniques and crop varieties suitable to the region. They published information from the *Dakota Farmer* and from the South Dakota Agricultural Experi-

For several years our funds have been somewhat less than in former times, but I think we are all conscious of the reason, and that we should feel consolation in the fact that whatever demand had been made we have always stood ready and willing to do our share.

Mrs. V. L. Ferguson,
President, New Century Club,
Midland, South Dakota, 1914

We have learned to follow the custom of the country, and get along as best we can with what we have.

Mrs. Theodore Jorgenson,
Thrall Academy,
Perkins County, 1914

ment Stations run by the state college at Brookings, as well as advice and testimonials from local farmers, who shared their successes and failures with their neighbors through the local paper. In December 1912 the Kadoka *Press* carried an article written by a Highmore man titled "The Lessons of 1910 and 1911." The author encouraged his readers to engage in diversified farming, treat the soil in accordance with the most recent scientific methods, rotate their crops, grow alfalfa, and milk more cows. He also urged farmers to take advantage of the farmer's institutes by attending the lectures and putting the advice given there to good use. In 1913 the *Press* printed an idea put forth by a Draper man that would have encouraged each nonresident landowner in Lyman County to provide five head of milk cows for each quarter section he or she owned to a resident farmer trying to succeed west of the river. In this way, the paper believed, the important goal of increased dairying could be more easily achieved. The nonresident owners would benefit because successful dairying in the region would increase land values generally. By 1915 the *Press* was reporting with interest the growth of alfalfa in the county. Experimental plots planted under the supervision of South Dakota State College professors had produced good yields, and the *Press* encouraged its readers to give the crop a chance. Kaoliang, a new forage crop, also did surprisingly well in the dry summer of 1914, and the *Press* editor hoped that it would "solve the winter feed question for our settlers."[1]

Harry Lovald of the Midland *Mail* advocated a similar program for the farmers of Stanley County. He wrote his own essays on the need for scientific farming and gave much of his space to farmers or rural correspondents who wrote on agricultural issues. In 1912, for example, the Elbon correspondent included detailed instructions on alfalfa planting and urged farmers to develop "fifty acres of seed alfalfa and a few good cows." Henry Jeffries of Sansarc wrote occasional epistles about his experiments with alfalfa and urged farmers to listen to the advice given by the professors at Brookings. Another farmer wrote a long technical article on techniques for ridding the land of the pesky Russian thistle, which established itself when absentee homesteaders broke their required five acres and then abandoned their claims. The weed flourished in the broken areas and spread to farmers' fields when the wind turned them into tumbleweeds. The author of the article also suggested that nonresidents be taxed for the care of their abandoned lands. Someone could then be paid, he argued, to eliminate the thistle from the empty quarter sections.[2]

Many people west of the river took decisive action to salvage what remained of their economy and find new directions for the future. Besides changing their farming practices to include new crops and the dairy cow, they banded together in associations devoted to the improvement of agriculture. In late 1912, the families of the Hayes-Sansarc area organized the Sansarc Agriculture Association. At one meeting a farmer gave a talk on "His Mistakes," while others spoke on "How to Succeed" and "Root Systems." In 1914, Ottumwa-area farmers organized the Farmer's Cooperative Society. The Midland area also organized a creamery association to help farmers ship their cream profitably. Representatives of this association travelled across the region spreading their message. In 1915 they helped Kadoka people, through the auspices of the town's Commercial Club (the successor of the Kommercial Klub), to organize their own association. About twenty farmers took part. Philip and Cottonwood had similar associations.[3]

The Kadoka *Press* chronicled the development of the Better Farming and Livestock Association in the neighboring town of Interior. The businessmen of the community and area farmers gathered frequently beginning in late 1915 to discuss methods and crops as well as to provide sociability and moral support. Organizers hoped for an attendance of 200 or more but never reached that goal. Reports of the meetings usually mentioned 50 or 60 in attendance. The group discussed a variety of issues, including such topics as the "Livestock Industry and

Its Improvement" and "Feed," presented by the men, and gardening, flowers, and chickens, presented by the women. When spring approached, the group met much less frequently, perhaps due to the pressures of spring work. In April the Interior correspondent included a list of crops area farmers intended to plant. The acres of forage crops mentioned indicate the success of the diversified crop message.[4]

Two memoirs also indicate the efforts that homesteaders made to succeed in the west river country. The William Miller family in Perkins County had begun their venture wisely in 1907. They came with dairy stock and had sold butter from the beginning. Their farm expanded slowly because they took few risks and considered every move carefully. After the crisis of 1911, which set them back as it did everyone, they resumed their slow progress. William Miller had purchased his brother-in-law's claim, which added to the potential cropland of the farm, and he also rented a number of other quarter sections for pasture. With more land, he believed, more machinery would quickly pay for itself, so he invested in a lister (a double-moldboard plow) and a cultivator for corn. The Millers did not plant much corn and they used what they had to feed the cows. William Miller had a stubborn streak that kept him experimenting with corn for many years, although his farm was really too far north for the varieties then available. But his son Henry remembered that "our dad had farmed in Iowa and raising corn in Dakota was just his kind of challenge." In 1916 William Miller learned to read English in addition to his native German, and from that point on he read the farm magazines avidly. Henry Miller did so, too, and in 1917, using techniques suggested by one such magazine, he kept the hens laying all winter, a major victory for the family. In the early twenties the family bought a tractor and mechanized their operation. When the Millers sold out to the government in the face of the Depression, drought, and grasshoppers of the thirties, they had accumulated ten quarter sections of their own and leased or rented another ten quarters.[5]

Grace Fairchild and her family also succeeded where others had failed. They did so because of her commitment to scientific agriculture and her willingness to experiment. In some ways her struggle to convince her husband to try the new ways serves as an example of the larger struggle in west river society. Shiloh Fairchild loved horses and hated farm work. Left to himself, he would have done nothing but raise stock on the open range. But Grace Fairchild had other ideas, and after the drought drove many of her neighbors away, she began to implement them. In 1912 when the county superintendent of schools tried to organize a 4-H club, Grace enrolled her ten-year-old son. He received experimental seed-corn varieties and instructions from South Dakota State College. Grace encouraged his work and ordered pamphlets for herself. She also heard of the work being done with alfalfa and ordered some seed to try on their claim, but her husband refused "to get that weed started on the place," and it sat unplanted for two years before the hired man mixed it with the oat seed and sneaked it into the ground in that way. "When Shy discovered that he had been tricked," Grace Fairchild remembered, "he was as mad as a wet hen. It gnawed at him all summer long. The next spring he hitched his team to the plow and plowed it all under." The alfalfa grew back and flourished and Shy Fairchild was finally convinced. Grace Fairchild continued to encourage her children to experiment with crops adapted to the dry west river climate. She also traded some of her husband's extra horses for a tractor, one of the first in the neighborhood. That allowed her boys to do more fieldwork in less time without the added labor of caring for horses. The family also bought a share in a cooperative creamery and maintained a herd of twenty-five cows. "As the years went by," Grace Fairchild commented, "I found that we could grow most anything adapted to this country, except in the drought years. The settlers who talked down 'text-book farming' either got out of the country or turned to other ways of making a living."[6]

The settlers remaining in the west river country had social problems to cope with in addition to their economic and psychological ones. Progressive educators on the national scene imparted their reforming ideals to local teachers and administrators, who were constantly frustrated by their inability to implement them, as schools were expensive and difficult to maintain. Students had to travel long distances to reach school. Those of high school age could not receive a full four-year course anywhere near their homes, and some families were forced to move away to provide their children with a good education.[7]

The schools received much attention in the local papers during the teens. The newspapers publicized teacher's institutes and a limited number of fund-raisers held to provide necessities for the districts. The sense that schools, especially in rural neighborhoods, had serious problems began to appear early. In February 1912 the Sansarc Township correspondent reported a plan to centralize the schools in that district and perhaps to provide a high school. "We can save much in a financial way by beginning now," wrote the correspondent in support of the plan. "Each year we are moving [school] houses and thereby adding expense to expense." The correspondent also saw the importance of a rural high school. It would be better for the farm children because they would be "in their natural environments" and would not "feel any shyness or hesitancy. . . . The broad open prairies with the beautiful sunshine . . . are much more conducive to the educational growth of children than the narrow crowded smoke-dimmed streets of the city with the noise and din of commercial life." The author concluded with an appeal for the best interests of the children but added a practical note as well: "Families coming here to make their future home will look long and favorably upon an institution of this kind and are sure to settle as near such as they possibly can."[8]

In March 1912 a farmer wrote of his experiences visiting the Prairie View school. He praised the dedication of the teacher, the competence of the children, and the discipline of both. The farmer recognized the need for dedicated, competent teachers and worried about the neighborhood's ability to keep them: "I cannot see . . . that it would be an enviable occupation to teach a country school. I do not wonder at teachers coming and going, year after year. If something could be done to retain a good teacher, like the one here now, for instance, during a term of years, it would be of untold benefit to our children."[9]

Salaries were an important factor in the failure of schools to get or keep good teachers. The Stanley County superintendent, W. W. Warner, spoke to Harry Lovald of the *Mail* about the problems the county faced. Lovald described Warner's plan to hold a six-week summer school to better educate some of the teachers. The need arose, Lovald explained, because schools paid too little to attract the quality teachers: "When our county was first settled up, and for several years thereafter, Stanley county was blessed with an unusual number of high grade teachers. We had more than our schools could use. They were here holding down claims and were glad of an opportunity to make some extra pocket money teaching school. . . . A large number of these teachers have left this country, presumably to go where wages are better. The result has been that, rather than not have school . . .

young girls, lacking the necessary training have been employed in some instances."[10]

The Nowlin correspondent, who claimed to speak from experience, commented on the departure of that community's teacher in August 1913. "She will take up her work as teacher of the Capa school," the reporter noted. "The Capa School Board seems to be right to the front in providing for their teacher, as they have built a little house on the school grounds and furnished free coal, besides paying $60.00 per month. . . . The sooner some school boards realize that they can't always hire a good teacher for $40 or $50 the sooner we will see an improvement in our schools. No one can keep abreast with the times and do good work on short rations." In the same column, the Nowlin correspondent commented on attitude problems prevalent in the region. He or she implored parents to recognize the importance of education: "Do not keep them home from school because you have a couple hours work in a day for them. Do not keep them home two days in the week, and expect them to keep up with their class—and if they do not, blame it on the teacher." The writer urged parents to be interested and progressive. "Parents, do not deny your children this chance. This is the richest inheritance you can leave them."[11]

The problems of education—and county services generally—were most acute in the reservation counties with large Indian populations. Indian peoples did not pay taxes, and white residents were generally poverty-stricken due to the drought and often did not yet hold title to their homesteads. As a result, tax revenues in these counties, and the services they financed, were meager. In Ziebach County, School Superintendent G. M. Drummond resigned his position to assume new duties at a higher salary as the principal of the Eagle Butte school. His successor, John R. Retz, resorted to putting up hay in the summers to supplement his income. The Dupree *Leader* reported his departure for this job and concluded "the superintendent of schools should be so compensated that their entire time could be devoted to that office, but the superintendent in this county can't exist on the salary paid."[12]

William W. Robertson, the county superintendent in Bennett County, another reservation county, described in detail his trials and tribulations in a letter to the state superintendent of public instruction. He listed conditions in the county that were "peculiar to itself," including "sparsely settled districts," and "the mixed population of White,

Mixed-bloods, and full-blood Indians." The mixed-bloods and full-bloods often lived too far from any school to attend and were governed by a combination of federal and state rules. They paid no taxes on their lands. Robertson also considered area school boards, poor communications, and low pay to be impediments to progress: "The widely separated members of the school boards who are farmers and ranchers and have but little time to spare from their farms and ranches to attend to school business, the limited or poor mail service, etc., etc., are rather discouraging conditions, to say the least, for a superintendent who receives a monthly pittance of $19.00, and, as he is allowed only five cents per mile while he has to pay five dollars a day for a livery conveyance that cannot average more than 30 miles a day while visiting the schools, it is easily seen that he is not 'in' very much."[13]

Robertson's letter went on to describe hardships and general disorganization at all levels. One district was so large that board members lived miles apart. Only three schools operated in Bennett County in 1913; by 1914, five new buildings were put up but because resources were so limited the districts had been forced to finance them through a bond issue. The lawyer who handled the bonds was incompetent, Robertson claimed, and had not yet sold them. Distances were so great that teachers could not meet regularly to share information or organize reading circles. Robertson did not want his superior to think he was a complainer, but he did want him to understand "some of the difficulties we have to contend with." He hoped that the coming years would bring some improvement.[14]

Voluntary organizations had a somewhat easier time in maintaining themselves than did schools because they were not as expensive. The Willard and Weta neighborhoods had a Grange that was organized in 1913 after area farm families decided it was too difficult to travel the distance to Cottonwood to meet with that group. The women of the Willard neighborhood, in fact, maintained an active social schedule. The area correspondent recorded the meetings of the Social R circle for women and told in great detail of the efforts of the ladies club to provide for the community as well as themselves. The ladies club celebrated its seventh anniversary in May 1914 but did not rest content with mere survival. In February of that year its membership began an ambitious plan to build a meeting hall for the Fairview Township community. The women organized box socials and dances to raise funds and enlisted the help of the *Dakota Farmer* and the Kadoka *Press* in their effort. Both newspapers donated a portion of each subscription from the neighborhood to the cause. In June an area farmer donated an acre of ground for the club's hall, provided that the club build a fence around it. In March 1915 the women held a special meeting to open the bids for lumber and supplies, and in April club members proudly announced that they had let the contract for a twenty-by-forty-foot hall to serve as an amusement center for "the west-central part of the county." The next year the Willard correspondent suggested that a stage for plays and entertainments would be a nice addition to the hall and that "two or three dances and box suppers would buy a nice addition to the hall." This prompted the author to urge: "Get busy at once." [15]

Townspeople also felt the effects of the drought and depopulation. The town of Kadoka, for example, went through difficult times in the years after 1911 but eventually revived and prospered. Forms of social organization remained the same as before the drought, but hard times limited the causes to which residents contributed. Groups like the Kadoka Kommercial Klub foundered and even disappeared temporarily. Some of the leaders left town and new people had to fill the gaps. Some members moved away for short periods but returned eventually and again made their homes in the town. The Kadoka Kommercial Klub disappeared from the news early in 1912. No mention is made of a businessmen's organization again until December 1913, when a group of men gathered to discuss reorganizing some kind of commercial club. The December 26, 1913, issue of the *Press* described the formation of a new group, the Kadoka Commercial Club, which hoped to "promote the interests of a live town." [16]

Church activities also dwindled. News of the Methodist church virtually disappeared from the columns of the *Press*. The Methodist ladies aid no longer held its fund-raisers and entertainments. The Presbyterians fared somewhat better. Although a note announcing the reelection of J. C. Pease to the post of Sunday school superintendent mentioned "many vicissitudes" and commented that "families have come and families have gone until there are only three families remaining who were among the workers at the organization of the school," the Presbyterian church met fairly regularly and often had a resident minister. One man, Reverend Shaw, revitalized the congregation with outstanding sermons, active youth organizations, and evening lectures.

He remained in town only briefly, however, and the church suffered through more acting pastors, visiting pastors, and short-term appointments. Its ladies aid continued to flourish but rarely held fund-raisers. An occasional election-day dinner or Christmas bazaar replaced the endless round of activities that prevailed before 1912. The Catholic church also survived and began a number of ambitious projects, including the erection of a Catholic school. The women of the church held fund-raisers for the proposed school beginning in May 1914.[17]

Secular groups suffered as well. The lodges continued to meet and a new one, the Royal Neighbors of America, was organized. The Dramatic Club faded into oblivion during the spring of 1912, although it was later reorganized in the happier days of 1916. The Tennis Club listed only eight members in May 1913. The Excelsior Club for women maintained its schedule and a new women's organization, the Park Embroidery Club, was formed to oversee the town park and encourage the members' interest in fancywork. The women met regularly, frequently travelling to the farm homes of members for their gatherings. Other organizations, like the WCTU, appear to have died or were incorporated into other groups. The opera house had occasional travelling shows or dances, but overall there appears to have been less activity in the town.[18]

Kadoka's fortunes changed when the voters of Stanley County chose to divide the huge county into three smaller ones. Kadoka ran a vigorous campaign for the county seat of the newly formed Jackson County and won that appointment in the January 1915 election. The Kadoka Commercial Club worked hard to achieve that victory; the campaign gave it issues and a purpose again. The club undertook a series of new projects, including the building of a courthouse, which it donated to the new county. By July 1915 the *Press* could report of a "Kadoka on a Boom"—a private residence, the Catholic school, and the courthouse were all under construction simultaneously. The men of the Commercial Club built the courthouse with their own hands, but they had financial help from many local organizations and individuals who held fund-raisers and donated the proceeds. The club's other ambitious projects included an effort to establish a ferry over the White River, the reorganization of the band, the establishment of a creamery association with twenty farmer members, and the beginning of a waterworks program expected to cost fourteen to fifteen thousand dollars.[19]

The year 1915 ushered in an era of new hopes and dreams. The growing season produced the first real crop in the region in four years. Although a hailstorm destroyed some of it in July, by fall many people were more prosperous than they had been since early settlement. The *Press* editor urged his readers to remember Kadoka merchants when it came time to buy. He was proud of the merchants for sticking by the country and the people during the hard times: "For the past four years, up to the present harvest—we had no harvest—the boys stayed with us, guess trusted a good many of us quite a bit." Now the stores were "completely filled with goods for the fall and winter trade" and there would be some money with which to buy. "Remember the past," he urged, buy your goods in Kadoka.[20]

The editor was also proud of the courthouse, and the new county seat and surrounding countryside alike shared his pride. In February 1916 the Kadoka Commercial Club held a banquet to celebrate. Nearly 350 people attended. Women from town and farm served dinner while the Kadoka Orchestra entertained. The crowd spent the evening listening to a succession of speakers, who addressed diversified farming, the development of silos, and the need for harmony and cooperation. Others spoke of their experiences as farmers over the past ten years, or of their faith in the future and of the need for a "live Commercial Club" to help the process along. One of the highlights of the evening came when Mrs. George Decker, president of the Park Embroidery Club, presented the Commercial Club with a check for twenty-five dollars for the courthouse fund. Each member of the club had earned a dollar in her own way and had donated it to help the county prosper. After the program ended, the people danced the night away. The future would bring new problems and trials, but for Kadoka the year 1915 marked the reemergence of energy and pride.[21]

The economic problems of the postdrought years in the west river country stemmed from the difficulties of practicing agriculture in a semiarid land with highly unpredictable weather patterns and unfamiliar soil types. The solutions lay in the application of scientific expertise and the willingness of farmers to adapt their traditional techniques to the needs of the land. In the years after 1911, the remaining farmers learned to follow the advice of experts. They formed groups to share information and boost morale as they struggled with slow, painful, and expensive experimentation. One county agent, writing about Stanley County in 1916, observed that the farmers in his jurisdiction were "more progressive than the farming classes farther east." He was pleased by their willingness to "take up with the new" and argued that the population in Stanley County, in 1916 just half of what it had been in 1910, "represent[ed] the select of the select." In reality it was the desperation of their agricultural situation that led them to such flexibility. In their fight for survival, west river farmers were willing to follow any advice that might allow them to succeed.[22]

The social problems of the postdrought years had no solutions. Poverty and depopulation were the enemies of complex and successful social organizations. People in the west river country became increasingly isolated as their neighbors left, their own farms expanded, and transportation and communication failed to improve. Money continued to be in short supply, and it was money, along with high hopes, that allowed schools, churches, and other social organizations to thrive. Only in towns like Kadoka, where winning the county seat provided new opportunities, did energy and hope revive to predrought levels. Without more money and a greater population, social institutions remained marginal. Despite that, the last great pioneers persevered.

11. CONCLUSION

On the sixth anniversary of his arrival on the last great frontier, James Stewart, editor of the Dupree *Leader*, reflected on the hopes and ambitions that had marked his first day in the west and contrasted them with the reality that he and his fellow settlers had faced since then. "We stood on the border of a new land and a new life," he remembered, "and knew not what lay before us. We had no gift of prophecy wherewith we might penetrate the future and read the history of the coming years, yet in every man's heart there was a stern determination that come what might, be the conditions whatever they may, he would, if humanly possible, prove himself equal to every occasion." The occasions had been trying. Drought had stalked the land; poverty and depopulation had followed. In 1916, after the first good year his country had known, Stewart admitted the hardships: "The history of those years [has] not been all we could have wished, all we did wish. . . . The valleys have not always stood thick with corn, nor our garners been filled when the first winter blast swept across our fields." But Stewart was grateful for the small successes—being "preserved alive," for one. The good crop year of 1915 had boosted his spirits, but not to the level of optimism he had known before the drought. Instead he was heartened and encouraged and believed that the settlers now felt "stronger to go forward, believing that our industry and patience will one day be adequately rewarded."[1]

His anniversary reflection says much about the west river frontier experience. Arriving in high hopes, battered by drought and hard times, the people who remained on their claims and in the towns had learned to expect less and be grateful for small favors. They had begun the venture with great ambitions. They had planned to build an empire overnight, complete the grand American frontier saga, and live prosperous lives of peace and contentment in a land built up with their own hands. The vagaries of nature had ended their dreams, and the lure of a more comfortable and secure life in the larger society had complicated their efforts. Along with the builders came large numbers of absentee homesteaders who came for personal profit, to see the West and participate in it but not to make long-term commitments. They helped build social institutions and made the land look crowded with settlers for a while, but they departed once their personal goals had been met, leaving those who remained to carry on the struggle alone and bitter at what they believed to be the misuse of the last frontier.

To justify their decision to stay and fight the hard fight, the settlers described city-dwellers and easterners in general as "soft" and implied that they were not as good as the pioneers who struggled bravely on. In 1916 the Philip *Pioneer* informed its readers that "Drones and idlers and good-for-nothings stay east, because they haven't the ambition or gumption or nerve to come west and try their luck. The cowards and those afraid to try stay east; while the ambitious, the hustlers, the real continent builders, come out to God's own good, free country." West river settlers, then, were humble in the face of nature but proud and defiant in confrontation with their fellow men.[2]

How and why had they become like this? This is but another way of inquiring into the whole history of west river settlement. Pioneers, both homesteaders and town-builders, began to arrive in the west river country in great numbers after 1904. Those who came to stay arrived with clear ideas of the kind of society they hoped to build. They would be landowning or merchant entrepreneurs, in on the ground floor of economic and social developments. They did not plan to depart radically from the basic structures they left behind, but they wanted to shape the direction in which their world would go. They would be economically successful and would fill in the continent, completing the American empire. Homesteaders worked hard to create farms from the grassland, devising patterns of work and family life that reflected traditional patterns and present goals. Men, women, and children worked together to wrest a living from the wilderness. With hard work and a little luck, farm families progressed a bit each year toward the realization of their dreams, just as other people on earlier frontiers had done before them.

Homesteaders quickly went beyond the family to forge social relations within neighborhoods and build organized institutions to foster social interaction and establish social order. In this, too, they had much in common with earlier agricultural frontiers. The social world the settlers occupied was highly personal, a place where the rigors of physical life and the vast loneliness of the plains mandated cooperation. In contrast to the anonymity of the growing city, where people could be lost in the crowd, individuals counted on the west river frontier. The highly motivated, committed individual was important to the development of informal sociability and the success of institutions as well. The close psychological proximity of such a personal world, however, sometimes generated tensions.

Among the homesteaders, women played vital roles in both economic and social developments. As wives they aided the family economy, selling butter and eggs, doing domestic work and often outdoor work as well. In the neighborhood, as members of ladies aids and "helping" societies and in their jobs as schoolteachers, women often created opportunities for sociability and led the way toward a more complex social organization. Their social involvements reflected the changes brought about in rural women's roles in the late nineteenth century, when the public sphere, at least in areas of the church and the school, became acceptable arenas for women's participation. By the twentieth century, women's involvement in the activities of the neighborhood, the school, and the church was the expected thing; it had become traditional behavior. West river farm women's lives combined the age-old patterns of farm life with the newer commitments to the society beyond the home.

Town-dwellers, men and women, participated in the last great frontier in their own ways. They worked to build homes and businesses where none had been before. They hoped to create "live" towns at the center of a vital economy. Factors beyond their control shaped their endeavors, however, and limited or defeated their chance for success. Railroad corporations, whose resources far exceeded those of the entire west river country, were a powerful factor in town building and in the town-dwellers' prospects for entrepreneurial success. Economic changes like standardization and specialization in the national economy also affected their operations, while offering little opportunity for local influence. But within these limitations, local political and institutional development was theirs to shape.

As part of this vision, town-dwellers created an active social world. In the boom years before the drought, town residents planned schools— including the high school grades, which at that time were typically associated with urban areas—built churches with the help of denominational mission funds, and founded lodges and clubs similar to those left behind. Men, in their organizations, worked to promote, protect, and entertain the town. Women worked to support the churches, aid the needy, and educate themselves on the important issues of the day. The fund-raisers and socials that women organized did much to create community within the town. Because most towns were small, relations within them remained highly personal. Just as in farm neighborhoods, the participation of individuals counted.

The drought of 1910 and 1911 dealt the developing societies of town and farm a fearful blow. The worlds the pioneers were in the process of building were predicated on the widely held belief that the west river country was similar to the humid lands of the middle western prairies. Settlers arrived with notions of success based on their own earlier experiences and those of their ancestors on earlier frontiers. The drought ended these assumptions and expectations. The settlers suffered physically from hot, dry winds, a lack of water, and often a lack of food. They also suffered spiritually, because they had hoped for so much and had received so little. They learned in 1910 and 1911 that doing good work did not necessarily bring rewards. In the early stages of the crisis, homesteaders had to endure the barbs of a few editors who accused them of laziness and poor agricultural techniques. As the crisis continued, however, even the complaining editors recognized disaster and worked together with farmers and townspeople to find solutions. The immediate need was for relief, and homesteaders and town-dwellers alike worked to provide aid to the destitute. That they failed to do so in any consistent fashion was due to the lack of resources and the philosophy of the times. No institution or agency was equipped to administer massive amounts of aid in an era of rugged independence, self-reliance, and laissez-faire.

The long-term consequences of the drought were many. Part of the population departed. Absentees who had never bargained for such hardship on their frontier "vacations" returned to more comfortable homes. Some homesteaders who had intended to stay permanently fled for the simple reason that the drought threatened their very survival. Some of them returned when the rains again fell, but many were gone for good. Farm neighborhoods suffered the worst losses, but towns withered as well.

In the grim aftermath of drought, the remaining west river settlers began a reevaluation of their goals and the means to achieve them. During the decade of the teens, the scientific development of dry-farming techniques began in earnest, primarily under federal auspices. Ironically, the same decade also witnessed the withering of local and regional institutions and ushered in a period of social disorganization. These larger developments were paralleled on the personal level as west river people created for themselves a new identity based on perseverance and self-reliance leavened with the faith that next year would be better.

It was the drought and the critical years following it that inducted west river settlers into the patterns of life on the Great Plains. Other areas of the plains had learned the truths of an uncertain climate a generation before, but these lessons had been lost on the west river people, who had to learn them on their own.[3] They found out the hard way that they were not exceptions to the rule of nature on the plains. Their desperate situation led them to experiment with new methods and new crops. The ideas they adopted were not new; some farmers had experimented from the beginning with crops suitable to semiarid lands. But the crisis of the drought compelled more farmers to adapt, and to do so on a large scale. Flexibility and a willingness to listen to experts corresponded with the severity of the threat to farm livelihoods.

This adaptability continued in the region over the ensuing decades. After the profitable years of World War I and with the development of affordable machinery in the 1920s, west river farmers turned increasingly to mechanization to cut their operating costs and to enable them to enlarge their farms. Agricultural experiment stations continued their work, developing new crop varieties better suited to the plains and better livestock breeds for faster gain and greater profit, endorsing new agricultural techniques to preserve moisture, and urging the adoption of fertilizers and insecticides to boost crop yields. Although such developments brought a small measure of economic success to farm families in the region, uncertain environmental factors continued to affect the future of farms on the plains. The terrible drought of the thirties was only the most extreme example of the uncertainties that farmers faced to a lesser degree every season. In 1943 an agricultural experiment station director spoke of the problems posed by the uncertainties of the climate and of the efforts of his organization to provide plains farmers with information adequate to meet the threat. He acknowledged that scientific farming had helped to improve the odds for plains farmers but cautioned that the experiment stations could not yet supply absolute certainty to farming. Until they could, he concluded, "we might just as well expect in-movements of a jubilant, optimistic, cultured population and out-movements of a cantankerous, impoverished society."[4]

The problem of social disorganization was less susceptible to technical solution. Social institutions required people and money to maintain them. Both were lacking after the drought, and the situation worsened as the west river country became increasingly a hinterland in ensuing decades. Adding to the difficulties was the adoption of urban standards for social institutions and services in the larger society. Those of the west river region could never measure up. Expenses for maintaining minimum standards exceeded their diminished resources. Schools were the most costly investment. Because 90 percent of the funding for the elementary schools came from district property taxes, poorer areas could not afford adequate facilities. Many districts continued to hold school in abandoned claim shacks or sod houses into the twenties. In 1918 a United States Bureau of Education report on education in South Dakota commented that "in some sections a condition of 'near illiteracy' prevails, due to scattered homesteading west of the Missouri River, with long distances to nearest schools, bad roads, and severe winters." High schools were generally unavailable to the majority of west river students. The South Dakota superintendent of education reported in 1920 that "owing to the scarcity of population and the low valuation of our pioneer sections of the state, proper high school advantages, within reasonable reach, are practically unknown to the boys and girls west of the river."[5]

Churches also suffered from a lack of funds, although membership continued to grow until the 1930s. But members alone were not the problem. Too many churches competed for too few members, yet distance and poor roads prevented consolidation. Church members had to contribute large sums for church upkeep and the ministers' salaries, especially after mission funds from the various denominations began to dry up. Many congregations solved the problem by maintaining only minimum facilities and sharing the services of a minister with one or a number of other congregations. Service, then, remained at the level of the early frontier days at a time when the larger society demanded well-equipped, efficiently run churches with strong programs of community social services.[6]

Another product of the drought and its aftermath was the redefinition of success and the creation of a new self-image for the remaining settlers that made a virtue of living with less. That west river settlers lived with fewer and poorer material goods was obvious. The Stanley County agent reported farm families in his county in 1916 living in "shacks that make the most insignificant pretension on the outside" while showing some signs of "culture and refinement within." Pictures published in county histories reveal the shabbiness of homes and farm buildings, many of a merely makeshift nature, well beyond the teens. Today, near Kadoka, one can visit such a home, a two-room combination dugout and tar-paper shack, inhabited by a farm family until 1941 and furnished now as it was in the teens and twenties. This site communicates without words the hardship and sacrifice of west river settlers.[7]

But for those who decided to stay in the country and live with less, there were other compensations. The pride they had in themselves for sticking with the "good work" in the face of risk and uncertainty was strong. While life was often hard, many loved the land and enjoyed the challenge that it posed. There was a heroic quality about "sticking," and settlers relished their image as heroes and heroines. They believed that they were more self-reliant, more independent, and more determined than those residing in long-settled areas. While they were humble in the face of nature's power, they were also optimistic about their long-range chance for success; each was convinced that the next year would be the turning point. As time went on and "next year" never came, bitter humor and cynicism became marked regional characteristics. Over the years the settlers redefined success to mean simple survival. As one rural correspondent reflected on Thanksgiving Day, 1915: "We should be thankful . . . that we are still living to try it again."[8]

Developments in the west river country did not occur in a vacuum, of course, and with the advantage of hindsight it is possible to see the effect of national issues and trends on west river settlement. By 1900 urbanization, industrialization, and rapid developments in technology were creating new American societies. West river settlers came from a settled world with higher standards of comfort and services than those of frontier generations before them. They left more behind them when they moved to the frontier, and they expected to regain their comfortable standard of living quickly. Thus they were easily disappointed by the crudeness of their new homes and by their failure to recreate rapidly the world they had left behind.

While west river settlers were relatively isolated, they maintained ties with settled areas through the railroad, magazines and papers delivered by mail or available at the stores in town, and even in some cases a telephone. They were always aware of the comforts known elsewhere, a fact that made living with less all the more difficult. The railroad and the automobile allowed settlers to travel to the frontier with relative ease but also made it easy for the disgruntled to escape. Those unhappy with the frontier experience also had a place to escape to— the growing cities with their job opportunities and social institutions and pleasures. The cities were less "free" than the frontier but they were more secure and required less effort to achieve a comfortable standard of living. These were factors that had not influenced earlier frontiers, and they made the last great frontier qualitatively different. A generation before, farmers on the frontier were on the cutting edge of American life; by the turn of the century, they were on the margins of American society. Farmers everywhere were losing status; their patterns of life could not match the excitement of the city. It was far harder to attract and keep settlers in a region where meeting even the minimum standard of farm life was difficult.

Ultimately, it was developments on the national scene that ended the frontier era in the west river country. The entry of the United States into World War I in 1917 was a turning point. Local papers devoted their attention to war-related issues, including the departures of draftees and volunteers from the area, their letters from Europe, and promotions for meatless and wheatless days. Red Cross chapters met to roll bandages. Liberty Bond drives easily filled their quotas and more. West river life revolved around the events of the war and the needs of the nation. When the war ended, life did not return to its pre-war pattern.[9] Boys returned from the military with new ideas and new goals. Farm families purchased automobiles with the money the higher prices of the war years had brought. Their increased mobility began to reshape trade patterns, condemning smaller towns to decline and decay. The drop in farm prices and real estate values after the war devastated the local economy and by 1921 many banks had failed and farm families were suffering. Although the old issues of agricultural adaptation and social disorganization remained only partially resolved, new issues had emerged, and national events and trends controlled life on the west river plains far more completely than they had before. The struggle now had new boundaries and new rules.

By 1900 the winning of the West had assumed mythic proportions in American imagination. Many of the people who settled the west river country moved west to help complete the glorious saga. They hoped to participate in the last frontier and win success as earlier generations had done before them. It was to be a grand conclusion to a three-hundred-year epic of conquest over man and nature. As it turned out, however, the west river settlers were to prove that the frontier saga, insofar as it entailed conquest and prosperity, had ended a generation earlier. Without knowing it, they had reenacted the failure of earlier plains frontiers in Kansas and Nebraska, but they did so finally and conclusively as twentieth century actors before a national audience. When the last great pioneers failed to live up to expectations, the spectators naturally soured on the play. Of course, the frontier myth has continued to thrive in American politics and imagination; the west river settlement from this perspective merits only an embarrassed, perhaps derisive, footnote. But where the nation saw foolish persistence in the face of failure, the west river people saw heroic struggle. The west river people created a new frontier myth that prized endurance, self-reliance, and irony rather than quick success, manifest destiny, and the march of progress. As the nation grew increasingly embroiled in its obsessive materialism and onrushing modernism, the west river pioneers continued the struggle to live their new frontier myth.

NOTES

INTRODUCTION

1. Frederick Jackson Turner, *The Significance of the Frontier in American History* (New York, 1963), 58.

2. Harold P. Simonson, *The Closed Frontier: Studies in American Literary Tragedy* (New York, 1970), 4–5.

3. The Black Hills area is not included in the term "west river" for the purposes of this study. The Black Hills had a very different history, based on mining rather than agriculture. Only the counties that are plains grasslands are included here. Some counties, like Pennington, are partially plains and partially Black Hills. The plains portions of those counties shared the history of agricultural settlement and are treated as part of the last frontier in this book.

4. Simonson, *The Closed Frontier*, 6.

1. MERELY THE PIONEERS

1. James E. Howard relates the Oglala folk tales that explain their crossing of the river and their association with the Cheyenne in "The Dakota or Sioux Indians, A Study in Human Ecology," *Anthropological Papers* (Vermillion, South Dakota) Number 2 (1966), 1. The French called the tribes the Sioux, a derivation of the Chippewa name for them, "Lesser Adders." The tribes called themselves the Dakota, but their differing dialects translated that into Dakota for the eastern group, Nakota for the Yankton and Yanktonai groups, and Lakota for the western, or Teton, division. When the Lakota moved west from Minnesota, their numbers increased and they eventually split into seven subtribes.

They were the Hunkpapa, the Minneconju, the Blackfoot, the Two Kettle, the Brulé, the Sansarc, and the Oglala. The Yankton and Yanktonai tribes remained east of the Missouri River, and the Santee tribes (the Dakota) remained farthest east, in Minnesota.

2. Herbert S. Schell, *History of South Dakota* (Lincoln, 1975), 18–23; Royal B. Hassrick, *The Sioux: Life and Customs of a Warrior Society*, in collaboration with Dorothy Maxwell and Cile M. Bach (Norman, 1964), 3. The Hassrick book is a thorough study of the Lakota people. James B. Howard, "The Dakota or Sioux Indians," 2–6, contains a very brief overview of Lakota culture. Two new books by James R. Walker provide documentary material as well as anthropological analysis: *Lakota Belief and Ritual*, edited by Raymond J. DeMallie and Elaine A. Jahner (Lincoln, 1980) and *Lakota Society*, edited by Raymond J. DeMallie (Lincoln, 1982). Both contain extensive introductions that explain the importance of Walker's contributions and interpretations of Lakota life.

3. The best book on the Oregon Trail itself is John Unruh, *The Plains Across: The Overland Emigrants and the Trans-Mississippi West, 1840–60* (Urbana, 1979). The military effort to defend travellers and settlers is described in Robert M. Utley's two books, *Frontiersmen in Blue: The United States Army and the Indian, 1848–1865* (New York, 1967) and *Frontier Regulars: The United States Army and the Indian, 1866–1891* (New York, 1973). An interesting essay on the changing image of the Great Plains is G. Malcolm Lewis's "Regional Ideas and Reality in the Cis–Rocky Mountain West" in James E. Wright and Sarah Rosenberg, eds., *The Great Plains Experience* (Lincoln, 1978), 27–33.

4. Rodman Paul, *Mining Frontiers of the Far West, 1848–1880* (New York, 1963), is the standard account. The warfare that engaged the Lakota is described in Schell, *History of South Dakota*, 65–77, as well as in George Hyde's books *Red Cloud's Folk: A History of the Oglala Sioux Indians* (Norman, 1937) and *Spotted Tail's Folk: A History of the Brulé Sioux* (Norman, 1961).

5. Schell, *History of South Dakota*, 125–133, 140–157, provides an overview of the gold rush. Watson Parker, *Gold in the Black Hills* (Norman, 1966) is the best account of the rush and the development of towns in the Black Hills.

6. Schell, *History of South Dakota*, 129–139; Hyde, *Red Cloud's Folk*, 221–308. George Hyde's *A Sioux Chronicle* (Norman, 1956) discusses the years immediately following the Sioux War.

7. Robert G. Athearn's *High Country Empire: The High Plains and Rockies* (New York, 1960) describes the movement of the cattle frontier into the northern plains, and a number of local histories tell the South Dakota story. Bob Lee and Dick Williams' *Last Grass Frontier: The South Dakota Stock Grower Heritage* (Sturgis, South Dakota, 1964) is a general history of the cattlemen's association. August H. Schatz, *Opening a Cow Country: A History of the Pio-*

neer's Struggle in Conquering the Prairies South of the Black Hills (Ann Arbor, 1939) and Longhorns Bring Culture (Boston, 1961) tell the story of the Anglo-American Cattle Company in Fall River County. Burt Hall, compiler, Round-Up Years: Old Muddy to Black Hills (Pierre, 1954) is a collection of interviews, autobiographies, and other pieces on the cattle frontier. The Pioneer Club of Western South Dakota has published a book of family stories titled Pioneers of the Open Range: Haakon County, South Dakota Settlers before January 1, 1906 (Midland, South Dakota, 1965) that includes many ranchers and cowboys. Two autobiographies are useful. W. H. Hamilton, "Dakota: An Autobiography of a Cowman," South Dakota Historical Collections 19 (1938): 475–637, describes the life of a small rancher in Butte County. Ike Blassingame, Dakota Cowboy (Lincoln, 1964) relates the adventures of a cowboy for the huge Matador ranch.

8. U.S., Census Office, Ninth Census of the United States, 1870: Compendium, 88; Schell, History of South Dakota, 159. Two excellent books on the expansion of the farmers' frontier are Allan G. Bogue, From Prairie to Cornbelt: Farming on the Illinois and Iowa Prairies in the Nineteenth Century (Chicago, 1963) and Gilbert Fite, The Farmers' Frontier, 1865–1900 (New York, 1966), which discusses the lands west of the Mississippi, including Minnesota, the plains states, the Rockies, and the Northwest.

9. Schell, History of South Dakota, 189–222, provides a detailed look at territorial politics and the campaign for statehood, while land entry data for 1878–1887 is discussed on p. 159. Schell also examines the Great Dakota Boom, the factors that contributed to it, and the lives the boom pioneers led (pp. 158–188). Another account of the boom is included in Fite, Farmers' Frontier, 94–112.

10. Lee and Williams, Last Grass Frontier, 127–153; and Schell, History of South Dakota, 242–247, describe the Dakotans' efforts to open the reservation to general settlement. Francis Paul Prucha, American Indian Policy in Crisis: Christian Reformers and the Indian, 1865–1900 (Norman, 1976) is an important source of information on reformers, and Robert F. Utley, The Last Days of the Sioux Nation (New Haven, 1963), 40–59, discusses the land agreement of 1889 and its devastating impact on the Lakota.

11. Wright and Rosenberg, Introduction to The Great Plains Experience, 9; John Wesley Powell, Report on the Lands of the Arid Regions of the United States (Washington, D.C., 1878).

12. Herbert Schell describes the topography of western South Dakota in his History of South Dakota, 4–8. A more technical account appears in E. P. Rothrock, A Geology of South Dakota, South Dakota Geological Survey, Bulletin No. 13 (Vermillion, 1943), 47–67.

13. Schell, History of South Dakota, 8–11. A technical discussion of South Dakota soil types can be found in Fred C. Westin, Leo F. Puhr, and George J.

Buntley, *Soils of South Dakota*, South Dakota Agricultural Experiment Station, Soil Survey Series, No. 3 (Brookings, South Dakota, March 1959). A good discussion of Great Plains soil types in general appears in Carl F. Kraenzel, *The Great Plains in Transition* (Norman, 1955), 24–41.

14. U.S. Department of Agriculture, *Climate and Man*, Yearbook of Agriculture, 1941, (Washington, D.C., 1941), 1110, 722; Mary W. Hargreaves, *Dry Farming in the Northern Great Plains, 1900–1925* (Cambridge, 1957), 8–10.

15. USDA, *Climate and Man*, 1110–1113, 1118.

16. Wright and Rosenberg, *Great Plains Experience*, 10.

2. THE LAST GREAT FRONTIER

1. Carl N. Degler, *The Age of Economic Revolution, 1876–1900*, 2d ed. (Glenview, Illinois, 1977), is an excellent short overview of late-nineteenth-century developments. See especially pages 1–14 and 73–85. George E. Mowry, *The Era of Theodore Roosevelt and the Birth of Modern America, 1900–1912* (New York, 1958) provides an excellent background on the social and material changes occurring at the turn of the century; see especially chapters 1 through 3. Mark Sullivan's *Our Times: The United States, 1900–1925*, 6 vols. (New York, 1926–35) is a detailed and useful study. Volumes 1 through 3 cover the pre–World War I period. An old but still helpful book on the women's role in the work force is Robert W. Smuts, *Women and Work in America* (New York, 1958). It should be supplemented with Alice Kessler-Harris, *Out to Work: A History of Wage-Earning Women in the United States* (New York, 1982).

2. A good overview of the Country Life Movement, which helped shape pro-rural views, is provided in William L. Bowers, *The Country Life Movement in America, 1900–1920* (Port Washington, New York, 1974). Bowers describes the Country Lifers as believers in the "yeoman myth." "To such people," he writes, "farmers represented the best in society, the energetic, intelligent, law-abiding mainstay. . . . The bulk of these reformers hoped to bring about a situation in which the ideals and values of a rural society could be preserved in a complex, urbanized world" (p. 4). They did not move to the country themselves, but their writings promoted the glories of rural life to others.

Two examples of articles that discuss the end of the frontier and its meaning are Frank Norris, "The Frontier Gone at Last," in *World's Work* 3 (February 1902): 1728–1731; and an editorial titled "The Passing of the Frontier" in *The Independent* 54 (May 15, 1902): 1201–1202.

3. An important source on the mythologizing of the west is G. Edward White, *The Eastern Establishment and the Western Experience: The West of Frederic Remington, Theodore Roosevelt, and Owen Wister* (New Haven, 1968). Owen

Wister, *Owen Wister Out West: His Journals and Letters*, edited by Fanny Kemble Wister (Chicago, 1958) adds more about the author of The *Virginian.* "Buffalo Bill" Cody wrote his autobiography, *True Tales of the Plains* (New York) in 1908, but other writers had popularized his exploits in the 1880s and 1890s. Two examples include James William Buel, *Heroes of the Plains; or, Lives and Wonderful Adventures of Wild Bill, Buffalo Bill . . . and other Celebrated Indian Fighters. . . .* (Philadelphia, 1886), and John M. Burke, compiler, *"Buffalo Bill" from Prairie to Palace: An Authentic History of the Wild West with Sketches, Stories of Adventure, and Anecdotes of "Buffalo Bill," the Hero of the Plains* (Chicago and New York, 1893).

4. These economic and cultural factors led to a new wave of migration of homesteaders and town-builders into the northern plains. In North Dakota, 250,000 latter-day pioneers settled in the state between 1898 and 1915. In Montana, the rush began somewhat later, but homesteaders there took up 45 million acres of land between 1910 and 1922. South Dakota showed similar activity. Between 1900 and 1920 its population increased from 401,570 to 636,547. In the nonmining lands west of the river, the population grew from approximately 17,000 in 1900 to approximately 107,000 in 1920. These figures do not reflect the settlers who only resided in the region for a short time, temporarily swelling the population to boom proportions but quickly moving on once they had proved up on a homestead or failed in business. Elwyn B. Robinson, *History of North Dakota* (Lincoln, 1966), 245; Joseph Kinsey Howard, *Montana: High, Wide, and Handsome* (New Haven, 1943), 169; Paul Landis, *The Growth and Decline of South Dakota Trade Centers, 1901–1933*, South Dakota Agricultural Experiment Station, Bulletin 279 (Brookings, April 1933), 7; Doane Robinson, *Doane Robinson's Encyclopedia of South Dakota* (Pierre, 1925), 990.

5. Charles Lowell Green, "The Administration of the Public Domain in South Dakota," *South Dakota Historical Collections* 20 (1940): 155–180. All data on South Dakota land openings come from this source.

6. *New York Times*, October 13, 1908; John A. Dixon, "Taking Chances on Indian Lands," *World Today* 15 (December 1908): 1239; *Yankton Press and Dakotaian*, July 25, 1904; Aberdeen *Daily News*, October 5, 1909; Sioux Falls *Argus-Leader*, July 5, 1904.

7. George Kingsbury, *History of Dakota Territory*, and *South Dakota: Its History and Its People*, ed. by George M. Smith (Chicago, 1915), 3: 97–98; Sioux Falls *Argus-Leader*, July 21, 1904.

8. Edith Eudora Kohl, *Land of the Burnt Thigh* (New York, 1938), 51, 150–158.

9. Lindsay Denison, "The Newest United States," *American Magazine* 67 (February 1909): 385.

10. A brief discussion of the extension of the Milwaukee Road lines across western South Dakota can be found in August Derleth, *The Milwaukee Road: Its First Hundred Years* (New York, 1948), 178–195. An example of railroad promotional literature is: Chicago, Milwaukee, St. Paul and Pacific Railroad Company, *Government Homesteads and How to Secure Them* (Chicago, n.d.). A copy is located in the special collections department of the University of Iowa Library. The Chicago and North Western's story appears in Robert J. Casey and W. A. S. Douglas, *Pioneer Railroad: The Story of the Chicago and North Western System* (New York, 1948), 234–242.

11. Robinson, *Encyclopedia of South Dakota*, 990.

12. Winner Chamber of Commerce, *Winner: Fiftieth Anniversary, 1909–1959* (Winner, South Dakota, 1959), 29; Elizabeth Henricksen, interview with author, Iowa City, Iowa, July 22, 1981; Kohl, *Land of the Burnt Thigh*, 5, 54–55.

13. Denison, "Newest United States," 385, 388, 394.

3. FIFTY MILES TO WATER, ONE HUNDRED MILES TO WOOD

1. Kohl, *Land of the Burnt Thigh*, 1–2, 4, 8.

2. Ibid., 26. Bess Corey, a woman homesteading alone in Stanley County, chose to build a larger home for herself because, as she put it, she did not "want to stand on end, sleep on edge, and walk in and back out for the rest of my days." Corey had a 12 × 16 two-room shack built to replace her "borrowed" 8 × 10. Paul Corey, ed., "Bachelor Bess: My Sister," *South Dakota Historical Collections* 37 (1974): 18.

3. Henry Miller, et al., *From a Soddy* (n.p., n.d.), 21–31; Fanny Malone, "A Michigan Family's Experiences on a Government Homestead," p. 4, Manuscript Collection, South Dakota Historical Resource Center (hereafter cited as SDHRC).

4. Kohl, *Land of the Burnt Thigh*, 18.

5. Ione Dunlap King, *On Our South Dakota Claim* (Pierre, 1977), 29–33; Mary W. M. Hargreaves, "Women in the Agricultural Settlement of the Northern Plains," *Agricultural History* 50 (January 1976), 185; this includes data on well-drilling costs, which were $1.00 per foot in 1914, with wells an average depth of 500 to 600 feet.

6. Miller, *From A Soddy*, 8, 9, 30; and Oscar Micheaux, *The Conquest: The Story of a Negro Pioneer* (College Park, Maryland, 1969; reprint of 1913 edition), 64, 72, for examples of positive responses to the prairie. The quoted statements are from Kohl, *Land of the Burnt Thigh*, 1, 12, 19. Other examples can be found in Book and Thimble Club, *Proving Up: Jones County History*

7. Faye Cashatt Lewis, *Nothing to Make a Shadow* (Ames, Iowa, 1971), 34; Ronald Rees, "Nostalgic Reaction and the Canadian Prairie Landscape," *Great Plains Quarterly* 2 (Summer 1982): 162–164; Wallace Stegner, *Wolf Willow: A History, a Story, and a Memory of the Last Plains Frontier* (New York, 1966), 268–273, describes the importance of "the making of paths" to the settlement process on the plains. Kohl, *Land of the Burnt Thigh*, 24, 16–17, 27–28.

8. Kohl, *Land of the Burnt Thigh*, 66–67. After the storm the sisters found their horse, still hitched to the buggy, calmly eating hay in his crude stable.

9. Corey, "Bachelor Bess," 22–28.

10. Ada Blayney Clarke, in "Pothook Pioneer: A Reminiscence," edited by Monroe Billington, *Nebraska History* 39 (March 1958): 55; *Western Star* (Midland, South Dakota), July 12, 1907.

11. *Western Star*, July 3, 1908.

12. Mildred Duckworth and Marjorie Clark, "The Claim Shanty," unpaged, uncatalogued manuscript, SDHRC.

13. Katherine Sprague Taylor, *A Shattered Dream* (Lusk, Wyoming, 1967), 31. Frieda Tupper, in *Down in Bull Creek* (Clark, South Dakota, n.d.), 23, describes how her family lost their entire ragged wardrobe in a sudden windstorm.

14. *Western Star*, August 19, 1904; September 8, 1905.

15. *The Coyote* (Moore, later Murdo, S.Dak.), January 23, 1904; Kohl, *Land of the Burnt Thigh*, 20. Other examples can be found in Avis McCoy, *Dakota Homestead* (Chicago, 1974), 50; and King, *On Our South Dakota Claim*, 11.

16. Walker Wyman, *Frontier Woman: The Life of a Woman Homesteader on the Dakota Frontier, Retold from the Original Notes and Letters of Grace Fairchild, a Wisconsin Teacher, Who Went to South Dakota in 1898* (River Falls, Wisconsin, 1972), 74.

17. Corey, "Bachelor Bess," 16.

18. *Western Star*, June 15, 1906; June 11, 1909; Kohl, *Land of the Burnt Thigh*, 138.

19. Clark, "Pothook Pioneer," 44, 46.

20. McCoy, *Dakota Homestead*, 33; *Cowboys and Sodbusters* (n.p., 1968), 233.

4. THRESHERS CAME RIGHT AFTER DINNER

1. Not all absentees were single. Families also moved to the west river country temporarily to gain land and then returned to their previous home or moved

on to a new venture. The Davidson family of Carthage, in eastern South Dakota, provides an example. They took up a claim near Newell in Meade County, but in the summer Mr. Davidson worked in town while his wife and children held down the claim. In the fall the whole family stayed in Newell so the children could attend school, but Mrs. Davidson and the children returned to the claim the following summer for their usual sojourn. The family eventually proved up and remained in Newell permanently. Myrtle Davidson Withrow, *The Claim* (New York, 1969), passim.

2. Hansen's list of canned goods included "several dozen tins of sardines, salmon, and roast beef." She also bought cookies and saltine crackers from Montgomery Ward. Erikka Hansen Ruste, "Homesteading in Lyman County, 1905–1908," p. 7, Daughters of Dakota Collection, SDHRC. Canned goods and processed foods were important staples for homesteaders who did not farm their land. Edith Ammons noted that the site of a transient's claim shack was usually marked by a pile of rusting tin cans. "And from the tin cans ye knew them," she later wrote. "Bachelor's huts were always surrounded; where there was a woman to do the cooking there were fewer cans. But as a rule the shack dwellers lived out of tin cans like city apartment dwellers" (Kohl, *Land of the Burnt Thigh*, 17). Not all people approved of the use of canned goods. Homemade foods were certainly more thrifty, and farm people accustomed to processing their own produce were slow to accept the change. Rhoda Davidson and her children made frequent use of canned goods during their summers on their claim in Meade County. Mrs. Davidson rarely made anything besides desserts from scratch. A neighbor woman who frequently visited them often criticized her extravagance and urged Mrs. Davidson to cook rice, beans, and macaroni and use stale bread for puddings. The neighbor also accused her of throwing "more out the back door than Malcom [Davidson, her husband] can bring in the front door" because she discarded any canned goods that were not perfect. Withrow, *The Claim*, 67.

3. Ruste, "Homesteading in Lyman County, 1905–1908," 1–47.

4. Ibid., 28.

5. T. A. Larson, "Women's Role in the American West," *Montana: The Magazine of Western History* 24 (July 1974): 5–6. The Dewitt data is from the *Thirteenth Census*, 1910, manuscript census schedules for Dewitt Township, Perkins County. Paula Marie Nelson, "No Place for Clinging Vines: Women Homesteaders on the South Dakota Frontier, 1900–1915 (Master's thesis, University of South Dakota, 1978), 41–43. Only 8 women of the 220 were engaged in farming as a full-time occupation. Three others combined farming with other occupations. Bess Corey, for example, always taught school yet tried to develop a farming and ranching operation besides. She took her farm seriously, hiring men to put in her crop or receiving her brother's help during his short

tenure in South Dakota. Most women homesteaders were not farmers, however, and they did not contribute to the agricultural development of the west river country, although they did much to aid social development, albeit temporarily. It could be argued that their long-term impact was negative because their commitment was limited. They helped form organizations that later had to be abandoned or greatly reduced due to a lack of membership, to the great resentment of people who stayed in the region. Agriculturally, their small plowed patches attracted weeds, especially Russian thistles, to the detriment of bona fide farmers. Yet the fact that women came alone to homestead tells us much about the changing status of women in the nation as a whole. Their contributions to the boom-time economy of the growing towns was also important, as was their role as schoolteachers. Most single women homesteaders did not remain on the farm as bona fide settlers.

6. Bormann, *Homesteading in the South Dakota Badlands*, 46–80; Old Stanley County Historical Society. *Prairie Progress in West Central South Dakota* (Sioux Falls, 1968), 24–25, 446–448.

7. Myrle George Hanson, "History of Harding County, South Dakota, to 1925," *South Dakota Historical Collections* 21 (1942): 537.

8. Bormann, *Homesteading in the South Dakota Badlands*, 25–46, 80–87.

9. Steam-powered tractors had been widely available by the 1890s but they were too expensive for most farmers to purchase. The peak of steam power came between the years 1908 and 1915, yet only 5 percent of the farmers nationwide owned a steam tractor. The gasoline tractor began to make inroads into the steam market by World War I, but it was not until 1924, when the Farmall tractor came on the market, that such tractors were widely affordable. R. Douglas Hurt, *American Farm Tools: From Hand-Power to Steam-Power* (Manhattan, Kansas, 1982), 112.

10. Lakeside Old Settlers Association, *Through the Years before 1966* (n.p., 1966), 174. Every issue of the Dupree *Leader* from July through December 1910 carried lists of possessions newcomers had brought; Winifred Reutter, *Mellette County Memories: Golden Anniversary Edition, 1911–1961* (Stickney, South Dakota, 1961), 15–18, 34–35.

11. Lewis, *Nothing to Make a Shadow*, 38.

12. Micheaux, *The Conquest*, 80–92.

13. Miller, *From a Soddy*, 49; Lewis, *Nothing to Make a Shadow*, 39.

14. Miller, *From a Soddy*, passim. American-born settlers predominated in Dewitt Township, where the Miller family lived. A survey of householders and their spouses indicated that 281 had been born in the United States, while only 80 had been born in a foreign country. Of those 80 immigrants, 20 came from Germany, 13 from Sweden, 9 from Canada, 8 from Denmark, and 7 each from Norway and Ireland. The remaining immigrant population was divided among

Finns, Swiss, Russians, English, and Hungarians. Many Americans had immigrant parents, of course. One hundred of the American-born settlers in Dewitt Township had at least one parent who had been born in a foreign land. Germany, Ireland, Norway, and Sweden, in that order, were the most frequent places of origin. *Thirteenth Census, 1910*, manuscript census schedules for Dewitt Township, Perkins County.

15. Carrie Miller continued to give birth regularly until 1923, twenty-three years after the birth of her first child. The remaining children and their birthdates were Billy, 1909; Ed, spring 1911; Lester, fall 1912; Ella, fall 1914; Donald, spring 1916; Edna, fall 1919; Alice, summer 1921; and George, spring 1923. Miller gives no exact dates for the births, so it is impossible to calculate exact birth intervals. In 1913, thirteen-year-old Christoff died of appendicitis enroute to a Mobridge hospital. George, born in 1923, was never healthy; he died suddenly in early 1924 before his first birthday. Miller, *From a Soddy*, 5, 11, 12, 68, 78, 91, 96, 105, 122, 131, 144, 145.

16. Information on the Millers' daily lives and work routine is from Miller, *From a Soddy*, 1–75.

17. Ibid., 49.

18. Ibid., 49, 54, 56, 63–64, 68, 72.

5. SOCIABILITY IS WHAT WE NEED IN THIS COUNTRY

1. Lewis, *Nothing to Make a Shadow*, 32; Miller, *From A Soddy*, 20–21; Kohl, *Land of the Burnt Thigh*, 14.

2. McCoy, *Dakota Homestead*, 27–30; Ruste, "Homesteading in Lyman County," 16.

3. Country Life reformers (see chapter 2, note 2) criticized the narrow social world of the rural community. Country Lifers believed that a new age had dawned and that "pioneer" social relations, as they called them, were now harmful to the community good and stood in the way of progress. In western South Dakota, "pioneer" traits were certainly present, and the undeveloped state of the country did not always allow for a broad social vision. There were urban people and well-educated and well-read people present who knew of the new trends in social relations, but practical considerations of money and distance forced social developments to follow tried and true directions. A "pioneer" society was better than no society, after all. Also, because the west river country was just being developed, there was a sense of excitement and push that made it seem that all things were possible. Older rural areas may have had pockets of stagnation that reformers could legitimately address as pathological. One settler who went home for a visit reported on his return that "back there [in

Illinois] the towns and villages seemed to be in the embrace of a peculiar atmosphere that made the population sit around on store boxes and hate themselves and their surroundings. He was glad to get back to a country where there is some pleasure in being alive." Midland *Mail,* April 11, 1912. The most important statement of the Country Life philosophy is the *Report of the Country Life Commission* (Washington, D.C., 1909), although the literature produced between 1900 and 1920 is voluminous. Rural sociologists also addressed the rural life problem and produced a wealth of information.

4. Corey, "Bachelor Bess," 26.

5. Ibid., 25.

6. Ibid., 30; pages 1–31 include the story of her first years in South Dakota.

7. Kadoka *Press,* November 19; May 13, 1910.

8. Kadoka *Press,* February 4, 25, March 4, 1910.

9. Kadoka *Press,* April 22, February 15, 1910.

10. The *Western Star* of June 7, 1907, reported that the ladies of Hayes and vicinity had signed a pledge not to dance with any man with liquor on his breath.

11. Owen Wister's novel *The Virginian,* published in 1902, includes the now-classic baby prank. The Virginian and a friend switched babies, and their joke was not discovered until some of the families reached home. Homesteaders mentioned similar jokes occurring in their neighborhoods or nearby. Dances were common entertainments for the whole family. The *Western Star,* for example, mentions at least one dance in the vicinity in practically every issue in fall and winter 1905.

12. George W. Mills, *Fifty Years a Country Doctor in Western South Dakota* (Wall, South Dakota, 1972). Dr. Mills' family homesteaded in the Wall area and he taught school there as a young man. He attended medical school and returned to Wall in 1919 to practice. His description of his experiences on distant farms in the twenties indicates that isolation, poverty, and crude "self-help" medical care continued for years after the homesteading period ended.

13. Lewis, *Nothing to Make a Shadow,* 63.

14. King, *On Our South Dakota Claim,* 19–29.

15. Wyman, *Frontier Woman,* 28–31. The "barbed wire telephone" used the barbed wire fences for wires to conduct the sound. They were not particularly dependable.

16. *Western Star,* June 29, 1906; July 29, 1910; Kadoka *Press,* November 13, 1908; True Joyce, ed., *Faith Country* (n.p., n.d.), 220.

17. Lewis, *Nothing to Make a Shadow,* 27.

18. Reutter, *Early Dakota Days,* 67; Book and Thimble Club, *Proving Up,* 148.

19. Lakeside Old Settlers, *Through the Years,* 223; Lewis, *Nothing to Make a Shadow,* 83–84; Book and Thimble Club, *Proving Up,* 55.

20. Book and Thimble Club, *Proving Up*, 41–42, 30–31; American Legion Auxiliary, *Eastern Pennington County Memoirs* (Wall, South Dakota, 1966), 19, 191–192.

21. Book and Thimble Club, *Proving Up*, 53.

22. Ibid., 54–55.

23. Ibid., 57.

24. Ibid., 44. The ladies aid eventually accumulated $1,700 and used it to build a church in 1923.

25. Mrs. Roy Roseth, *Chronicles of the Deep Creek Church and Community* (Pierre, 1955), 35–36.

26. Ibid., 37.

27. Old Stanley County Hist. Soc., *Prairie Progress*, 615–616; Roseth, *Chronicles of the Deep Creek Church*, 37.

28. U.S. Department of the Interior, Bureau of Education, *The Educational System of South Dakota*, Department of the Interior Bulletin, 1918, no. 31 (Washington, D.C., 1918), 8–50.

29. *Western Star*, February 5, 1909.

30. *Western Star*, June 19, July 3, 1908.

31. Quoted in *Western Star*, November 18, 1910. See Wayne Fuller, *The Old Country School: The Story of Rural Education in the Middle West* (Chicago, 1982), for a thorough discussion of rural school development in the Midwest.

32. Corey, "Bachelor Bess," 20.

33. Ibid., 16–42.

34. Lewis, *Nothing to Make a Shadow*, 107–118. Although teachers played an important role in the community, this does not mean that teaching was well paid or always pleasant. Bess Corey began her teaching career in Stanley County, earning forty dollars a month for an eight-month term. She was paid in warrants, which had to be signed by each board member. Corey rode to the home of each to collect the signatures and then cashed her warrant at the bank. Banks discounted warrants up to as much as 10 percent, so a teacher's pay was often less than the contract specified. On one occasion an outbreak of scarlet fever closed the school two days before payday. With the school closed for a month, Corey could not collect her salary and was left with $1.32 to live on. Apart from this, the situation at two of her schools proved difficult. In one, the Speers family took a dislike to her and worked to have her contract go unrenewed. In a second school she was forced to expel a difficult student and because she boarded at the student's home, she had to seek a bed for the night somewhere else. Corey, "Bachelor Bess," 28, 36–37, 40, 43.

35. Kadoka *Press*, January 28, 1910.

36. Ibid., July 17, 24, 1908. There was a court system in the west river country that settlers could turn to if the situation warranted it. Most towns had justices of the peace, who heard testimony on local matters and awarded judg-

ments. County governments had been established in the region in 1890, and county seat towns had sheriffs and state's attorneys and held district court sessions where matters of this sort could be heard. The problem was one of distance and expense. The sheriff could not make his presence known throughout the district because of the size of his domain. Until it was divided up in 1914, for example, Stanley County was 100 miles long and 70 miles wide. Towns like Kadoka did not have direct train connections to Fort Pierre, the county seat, because the Milwaukee Road went to Chamberlain instead. Someone wanting to travel to Fort Pierre would either have to go cross-country at least fifteen miles to a town on the Chicago and North Western line and travel to Fort Pierre from there, or go west to Rapid City, a distance of 92 miles, change train lines there, and then travel east 169 miles to Fort Pierre. Farm people had poor roads (usually mere trails) that made travel difficult at all times and nearly impossible in rainy or winter weather. They had to travel to the nearest railhead and then make connections to Fort Pierre from there.

37. Kadoka *Press*, November 5, 1909.

38. Ibid., June 12, 1908.

39. Ibid., November 6, 1908.

40. Wyman, *Frontier Woman*, 41–42.

41. Ruste, "Homesteading in Lyman County," 45. Another case in which local residents worked out their own problems occurred when Bess Corey took a new school near Van Metre one school year and boarded with a family in the district. After two months on the job, one of the parents asked Corey to mediate a local dispute. Corey visited the two feuding families and solved the problem. "This isn't the first time I've been asked to pour oil on the troubled neighborhood waters," Corey told her mother. When she was offered a contract for the next year, however, she hesitated. The neighbors continued to feud, and she related an incident where a woman chased a male neighbor around and around a wagon with either a butcher knife or a hatchet. "How would you like to be where they fight with knives, hatchets, and guns, to say nothing of rocks and clubs?" she wrote. She agreed to return because the board built her a house with a stove and other furnishings right on the school grounds, built walks for her, and cut her stovewood. They also paid her sixty-five dollars a month with no discount. When the residents of the district decided to form a "Social Service Society," they unanimously elected Corey their president. Corey, "Bachelor Bess," 82, 83, 87.

6. THE BEST AND MOST PROGRESSIVE TOWN

1. For more information on the importance of the railroad to Great Plains development, see Robert R. Dykstra, "Cities in the Sagebrush: Great Plains Ur-

banization, 1865–1890," and Kenneth Hammer, "Railroads and Towns," both in Wright and Rosenberg, eds., *The Great Plains Experience*, 209–221 and 227–232.

2. John C. Hudson, "The Plains Country Town," in Brian W. Blouet and Frederick C. Luebke, eds., *The Great Plains: Environment and Culture* (Lincoln, 1979), 99–118.

3. Automobiles were present in limited numbers from the beginning of the land rushes in 1904. Land locators and real estate men found them particularly useful as they travelled over wide territories with eager homeseekers. Edith Kohl reported on the arrival of registrants for the 1907 Lower Brule lottery: "Into the little town of Pierre they swarmed—by train, by stagecoach, by automobile, by wagon, on foot." Potential homesteaders travelled to the reservation to see the available land. As a result, "all night, vehicles rattled over the hard prairies. . . . Flivvers bumped over the rough ground, chugging like threshing machines." Kohl, *Land of the Burnt Thigh*, 50, 56.

4. See the *Western Star* issue of September 9, 1904, for a stage schedule; the issue of July 8, 1904, for publishing problems; and the issue of March 29, 1907, for railroad mail services. The Pioneer Club of Western South Dakota's *Pioneers of the Open Range* includes J. C. Russell's story (pp. 6–7), as does the July 15, 1904, issue of the *Western Star*. Freighting problems are discussed in the *Western Star* of March 30, 1906, when J. C. Russell had 30,000 pounds of freight to be hauled with roads too muddy for travel. The July 29, 1904, issue carries a note on D. Bastion's travels. Drummer visits are discussed in the September 9, 1904, and March 2, 1906, issues and others.

5. The "team-haul principle" was based on the practical limitations of horse-and-wagon technology. The railroads' effort to plat towns at distances that would allow most farmers in a trade area to reach town by wagon and return home again the same day meant that towns could be no more than six to ten miles apart. Once automobiles became common, towns were unnecessarily close and there were too many of them; people could travel to their destination more rapidly and were willing to go farther.

6. Hudson, "Plains Country Town," 103–105.

7. The Herrick plat is included in Adeline S. Gnirk, *Saga of Ponca Land* (Gregory, South Dakota, 1979), 53; the Kadoka plat is included in the Kadoka *Press*, 75th year, Diamond Anniversary Edition, June 18, 1981. A plat of Dallas shows it to be a T town with a small development or addition named North Dallas on the north end. There are photographs of Philip, another T town, in Curt Satzinger, ed., *First Half Century: Philip, South Dakota, 1907–1957* (Philip, South Dakota, 1957), 4.

8. Kadoka *Press*, May 15, 1908.

9. *Western Star*, September 21, 28, December 12, 1906; February 8, March 22, 1907.

10. Mrs. Lloyd I. Sudlow, *Homestead Years, 1908–1968* (Bison, South Dakota, 1968), 52, 59, 151–152.

11. Hudson, "Plains Country Town," 112–115.

12. *Building an Empire: A Historical Booklet on Harding County, South Dakota, Prepared Especially for the Fiftieth Anniversary of Harding County to be Observed on September 6–7, 1959 at Buffalo, South Dakota* (Buffalo, South Dakota, 1959), 27.

13. Hudson, "Plains Country Town," 112.

14. *Coyote*, May 25, 1906.

15. Reverend William Reitmeir, *Golden Anniversary, Newell, S. Dak., 1910–1960* (n.p., 1960), 14.

16. The drugstore in Dupree advertised the list of magazines they carried in the store. They sold nineteen titles, including the *Saturday Evening Post, The Ladies Home Journal, Collier's, Cosmopolitan, and McClure's*. The Dupree library, a project of the local women, also listed all of its books, as did the Doty Circulating Library in Kadoka. The Doty library contained 106 titles, including books by Kipling, George Eliot, Dickens, James Fenimore Cooper, Booth Tarkington, Winston Churchill, and Owen Wister. A local businessman purchased the library in lieu of his usual advertising calendars and made the books available to the public. Dupree *Leader*, March 23, 1911, July 25, 1912, November 13, 1913.

17. Kadoka *Press*, October 16, 1908; July 29, 1910; January 5, March 22, 1912.

18. Ibid., July 22, 29, December 16, 1910; November 26, 1909; January 26, December 20, 1912.

19. Ibid., March 11, 18, April 8, 1910; *Western Star*, February 4, March 4, 1910.

20. *Range-Gazette* (Camp Crook, South Dakota), December 31, 1908.

21. Sudlow, *Homestead Years*, 2.

22. Robert James Maule, "A History of Tripp County, South Dakota" (Master's thesis, University of South Dakota, 1953), 29–31.

23. Micheaux, *The Conquest*, 182–192, 208–215.

24. Maule, "History of Tripp County," 36–37.

25. Kadoka *Press*, May 15, 22, 29, June 5, 19, 26, 1908.

26. Kadoka *Press*, April 14, 1911; July 3, August 7, October 9, November 13, 1908; February 19, March 19, May 28, 1909. Sometimes Kommercial Klub activity led to action by the town at large. The issuance of waterworks bonds, a project pushed by the Klub, was voted on and passed; Kadoka *Press*, March 19, 1909. The *Press* of March 26, 1909, discusses band funds, and that of December 3, 1909, discusses regional commercial clubs.

27. Kadoka *Press*, February 12, 19, 1909.

28. Ibid., January 8, 1909.

29. Ibid., May 15, 23, 1908; March 19, 1909; April 15, 22, 1910. The liquor law issue is discussed in the *Coyote*, March 22, 1907. The number of saloons in Kadoka is discussed in the Kadoka *Press*, 75th Anniversary Edition, June 18, 1981, article reprinted from *Jackson-Washabaugh Counties, 1915–1965*. See the Kadoka *Press* of December 11, 1908, for the Black Pipe Saloon. Dupree provides the clearest example of factionalism. During the early months of 1910, reports of a gang or "ring" committed to vice and general lawlessness made the local news. The newly elected county sheriff and state's attorney closed down some local gambling and prostitution dens under the banner of reform. Factions developed around those representing the old "wide-open" days and men chosen by the homesteaders. The battle continued for years. In 1912 the factions fought over the postmaster's appointment, held by James Stewart, the editor of the *Leader* and an outspoken advocate of law and order, homesteader style. Only Stewart's arguments survive, but from their tone it is clear that the battle was vitriolic. At one point, Stewart alleged that in the fall of 1911 an arsonist's attempt to burn the whole town was instigated by the gambler-horsethief ring. The editor of the opposing *Ziebach County News* supported the "ring," at least according to Stewart, and gave them an opportunity to assail their opponents in print. He also spearheaded the drive to run Stewart out of the postmaster's office and attempted to run for the Republican State Central Committee. A continuing issue in Dupree, and one tied in to the fray described above, was the problem of liquor. The reservations were off-limits to alcohol. Even white towns like Dupree were not allowed to have saloons or liquor available. There were always individuals in trouble over this provision of federal law, and many in the "ring" were active in importing liquor as well, or at least so it seems. Dupree *Leader*, March 30, May 18, 1911; May 16, 23, 30, 1912.

30. Maule, "History of Tripp County," 36–37.

31. Kadoka *Press*, September 3, 1909.

32. Ibid., June 19, August 7, 1908; February 19, July 23, 1909. Rumors started easily in small towns, and a person's reputation could be badly damaged if he did not act as the town felt he should. On May 4, 1909, the Kadoka *Press* felt obliged to print a note defending the water man, George Nott, who apparently was being accused of failing to haul water to a prairie fire that threatened the town. The editors informed their readers that Nott had hauled water and had fought the fire just as vigorously as had the rest of the community.

7. HAPPY HOMES, FINE RESIDENCES, AND GOOD SCHOOLS AND CHURCHES

1. Lewis Atherton, *Main Street on the Middle Border* (Bloomington, 1954), 183.

2. Harlan Douglass, *The Little Town* (New York, 1970; reprint of 1919 edition), 1–21. West river town populations are difficult to compute because so many remained unincorporated in 1910 and therefore were not counted apart from their townships. Of the twenty-three that were incorporated, eleven, or 48 percent, had fewer than 300 people. Five, or 21.7 percent, of the communities had between 300 and 600 people, while there were three, or 13 percent, that had populations over 600 but fewer than 1,000. Four towns had over 1,000 inhabitants. They were Belle Fourche, in Butte County, with 1,352; Dallas and Gregory, both in Gregory County, with 1,277 and 1,142 people respectively; and Lemmon, in Perkins County, which had 1,255 residents in 1910. Towns in the Black Hills, such as Rapid City, Sturgis, and Spearfish, also had over 1,000 residents, but they were not founded in the homestead rush and had other economic bases beyond farming. Belle Fourche could perhaps be considered in the latter category as well, as it was founded in 1890 as a cattle market center when the Fremont, Elkhorn, and Missouri Valley Railroad reached it from Nebraska via Rapid City. Robinson, *Encyclopedia of South Dakota*, 991–994; Schell, *History of South Dakota*, 125–157, 250.

Besides the towns' very small populations, the living patterns in the area also promoted town-country harmony. Many people lived on claims part of the year and in town the remainder, or part of the family stayed in town and part on the claim. The Kadoka *Press* of August 20, 1909, explained the living arrangements of the Kadoka school principal. His wife and child lived on the claim, while he resided in town during the week. Withrow, in *The Claim*, 61–65, describes the Davidson family pattern. The father worked in the town of Newell, while the mother and children lived on the claim in the summer and in town with him in the fall and winter.

The Franklin Creek schoolhouse fund-raiser discussed in chapter 6 is one example of shared sociability, as is the story about the "Big bunch at the dance at the Willard Hall, including many from Kadoka," referred to in the Kadoka *Press* of February 11, 1910. On another occasion the Willard people came to Kadoka to give a play. The play was "well received" and the Kadoka Band played. Kadoka *Press*, May 14, 1909.

3. Atherton, *Main Street on the Middle Border*, 181–216, 285–329.

4. Kadoka *Press*, May 8, 15, July 3, 31, 1908.

5. The following census data is from the *Thirteenth Census of the United States, 1910*, manuscript census schedules of Kadoka, Stanley County.

6. Ibid.

7. Ibid. The enumerator clearly indicated where people lived, unlike other enumerators, who listed many streets and many people and did not distinguish who lived where. Also, an early photograph of the town was published in the Kadoka *Press*, 75th Anniversary Edition, June 18, 1981. The picture is undated but no automobiles are present and many of the houses are no more than

shacks, a situation that existed until the teens. Another photograph in the 1981 edition, taken in 1928, shows many more substantial dwellings, and many are built more closely together, although many empty lots remain and in places large gaps still exist between the business district and the residential areas.

8. Most early issues of the Kadoka *Press* provide some indirect information about home life. A note in the January 22, 1909, issue, for example, describes a fire caused by the current methods of cooking, lighting, and heating and urges caution. The *Press* mentioned odor and sanitation problems on occasion as well. The issues of June 5 and 26, 1908 (when the Board of Health was established), and July 31, 1908, are examples. Stray pigs in town are discussed in the November 20, 1908, issue, although they appear to have wandered in from the country. On gardens and cleanup see the *Press* of April 15, 1910.

9. Kadoka *Press*, July 24, August 28, 1908. The Dupree *Leader* of February 6, 1913, carried an announcement that H. E. Keller would close his store on Sundays beginning February 9. The Isabel *News* carried a note congratulating Dupree for cooperating on Sunday closings without a law; reprinted in the Dupree *Leader*, February 27, 1913.

10. *Thirteenth Census, 1910*, manuscript census schedules of Kadoka, Stanley County.

11. Kadoka *Press*, July 31, August 14, 28, September 18, December 12, 1908; April 2, 1909; January 7, October 7, 1910; April 1, 1909; September 9, 1910. Women did not vote in school elections in South Dakota as they did in states like Colorado.

12. Ibid., July 3, 1909. The Presbyterians dedicated their church and a resident Catholic priest arrived during this week. "Union" churches and Sunday schools that combined Presbyterians, Methodists, and Congregationalists or other "liberal" Protestant denominations were common in towns or rural areas without the numbers or money to support a denominational church. In Kadoka all Protestants were welcome in the Presbyterian church when that was the only church available. Protestants appeared to attend any service that was available at the time, as long as it was mainline Protestant, of course. A general Gospel message and a code of personal behavior that emphasized self-reliance, good citizenship, and strong morals were all that was necessary for many. People may have preferred their own denomination, but in its absence they mingled with the general Protestant community.

13. Kadoka *Press*, November 13, 1908.

14. Ibid., August 28, 1908.

15. Ibid., July 3, 1908; February 19, 1909; February 25, 1910.

16. The Kadoka *Press* of July 17, 1908, carries the first column on the Catholic faith written by the local priest. His goal, he wrote, was to present the

truth about Catholic doctrine and combat untruths that were in circulation. In the column he compared the Catholic church to the South after the Civil War. The July 24, 1908, edition carried a column written by James Cardinal Gibbon aimed at the "prodigal sons" who had left the faith four hundred years before. The same issue described Father McNaboe's work. While he resided in Kadoka, he was in charge of all Catholic churches between Okaton and Rapid City, a distance of 130 miles. The Kadoka *Press* of August 21, 1908, described the laying of the cornerstone.

17. The activities of Frank Reidinger appeared in practically every issue of the *Press*. His wife was listed as a committee member for a Catholic fundraiser, and he donated a town lot to be sold for the church; October 1, July 30, 1909. The Hughes men appeared frequently because of their active participation in business and farming. Louis Determan, the manager of the elevator, was also mentioned frequently.

18. The Catholics' sense of their minority status appears to have been strong. A history of the Catholic church in Minnesota, North Dakota, and South Dakota included the statement: "Little did the people realize as they trudged over dry grass and through thick gumbo, the battle that lay ahead with the arid soil and severe weather. Catholics found themselves a small minority in this western world; the one thing they shared with their non-Catholic brothers was the poverty of the times" (from *Catholic Heritage: Minnesota, North Dakota, and South Dakota*, quoted in Book and Thimble Club, *Proving Up*, 41–42). In 1916 in the three counties formed from old Stanley County, there were 796 Catholics out of 1,867 total church members. In Jackson County, where Kadoka was located, there were 159 Catholics out of a total church population of 480. The numbers of actual church members are small compared to the total population. Old Stanley County had a population of 14,975 in 1910 and 7,881 in 1915 (divided among the three new counties made from the old). The remaining population appears to have been vaguely Protestant. *Federal Census of Religious Bodies, 1916.*

19. Kadoka *Press*, June 18, 1909.

20. Ibid., September 10, 17, 1909; April 1, 1910.

21. Ibid., February 11, 25, April 8, 1910.

22. Ibid., January 29, March 19, April 16, May 21, July 30, October 15, December 10, 1909; January 28, February 11, 18, March 11, April 8, July 29, October 21, 28, November 11, 1910.

23. Ibid., December 10, 1909; March 11, 1910.

24. In spite of the relative homogeneity of the town, voluntary associations remained important. Kadokaites were strangers with no common history in the early years. The voluntary associations held people together and created a common culture for them, which became a common history as time went on.

The list of organizations and their meeting schedules comes from the Kadoka *Press*, May 1908 to June 1911. The identification of individuals comes from the *Press* as well, with some assistance from the manuscript population schedules of the *Thirteenth Census, 1910*.

25. Kadoka *Press*, October 9, 1908; December 31, 1909; March 18, 1910.

26. Ibid., December 4, 1908; April 23, December 10, 17, 1909; February 11, 18, May 20, December 23, 1910.

27. Ibid., May 13, 20, December 9, 1910.

28. Ibid., June 5, 1908; September 10, 1909; March 18, 1910.

29. Ibid., October 1, May 7, 1909.

30. Ibid., May 29, June 5, 1908; November 19, 1909; June 19, 1908; June 17, 1910.

31. Ibid., September 11, 18, October 2, 1908; February 18, 1910; *Thirteenth Census, 1910*, manuscript census schedules of Kadoka, Stanley County.

32. Kadoka *Press*, March 18, February 25, May 20, 27, October 28, November 18, 1910.

33. Ibid., April 15, 22, October 21, 28, November 18, 1910.

34. Ibid., March 11, 1910.

35. Ibid., February 11, 25, April 11, 1910.

36. Ibid., August 6, 1909.

37. Ibid., April 1, 1910.

38. Ibid., January 15, 1909; January 27, 1911.

39. Ibid., May 20, 1910.

40. Ibid., January 14, March 4, 11, April 8, 1910; April 1, 1910; January 28, 1910. The new opera house opened in mid-November 1909 and announced that it planned to have "a full complement of shows," the first of which was the Clifton Comedy Company; Kadoka *Press*, November 19, 1909. In January a travelling company presented a play. In March a harpist presented "Ireland in Music and Song." A dramatic reader appeared in April, and a variety of local dances and entertainments filled the hall's calendar.

8. WE'VE REACHED THE LAND OF DROUTH AND HEAT

1. As reported by the federal census of 1910, the development of the west river country was well under way. The population of the homesteading counties had increased threefold from 33,616 in 1905 to 108,666 in 1910. Farmers were breaking and planting more acres every year, and town populations were stabilizing and prospering after the first hectic years of the rush. The number of speculative homesteaders (absentees) remained high. One federal census enumerator working in Stanley County carefully distinguished between farmers or

ranchers and homesteaders just living on their claims. Figures from her ten townships reveal that out of 451 heads of households, 186 were homesteaders only. The enumerator filed no farm schedules for people listed as homesteaders; apparently they were not engaged in any farm work. Although they occasionally attracted criticism, the presence of so many speculators made the land look thickly settled. The demand for land generated by the speculators, along with the progress made by bona fide farmers, drove land values up. Stanley County land rose from an average of $1.91 per acre in 1900 to $14.09 per acre in 1910. Perkins County land appreciated from an average of $3.55 per acre to $12.38. Accessibility to rail lines, rainfall totals, and length of settlement all influenced land values. The region's progress appeared real.

Population figures were computed from Robinson, *Encyclopedia of South Dakota*, 990. These figures do not include counties in the Black Hills. The *Thirteenth Census of the United States, 1910, Agriculture*, 7: 543, 557, provides information on land values. It also discusses crop production by county in 1909 and 1910. Those figures indicate that Stanley County farmers planted 47,209 acres of corn, more acres than for any other cultivated crop. Oats were the second most frequently planted crop, with 16,618 acres. Wild hay was the largest crop, however, with 195,398 acres of Stanley County land producing natural grasses. The pattern was the same in Perkins County.

2. *Western Star*, June 18, July 16, 1909.

3. Ibid., September 11, 1908.

4. Ibid., August 8, 13, 20, November 19, 1909.

5. Ibid., January 14, April 15, 1910; March 11, 1910.

6. *Fairplay* (Ft. Pierre, South Dakota), July 2, 8, 1910.

7. *Coyote*, July 24, 1910; *Fairplay*, July 29, 1910.

8. Miller, *From a Soddy*, 75; Lakeside Old Settlers, *Through the Years*, 224; American Legion Auxiliary, *Eastern Pennington County*, 172. According to the *Thirteenth Census, 1910, Agriculture*, 533, 552, 557, the average yield of wheat statewide in South Dakota in 1909 was 14.6 bushels per acre. For oats the figure was 28 bushels per acre, and for speltz it was 23.5. In Brookings County, South Dakota, on the eastern border with Minnesota, the average number of bushels of wheat per acre was 16.4. The figure for oats was 31.1 bushels per acre, while the figure for speltz in Brookings County was 21.4. The Hayes family grew no corn, but other west river homesteaders did. In Stanley County the average number of bushels of corn per acre in 1909 was 8.77, compared to a statewide average of 27.3 bushels per acre. In Iowa County, Iowa, that same year an average yield of corn was 43.57 bushels; *Thirteenth Census, 1910, Agriculture*, 6: 545.

9. Dupree *Leader*, November 24, 1910.

10. *Fairplay*, July 29, 1910. For a discussion of the history of the "rain fol-

lows the plow" theory, see David M. Emmons, *Garden in the Grasslands: Boomer Literature of the Central Great Plains* (Lincoln, 1971), 128–161.

11. *Coyote*, August 12, 1910, quoting the Philip *Weekly Review*.

12. *Western Star*, January 20, 1911.

13. Ibid., January 20, March 17, 1911.

14. Ibid., July 7, 1911. The Cottonwood Agricultural Experiment Station received 6.95 inches of precipitation between July and December 1909, but it received only 9.95 inches during the entire year of 1910. In 1911 the Cottonwood station received only 3.83 inches between January and late August. After the crops had dried up and the growing season had ended, Cottonwood received 2.41 inches of rain in late August and 3.59 inches in September, breaking the worst of the drought. U.S. Weather Bureau, *Monthly Weather Review*, vols. 37–39 (Washington, D.C., 1909–11).

15. Micheaux, *The Conquest*, 287–289.

16. Ibid., 290.

17. Miller, *From a Soddy*, 78–84, 89.

18. Book and Thimble Club, *Proving Up*, 144, 432.

19. Micheaux, *The Conquest*, 289; Book and Thimble Club, *Proving Up*, 144; Wasta *Gazette*, August 4, 1911; Wyman, *Frontier Woman*, 88–89.

20. *Western Star*, July 7, 1911; Book and Thimble Club, *Proving Up*, 403; American Legion Auxiliary, *Eastern Pennington County*, 133–134.

21. Old Stanley County Hist. Soc., *Prairie Progress*, 62; Robinson, *Encyclopedia of South Dakota*, 990.

22. *Western Star*, July 21, 1911; Wasta *Gazette*, July 28, 1911; Sudlow, *Homestead Years*, 104; *Western Star*, October 20, 1911; Dupree *Leader*, January 18, 1912.

23. Miller, *From a Soddy*, 78–86; Wyman, *Frontier Woman*, 89.

24. Olaf Olseth, *Mama Came from Norway* (New York, 1955), 60–61, 77, 79.

25. Quoted in *Western Star*, July 21, 1911; quoted in Isabel *News*, August 3, 1911; quoted in Kadoka *Press*, June 20, 1911; quoted in *Western Star*, July 7, 1911.

26. Kadoka *Press*, August 4, 1911; quoted in the *Coyote*, August 4, 1911; quoted in Kadoka *Press*, June 30, 1911.

27. Quoted in Dupree *Leader*, July 13, 1911; quoted in *Western Star*, July 28, 1911.

28. Quoted in *Western Star*, July 28, 1911; quoted in Dupree *Leader*, July 13, 1911; quoted in the *Coyote*, August 4, 11, 1911.

29. Quoted in *Western Star*, July 28, 1911.

30. The Kadoka *Press* of February 24, 1911, has an article on dry farming. The March 3, 1911, issue has an article on alfalfa, as does the issue of April 21, 1911. On April 7, 1911, an article on hamus appeared. The article on diver-

sification appeared on August 18, 1911. E. L. Keith's statement is from the Kadoka *Press*, August 18, 1911.

31. Dupree *Leader*, July 20, 1911.

32. Isabel *News*, July 27, August 3, 31, 1911; Dupree *Leader*, August 10, 1911.

33. Dupree *Leader*, July 20, August 3, 10, 17, 24, 1911; February 22, 29, 1912; Isabel *News*, July 27, August 3, 10, 1911; January 18, 25, February 15, 22, 29, 1912.

34. Dupree *Leader*, August 17, 1911.

35. Isabel *News*, December 21, 1911; January 25, 1911; February 22, April 4, 18, 1912.

36. *Western Star*, September 15, 1911.

37. *Western Star*, August 19, 1911; August 11, 1911; Wasta *Gazette*, September 18, 1911.

38. Wyman, *Frontier Woman*, 88; Kadoka *Press*, January 15, March 1, 1912.

39. Wyman, *Frontier Woman*, 88.

40. Quoted in the Kadoka *Press*, January 15, 1912; Kadoka *Press*, March 1, 1912.

41. *Western Star*, October 13, 1911.

9. LET THE GOOD WORK GO ON

1. Midland *Mail*, April 25, 1912.

2. Ibid., May 9, 1912.

3. Midland *Mail*, March 7, 1912. Harry Lovald purchased the Midland *Mail* in January 1912. He had edited the *Cheyenne Valley News* in the tiny hamlet of Davenport in the northern part of old Stanley County and had conducted a forceful campaign against the settler exodus in 1911.

4. Midland *Mail*, March 28, 1912.

5. Ibid., March 7, 1912.

6. Ibid., June 20, 1912.

7. Ibid., October 1, 1914.

8. Ibid., August 1, 1912.

9. Ibid., April 24, June 5, 1913.

10. Kadoka *Press*, January 14, 1916.

11. Ibid., October 3, 31, 1913.

12. Midland *Mail*, February 22, December 5, 1912, May 1, 1913; Kadoka *Press*, July 11, 1913.

13. Midland *Mail*, August 6, 1914.

14. Ibid., February 8, 1912.

15. Ibid., February 15, 1912.

16. Ibid., March 14, 1912.

17. Ibid., March 6, 1913.

18. Ibid., December 4, 1913.

19. Ibid., March 14, 1912.

10. TO OVERCOME THE DRAWBACKS AND FAILURE

1. Kadoka *Press*, December 6, 1912; October 3, 1912; May 14, 21, 1915; April 9, 1915.

2. Midland *Mail*, July 11, 1912; February 13, 1913; February 27, April 10, 1912; February 5, 1914.

3. Ibid., December 26, 1912; May 17, 1914; Kadoka *Press*, June 4, 1915. The Kadoka *Press* of March 29, 1912, reported that A. G. Granger, a local attorney and scientific farming advocate, had addressed a farmer's club from the country south of Ft. Pierre. The club had over a hundred members and tried to "solve some of the problems of development of a new country." By 1915 some counties had county agents, who worked to perfect organizations that would promote better farming techniques. Lyman County organized an association in 1915, and the county agent reported that he visited 189 farms and addressed nineteen meetings on farm problems. The agent also assisted at six "short courses" in the county. Stanley County agent Vey J. Valentine went to work there in April 1916. Although he did not perfect an organization of adults, he did establish Boys and Girls clubs and worked to distribute information and pure seed to farmers. Meetings were held in Jackson County at Kadoka and seventy-five people attended. In Jones County only twenty-five attended the first meeting. In both Jackson and Jones counties, those in attendance voted to organize agricultural associations and work was begun. Reports from the Third Congressional District, June 1915, and Lyman and Stanley counties, 1916, in *Extension Service Annual Reports: South Dakota, 1913–1944*, National Archives, Microcopy T-888, roll 1. Kadoka-area farmers organized a Farmer's Equity Union Association in March 1916, the first chapter west of the river; Kadoka *Press*, March 17, 1916.

4. Kadoka *Press*, December 31, 1915; February 11, March 3, 17, April 14, 1916.

5. Miller, *From a Soddy*, 94, 121, 125, 130. Henry Miller attributed his father's success to his "big family of boys" and his "hard-working wife." The Miller land "is now part of the West River National Grasslands, and there is not even a windmill tower to mark where the homestead once was" (p. 150).

6. Wyman, *Frontier Woman*, 104–111; quoted statements are from 104–105, 107.

7. Hargreaves, *Dry Farming in the Northern Great Plains*, 486. Hargreaves quotes the report of the superintendent of public instruction in 1918: "proper high school advantages, within reasonable reach, are practically unknown to the boys and girls west of the river." South Dakota did not provide much aid to local education until 1917, when "small payments scaled to the amount of state-owned indemnity and endowment lands within the various school districts" were authorized by the legislature. In 1919 South Dakota "granted funds for rural and graded elementary schools"; in the twenties the state provided aid for high schools. Hargreaves, 488. Elementary school aid continued to be very low until the mid-1930s. Mary Hargreaves' essay "Space: Its Institutional Impact" in Blouet and Luebke, eds., *The Great Plains: Environment and Culture*, states that 90 percent of such funding came from local property taxes. The result was poor facilities, "frequently sod houses and abandoned claim shacks" (p. 209). Private schools were scarce and did not fare much better. The Congregationalists established Thrall Academy near Sorum in Perkins County in 1913. The school was located fifty-five miles from a railroad in the center of a four-county area served by only two high schools. Money was scarce and facilities poor. While the circumstances were hard, the director noted, "We have learned to follow the custom of the country, and get along as best we can with what we have" (Mrs. Theodore Jorgenson, "Young People of the Prairie," typescript, SDHRC). The *South Dakota Congregationalist* of April 1, 1914, described the founding of the Academy.

8. Midland *Mail*, February 22, 1912.

9. Ibid., March 14, 1912.

10. Ibid., February 27, 1913.

11. Ibid., August 28, 1913.

12. Dupree *Leader*, August 12, 1915. Money was so scarce that county citizens resented any tax burden for any services. At one point a potential candidate for sheriff published a letter to the public on the front page of the *Leader* denying that he had "fallen heir to considerable money" and would "not stand in need of holding the office of sheriff." The public apparently believed that anyone with a means of livelihood should not take a public job. The candidate opposed such an idea. "It is claimed I am a good machinist," he wrote, "and capable of making a living, and therefore the county offices should be given to men who are not in a position to do as I can do. Is this just? Are county offices only for charitable purposes? If men are capable in the several callings of life, are the public offices closed to them?" (Dupree *Leader*, October 22, 1914).

13. Bennett County Historical Society, *70 Years of Pioneer Life in Bennett County* (Pierre, 1981), 129–130.

14. Ibid., 129–130. Town schools in settled counties did not suffer as much as those in rural districts. In 1913 Kadoka added grade 11. Fewer people voted in school elections, however, indicating a waning interest in the district's direc-

tion. Midland maintained a four-room school with fourteen students enrolled in the high school grades. Subjects taught included English, Latin, math, history, botany, and physical geography. Kadoka *Press*, August 8, June 20, 1913; June 19, 1914; Midland *Mail*, January 14, 1915.

15. Kadoka *Press*, July 19, August 9, 1912; February 7, 1913; February 6, April 10, 17, June 5, 19, 26, 1914; April 23, 1915; March 10, 1916.

16. Kadoka *Press*, December 5, 12, 26, 1913. Mortgage foreclosure notices published in the *Press* include the names of some of the most prestigious businessmen from the predrought years. R. G. Skrove lost his quarter section by sheriff's sale to retire a debt of $234.76. William Durkee, former coeditor of the *Press*, lost his homestead as well. Another leader, A. C. Zemanek, faced a chattel mortgage sale because he owed International Harvester $845.40. The company sold Zemanek's town lots to recover the debt. G. G. Inman, another early town leader, allowed the Kadoka State Bank to foreclose on his butcher shop equipment for his debt of $675. Nat Stevenson also faced the sale of two town lots for nonpayment of his debts. W. D. Vice, another early name, also lost his quarter section through foreclosure, though he continued to live in Kadoka in spite of his financial troubles. The others had moved away by the time the notices were printed. Two lawsuits were filed to force payment of debts. J. H. Dithmer, the blacksmith, sued the druggist, S. B. Dorn, for fifteen dollars for labor performed. G. G. Inman and Harry French sued W. G. Bailey and Albert Wiltfang for ninety-eight dollars for feed and pasture for two horses. Kadoka *Press*, July 19, 1912; October 31, November 7, 1913; March 6, 1914; May 1, 1913; March 5, November 5, 1915; October 3, 1913; July 19, 1912.

17. Ibid., April 5, 1912; May 1, 1914.

18. Ibid., January 24, March 7, September 26, 1913; January 30, April 10, 1914.

19. Ibid., January 1, 8, 15, 22, 29, 1915; July 9, 1915; April 2, May 28, June 4, 1915; February 25, 1916.

20. Ibid., October 1, 1915.

21. Ibid., February 11, 1916.

22. *Extension Service Annual Reports*, T-888, roll 1.

11. CONCLUSION

1. Dupree *Leader*, June 15, 1916.

2. Quoted in Kadoka *Press*, March 3, 1916.

3. Bradley H. Baltensperger, in "Agricultural Adjustments to Great Plains Drought: The Republican Valley, 1870–1900" in Blouet and Luebke, eds., *The Great Plains: Environment and Culture*, 46–51, indicates that new migrants

without agricultural experience on the plains tried to duplicate the methods of their previous homes (usually in the Corn Belt) until hard evidence in the form of drought made change or out-migration inevitable. The accumulated wisdom of earlier arrivals was repeatedly submerged in the ignorance of each successive wave of migrants.

4. Northern Plains Conference, *Digest of the Billings Conference, Billings, Montana, November 12 and 13, 1943* (Billings, 1943), 66.

5. Hargreaves, "Space: Its Institutional Impact," 209, 210; U.S. Bureau of Education, *The Educational System of South Dakota*, 8.

6. Old Stanley County provides one example of overchurching. In 1935 the Catholics had one church for every sixty-six members, the Presbyterians had an average of one church for every forty-four communicants, and the Lutherans one church for every forty-seven members. The National Home Mission Board at the time advised a minimum of 1,000 members per church for maximum efficiency. West river people would have had to travel tremendous distances to attend a consolidated church of that size. Studies of rural church attendance on the plains have indicated that farm families would not travel more than ten miles or so to attend church. In western North Dakota, for example, only 9 percent of those who lived ten or more miles away from church attended. *Federal Census of Religious Bodies, 1936*; W. F. Kumlien, *The Social Problem of the Church in South Dakota*, South Dakota Agricultural Experiment Station Bulletin 294 (Brookings, 1935), 18, 19; E. A. Wilson, H. C. Hofsommer, and Alva H. Benton, *Rural Changes in Western North Dakota*, North Dakota Agricultural Experiment Station Bulletin 214 (Fargo, 1931), 75–84.

7. *Extension Service Annual Reports*, Microcopy T-888, roll 1. The Prairie Homestead is a registered national historic place. For an admission fee, one is free to roam through the home and outbuildings, observing firsthand the household and barnyard furnishings available to homesteaders in 1910. Although no study has been done of amenities available in the west river country in the decades after the drought, the North Dakota Agricultural Experiment Station did a comparative survey in 1925 of farm families east and west of the Missouri River in that state. They discovered important differences in almost all categories. The eastern townships had only 7.4 percent of their farms equipped with running water, but 62.9 percent had sinks, 38.8 percent had electricity, and 44.4 percent had power washers. West of the river only 3.5 percent had running water, 11.8 percent had sinks, 2.9 percent had electricity, and only 16.1 percent had power washers. When homes and buildings were evaluated, the differences were also extreme. East of the river, 65.7 percent had "good" homes, compared to 41.9 percent in the west. Sixty percent of the eastern farmers evaluated their farm buildings as "good," while 66.6 percent believed their barnyards to be "good." The comparative figures for the western

farmers were 35.5 percent and 37.1 percent. The cultural factors showed similar differences. East of the river, 88.8 percent of the farmers were church members and 95.6 percent attended church. West of the river, only 49 percent belonged to a church and only 72.7 percent attended a church. Wilson, Hofsommer, and Benton, *Rural Changes in Western North Dakota*, 106.

8. Kadoka *Press*, December 3, 1915. Howard Lamar has suggested that historians do more to tell the story of those who stayed in the plains, because it was people's "persistence in the Plains [that] created the very toughness we think of as being truly Western" ("The Unsettling of the American West: The Mobility of Defeat," in Dick Harrison, ed., *Crossing Frontiers: Papers in American and Canadian Western Literature* [Edmonton, Alberta, 1979], 45). Thomas Saarinen, a geographer, studied the perception of drought and related personality characteristics in Great Plains farmers in the 1960s. He found that "although Great Plains wheat farmers are aware of the drought hazard, they appear to underestimate its frequency and to overestimate the number of very good years and the average crop yields in such years. They are eternally optimistic." When Saarinen tested other areas of the farmers' perceptions, he discovered that they saw themselves as "extremely resolute, determined individuals standing up to the environmental buffeting, fighting back, refusing to give in." The farmers stressed "the importance of will power and spirit in overcoming the great odds against them." Thomas F. Saarinen, *Perception of the Drought Hazard on the Great Plains*, University of Chicago, Department of Geography Research Paper, No. 106 (Chicago, 1966), 63, 110, 113.

9. The Dupree *Leader* of 1917 and 1918 provides a number of examples of this transition from self-interest to national interest. By midsummer 1917 the paper carried articles on the draft, local volunteers, the Red Cross, and the committee on draft exemption. By August, Dupree had organized a local Red Cross chapter. From that point on, at almost every social function where money was raised it was turned over to the Red Cross or to Liberty Bond drives. By mid-August 1917 the first long letter from a serviceman was printed on the front page, starting a custom that continued throughout the war and in fact well into 1919. The editor occasionally commented on how different the west river country would look to the boys who had been in the service. He speculated that west river life would not be exciting for them. Dupree *Leader*, May 31, June 21, July 5, August 2, 9, 1917; December 19, 1918.

BIBLIOGRAPHY

PRIMARY SOURCES

Newspapers and Periodicals

Aberdeen (South Dakota) *Daily News.*
The Coyote (Moore, later Murdo, South Dakota).
Dupree (South Dakota) *Leader.*
The Fairplay (Ft. Pierre, South Dakota).
Isabel (South Dakota) *News.*
Kadoka (South Dakota) *Press.*
Midland (South Dakota) *Mail.*
New York Times.
The Range-Gazette (Camp Crook, South Dakota).
Sioux Falls (South Dakota) *Argus-Leader.*
South Dakota Congregationalist (Pierre), April 1, 1914.
Wasta (South Dakota) *Gazette.*
Western Star (Midland, South Dakota).
Yankton (South Dakota) *Press and Dakotaian.*

Manuscripts

Bates, C. H. "Forty Years in South Dakota." Unpublished manuscript in the possession of the author.
Duckworth, Mildred, and Marjorie Clark. "The Claim Shanty." South Dakota Historical Resource Center, Pierre, South Dakota.

Jorgenson, Mrs. Theodore. "Young People of the Prairie." South Dakota Historical Resource Center, Pierre, South Dakota.

Malone, Fanny. "A Michigan Family's Experiences on a Government Homestead." South Dakota Historical Resource Center, Pierre, South Dakota.

Ruste, Erikka Hansen. "Homesteading in Lyman County, 1905–1908." Daughters of Dakota Collection. South Dakota Historical Resource Center, Pierre, South Dakota.

Interview

Henricksen, Elizabeth. Interview with author, Iowa City, Iowa, July 22, 1981.

Autobiographies, Memoirs, and Letters

Blassingame, Ike. *Dakota Cowboy.* Lincoln, 1964.

Bormann, Ernest. *Homesteading in the South Dakota Badlands, 1912.* Stickney, South Dakota, 1971.

Clarke, Ada Blayney. "Pothook Pioneer: A Reminiscence." Edited by Monroe Billington. *Nebraska History* 39 (March 1958): 39–56.

Cody, William F. (Buffalo Bill). *True Tales of the Plains.* New York, 1908.

Corey, Paul, editor. "Bachelor Bess: My Sister." *South Dakota Historical Collections* 37 (1974): 3–101.

Hamilton, W. H. "Dakota: An Autobiography of a Cowman." *South Dakota Historical Collections* 19 (1938): 475–637.

King, Ione Dunlap. *On Our South Dakota Claim.* Pierre, 1977.

Kohl, Edith Eudora. *Land of the Burnt Thigh.* New York, 1938.

Lewis, Faye Cashatt. *Nothing to Make a Shadow.* Ames, Iowa, 1971.

McCoy, Avis. *Dakota Homestead.* Chicago, 1974.

McKillip, Mabel. *Prairie Bride.* Typed copy, 1979. In South Dakota Historical Resource Center Library. Pierre, South Dakota.

Micheaux, Oscar. *The Conquest: The Story of a Negro Pioneer.* College Park, Maryland, 1969. Reprint of 1913 edition.

Miller, Henry, et al. *From a Soddy.* N.p., n.d.

Mills, George W. *Fifty Years a Country Doctor in Western South Dakota.* Wall, South Dakota, 1972.

Olseth, Olaf. *Mama Came from Norway.* New York, 1955.

Taylor, Katherine Sprague. *A Shattered Dream.* Lusk, Wyoming, 1967.

Tupper, Frieda. *Down in Bull Creek.* Clark, South Dakota, n.d.

Withrow, Myrtle Davidson. *The Claim.* New York, 1969.

Wyman, Walker. *Frontier Woman: The Life of a Woman Homesteader on the Dakota Frontier, Retold from the Original Notes and Letters of Grace Fair-*

child, a Wisconsin Teacher, Who Went to South Dakota in 1898. River Falls, Wisconsin, 1972.

County and Local Histories

American Legion Auxiliary. Carrol McDonald Unit, Wall, South Dakota. *Eastern Pennington County Memories.* Wall, South Dakota, 1966.

Bennett County Historical Society. *70 Years of Pioneer Life in Bennett County.* Pierre, 1981.

Book and Thimble Club. *Proving Up: Jones County History.* Murdo, South Dakota, 1969.

Building an Empire: A Historical Booklet on Harding County, South Dakota, Prepared Especially for the Fiftieth Anniversary of Harding County to be Observed on September 6–7, 1959 at Buffalo, South Dakota. Buffalo, South Dakota, 1959.

Cowboys and Sodbusters. N.p., 1968.

Dallas Historical Society. *Dallas, South Dakota: The End of the Line.* Dallas, South Dakota, 1971.

Fall River County Historical Society. *Fall River County Pioneer Histories.* N.p., 1976.

Gnirk, Adeline S. *Saga of Ponca Land: Comprising Ellston, Union, Spring Valley, St. Charles, West Half of Schriever Townships, and the Community of Milk Camp in Gregory County, South Dakota.* Gregory, South Dakota, 1979.

Hall, Bert, compiler. *Round-Up Years: Old Muddy to Black Hills.* Pierre, 1954.

Hanson, Myrle George. "History of Harding County, South Dakota, to 1925." *South Dakota Historical Collections* 21 (1942): 515–565.

Joyce, True, editor. *Faith Country.* N.p., n.d.

Lakeside Old Settlers Association. *Through the Years before 1966.* N.p., 1966.

Old Stanley County Historical Society. *Prairie Progress in West Central South Dakota.* Sioux Falls, 1968.

Pioneer Club of Western South Dakota. *Pioneers of the Open Range: Haakon County, South Dakota Settlers Before January 1, 1906.* Midland, South Dakota, 1965.

Reitmeir, Reverend William. *Golden Anniversary, Newell, S. Dak., 1910–1960.* N.p., 1960.

Reutter, Winifred, editor. *Early Dakota Days: Stories and Pictures of Pioneers, Cowboys, [and] Indians.* Stickney, South Dakota, 1962.

Reutter, Winifred. *Mellette County Memories: Golden Anniversary Edition, 1911–1961.* Stickney, South Dakota, 1961.

Roseth, Mrs. Roy. *Chronicles of the Deep Creek Church and Community.* Pierre, 1955.

Satzinger, Curt, editor. *First Half Century: Philip, South Dakota, 1907–1957.* Philip, South Dakota, 1957.

Sudlow, Mrs. Lloyd I. *Homestead Years, 1908–1968.* Bison, South Dakota, 1968.

Winner Chamber of Commerce. *Winner: Fiftieth Anniversary, 1909–1959.* Winner, South Dakota, 1959.

SECONDARY SOURCES

Government Publications

Country Life Commission. *Report of the Country Life Commission.* Washington, D.C., 1909.

Extension Service Annual Reports: South Dakota, 1913–1944. National Archives, Microcopy T-888, roll 1.

Federal Census of Religious Bodies, 1916, 1936.

Kumlien, W. F. *The Social Problem of the Church in South Dakota.* South Dakota Agricultural Experiment Station Bulletin 294. Brookings, 1935.

Landis, Paul. *The Growth and Decline of South Dakota Trade Centers, 1901–1933.* South Dakota Agricultural Experiment Station Bulletin 297. Brookings, April 1933.

Powell, John Wesley. *Report on the Lands of the Arid Regions of the United States.* Washington, D.C., 1878.

Rothrock, E. P. *A Geology of South Dakota.* South Dakota Geological Survey Bulletin No. 13. Vermillion, 1943.

U.S. Bureau of the Census. *Thirteenth Census of the United States, 1910, Agriculture.*

U.S. Bureau of the Census. *Thirteenth Census of the United States, 1910, Manuscript Census of Population.*

U.S. Department of Agriculture. *Climate and Man.* Yearbook of Agriculture, 1941. Washington, D.C., 1941.

U.S. Department of the Interior. Bureau of Education. *The Educational System of South Dakota.* Department of the Interior Bulletin, 1918, no. 31. Washington, D.C., 1918.

U.S. Weather Bureau. *Monthly Weather Review.* vols. 37–39. Washington, D.C., 1909–11.

Westin, Fred C., Leo F. Puhr, and George J. Buntley. *Soils of South Dakota.* South Dakota Agricultural Experiment Station, Soil Survey Series No. 3. Brookings, South Dakota, March 1959.

Wilson, E. A., H. C. Hofsommer, and Alva H. Benton. *Rural Changes in West-*

ern North Dakota. North Dakota Agricultural Experiment Station Bulletin 214. Fargo, 1931.

Theses

Maule, Robert James. "A History of Tripp County, South Dakota." Master's thesis, University of South Dakota, 1953.

Nelson, Paula Marie. "No Place for Clinging Vines: Women Homesteaders on the South Dakota Frontier, 1900–1915." Master's thesis, University of South Dakota, 1978.

Articles

Baltensperger, Bradley H. "Agricultural Adjustments to Great Plains Drought: The Republican Valley, 1870–1900." In Brian W. Blouet and Frederick C. Luebke, editors, *The Great Plains: Environment and Culture.* Lincoln, 1979.

Denison, Lindsay. "The Newest United States." *American Magazine* 67 (February 1909): 384–394.

Dixon, John A. "Taking Chances on Indian Lands." *World Today* 15 (December 1908): 1236–1240.

Dykstra, Robert R. "Cities in the Sagebrush: Great Plains Urbanization, 1865–1890." In James E. Wright and Sarah Rosenberg, editors, *The Great Plains Experience*, pp. 209–221. Lincoln, 1978.

Green, Charles Lowell. "The Administration of the Public Domain in South Dakota." *South Dakota Historical Collections* 20 (1940): 7–280.

Hammer, Kenneth. "Railroads and Towns." In James E. Wright and Sarah Rosenberg, editors, *The Great Plains Experience*, pp. 227–232. Lincoln, 1978.

Hargreaves, Mary W. "Space: Its Institutional Impact." In Brian W. Blouet and Frederick C. Luebke, editors, *The Great Plains: Environment and Culture.* Lincoln, 1979.

———. "Women in the Agricultural Settlement of the Northern Plains." *Agricultural History* 50 (January 1976): 179–189.

Howard, James H. "The Dakota or Sioux Indians, A Study in Human Ecology." *Anthropological Papers* (Vermillion, South Dakota) Number 2 (1966), 1–6.

Hudson, John C. "The Plains Country Town." In Brian W. Blouet and Frederick C. Luebke, editors, *The Great Plains: Environment and Culture*, pp. 99–118. Lincoln, 1979.

Lamar, Howard R. "The Unsettling of the American West: The Mobility of Defeat." In Dick Harrison, editor, *Crossing Frontiers: Papers in American and Canadian Western Literature.* Edmonton, Alberta, 1979.

Larson, T. A. "Women's Role in the American West." *Montana: The Magazine of Western History* 24 (July 1974): 2–11.

Lewis, G. Malcolm. "Regional Ideas and Reality in the Cis-Rocky Mountain West." In James E. Wright and Sarah Rosenberg, editors, *The Great Plains Experience*, pp. 27–33. Lincoln, 1978.

Norris, Frank. "The Frontier Gone at Last." *World's Work* 3 (February 1902): 1728–1731.

"The Passing of the Frontier." *Independent* 54 (May 15, 1902): 1201–1202.

Rees, Ronald. "Nostalgic Reaction and the Canadian Prairie Landscape." *Great Plains Quarterly* 2 (Summer 1982): 157–167.

Voisey, Paul. "Boosting the Small Prairie Town, 1904–1931: An Example from Southern Alberta." *Canadian Plains Studies* (Regina) 10 (1981): 147–176.

Books

Athearn, Robert G. *High Country Empire: The High Plains and Rockies*. New York, 1960.

Atherton, Lewis E. *Main Street on the Middle Border*. Bloomington, Indiana, 1954.

Bogue, Allan G. *From Prairie to Cornbelt: Farming on the Illinois and Iowa Prairies in the Nineteenth Century*. Chicago, 1963.

Bowers, William L. *The Country Life Movement in America, 1900–1920*. Port Washington, New York, 1974.

Bremer, Richard G. *Agricultural Change in an Urban Age: The Loup Country of Nebraska, 1910–1970*. Lincoln, 1976.

Buel, James William. *Heroes of the Plains; or, Lives and Wonderful Adventures of Wild Bill, Buffalo Bill . . . and other Celebrated Indian Fighters. . . .* Philadelphia, 1886.

Burke, John M., compiler. *"Buffalo Bill" from Prairie to Palace: An Authentic History of the Wild West with Sketches, Stories of Adventure, and Anecdotes of "Buffalo Bill," the Hero of the Plains*. Chicago and New York, 1893.

Casey, Robert J., and W. A. S. Douglas. *Pioneer Railroad: The Story of the Chicago and North Western System*. New York, 1948.

Chicago, Milwaukee, St. Paul and Pacific Railroad Company. *Government Homesteads and How to Secure Them*. Chicago, n.d.

Degler, Carl N. *The Age of Economic Revolution, 1876–1900*. 2d ed. Glenview, Illinois, 1977.

Derleth, August. *The Milwaukee Road: Its First Hundred Years*. New York, 1948.

Douglass, Harlan. *The Little Town*. New York, 1970. Reprint of 1919 edition.

Emmons, David M. *Garden in the Grasslands: Boomer Literature of the Central Great Plains*. Lincoln, 1971.

Fite, Gilbert. *The Farmers' Frontier, 1865–1900*. New York, 1966.

Fuller, Wayne. *The Old Country School: The Story of Rural Education in the Middle West.* Chicago, 1982.

Hargreaves, Mary W. *Dry Farming in the Northern Great Plains, 1900–1925.* Cambridge, 1957.

Hassrick, Royal B. *The Sioux: Life and Customs of a Warrior Society.* In collaboration with Dorothy Maxwell and Cile M. Bach. Norman, 1964.

Howard, Joseph Kinsey. *Montana: High, Wide, and Handsome.* New Haven, 1943.

Hurt, R. Douglas. *American Farm Tools: From Hand-Power to Steam-Power.* Manhattan, Kansas, 1982.

Hyde, George E. *Red Cloud's Folk: A History of the Oglala Sioux Indians.* Norman, 1937.

———. *A Sioux Chronicle.* Norman, 1956.

———. *Spotted Tail's Folk: A History of the Brulé Sioux.* Norman, 1961.

Kessler-Harris, Alice. *Out to Work: A History of Wage-Earning Women in the United States.* New York, 1982.

Kingsbury, George. *History of Dakota Territory;* and *South Dakota: Its History and Its People,* edited by George M. Smith. 5 vols. Chicago, 1915.

Kraenzel, Carl F. *The Great Plains in Transition.* Norman, 1955.

Lee, Bob [Robert H.], and Dick Williams. *Last Grass Frontier: The South Dakota Stock Grower Heritage.* Sturgis, South Dakota, 1964.

Mowry, George E. *The Era of Theodore Roosevelt and the Birth of Modern America, 1900–1912.* New York, 1958.

Northern Plains Conference. *Digest of the Billings Conference, Billings, Montana, November 12 and 13, 1943.* Billings, 1943.

Parker, Watson. *Gold in the Black Hills.* Norman, 1966.

Paul, Rodman. *Mining Frontiers of the Far West, 1848–1880.* New York, 1963.

Prucha, Francis Paul. *American Indian Policy in Crisis: Christian Reformers and the Indian, 1865–1900.* Norman, 1976.

Robinson, Doane. *Doane Robinson's Encyclopedia of South Dakota.* Pierre, 1925.

Robinson, Elwyn B. *History of North Dakota.* Lincoln, 1966.

Rothman, Sheila. *Woman's Proper Place: A History of Changing Ideals and Practices, 1870 to the Present.* New York, 1978.

Saarinen, Thomas F. *Perception of the Drought Hazard on the Great Plains.* University of Chicago, Department Geography Research Paper, No. 106. Chicago, 1966.

Schatz, August H. *Longhorns Bring Culture.* Boston, 1961.

———. *Opening a Cow Country: A History of the Pioneer's Struggle in Conquering the Prairies South of the Black Hills.* Ann Arbor, 1939.

Schell, Herbert S. *History of South Dakota.* Lincoln, 1975.

Simonson, Harold P. *The Closed Frontier: Studies in American Literary Trag-edy.* New York, 1970.

Smuts, Robert W. *Women and Work in America.* New York, 1958.

Stegner, Wallace. *Wolf-Willow: A History, a Story, and a Memory of the Last Plains Frontier.* New York, 1966.

Sullivan, Mark. *Our Times: The United States, 1900–1925.* 6 vols. New York, 1926–35.

Turner, Frederick Jackson. *The Significance of the Frontier in American History.* New York, 1963.

Unruh, John. *The Plains Across: The Overland Emigrants and the Trans-Mississippi West, 1840–60.* Urbana, 1979.

Utley, Robert M. *Frontier Regulars: The United States Army and the Indian, 1866–1891.* New York, 1973.

———. *Frontiersmen in Blue: The United States Army and the Indian, 1848–1865.* New York, 1967.

———. *The Last Days of the Sioux Nation.* New Haven, 1963.

Walker, James R. *Lakota Belief and Ritual.* Edited by Raymond J. DeMallie and Elaine A. Jahner. Lincoln, 1980.

———. *Lakota Society.* Edited by Raymond J. DeMallie. Lincoln, 1982.

White, G. Edward. *The Eastern Establishment and the Western Experience: The West of Frederic Remington, Theodore Roosevelt, and Owen Wister.* New Haven, 1968.

Wister, Owen. *Owen Wister Out West: His Journals and Letters.* Edited by Fanny Kemble Wister. Chicago, 1958.

Wister, Owen. *The Virginian: A Horseman of the Plains.* New York, 1902.

Wright, James E., and Sarah Rosenberg, editors. *The Great Plains Experience.* Lincoln, 1978.

INDEX

Adams, S., 79

Agriculture: ideas of, 15, 151; practice, 50–52, 54, 58–60; crops, 199; yields, 199

Alkali Divide, 13

Allotments, 9

Ammons, Edith, 20, 22, 27–28, 30, 32, 33, 34, 35, 38, 39, 63, 192

Attitudes and perceptions, xiv–xvi, 22, 51; town-builders, 82, 98–99, 118; doubt and failure, 120, 122, 125; editors on crisis, 123–124; postdrought adjustments, 144–149, 153–154, 169–177, 204; demoralization, 149–151; farming vs. stock-raising, 151–153; Great Plains residents, 206

Automobiles, 83, 115, 192

Badlands, 10–11, 61

Bailey, W. G., 204

Barbed wire telephones, 69, 189

Bartels, Mary, 22

Bastion, Dan, 84, 192

Belle Fourche, 88

Belvidere, 1, 107, 155

Belvidere *Times*, 132

Bennett County, 19, 162–163

Better Farming and Livestock Association, 158

Bison, 92

Bonesteel, 17, 20

Boosterism, 83, 84, 98

Bork, Otto, 148

Boyden, Edward, 63

Brave Bull school, 77

Brown, Rev. D. S., 109

Buffalo, 88, 92

Bull Creek, 39

Busy Creek, 67

Butte County, 21, 88, 129

Camp Crook, 92, 125

Capa, 39, 46, 162

Cashatt, Faye, family, 51, 62, 69
Catholics, 72, 108, 109, 110, 112,
    114–115, 165, 196, 197
Cattle frontier, 6–7, 9, 26, 120
Chamberlain, 17, 18, 21
Character, of west river settlers, xv–
    xvi, 154, 169–177, 206
Cheyenne River Reservation, 19, 135
Cheyenne Valley News, 132, 135
Chicago, Milwaukee, St. Paul and
    Pacific Railroad (Milwaukee Road),
    21, 84, 86, 88, 116, 137, 184
Chicago and North Western, 21, 84,
    92, 94
Childbirth, 68–69
Churches and Sunday schools, 70–
    73; in Kadoka, 108–111, 174–
    175; overchurching, 205
Clark, Ada Blayney, 39, 42
Clark, Marjorie, 37
Climate, 11–12, 34–37, 200
Colome, 94, 119
Congregationalists, 196, 203
Corey, Bess, 35–36, 39, 63–66, 76–
    78, 184, 186, 190, 191
Corson County, 138
Cottonwood, 79, 158, 163
County agents, 167, 202
County seat contests, 91–94, 165–
    166
Court system, 190–191
Coyotes, 38, 46
Crawford, Ella, 115
Crawford, Maria, 115

Dallas, 18, 19, 20, 23, 94, 192
Jack Daly neighborhood, 129
Dances, 67–68, 189
Davenport, 146, 153, 201
Davenport, Frank, Mr. and Mrs., 44,
    46

Davenport *News*, 121, 132, 133
Daviston, 86
Decker, Mrs. George, 166
Dewey County, 138
DeWitt Township, Perkins County,
    48, 186, 187–188
Dithmer, J. H., 204
Domestic service, 48, 106
Dorn, Mrs. S., 116
Dorn, S. B., 204
Draper, 73, 157
Driggers neighborhood, 122
Drought of 1910–1911, xv, 120–
    141; relief efforts, 135–141, 172–
    173
Drummond, G. M., 162
Dunlap, Otto, family, 32, 69
Dunn, George H., 144
Dunn, Huey, 32
Dupree, 130, 136, 193, 196, 203
Dupree *Leader*, 136, 162, 169
Durkee, William, 95, 204

Eagle Butte, 162
Eastern Star lodge, 116
Elbon, 158
Eureka neighborhood, 130
Excelsior Club, 115, 165

Factionalism, towns, 84, 97, 194
Fairchild, Grace, 38, 69, 79–80, 132,
    140, 159–160
Fairfax, 17
Fairview Township, 163–164
Faith, 86
Faith *Gazette*, 132
Fall River County, 42
Farm equipment, 50–51, 53, 54,
    58–60, 187
Farmer's clubs, 158, 202
Farmer's Cooperative Society, 158

Farmer's frontier, 7–8, 12, 20, 26–27, 120
Fence problem, 151–153
Ferguson, Mrs. V. L., 157
Ft. Pierre, 21, 49, 79, 84, 129, 202
Ft. Pierre *Fairplay,* 123, 124, 125
Ft. Pierre *News,* 140
Franklin Creek school, 78, 195
Freemole, Ed, 67
French, Harry, 204
Frontier: meaning of, xi, 169–177; lure of, 14–15, 21–23; myth of, 16

Gardner, Albert, 90
Graham, Elizabeth, 70
Grandfield Township, 152
Great Dakota Boom, 7–9
Great Plains physiography, 10–12
Great Sioux Reservation, 6
Gregory, 18, 20
Gregory County, 17, 85, 92, 94, 127, 128, 130
Gueffroy, Francis, 86
Gumbo, 11, 39–40

Hammond, Harry, 109
Hansen, Erikka, 43–47, 63, 80, 186
Harding County, 48, 88–89, 92, 132
Harrington school, 73
Harris, Mrs. C. J., 129
Haulman, Harry, 90
Hayes, 146, 158, 189
Hayes, Rettie, 43, 125
Helping Hand Society, 73
Henricksen, Elizabeth, 22
Herrick, 85, 192
Highland school, 73
Homesteaders: single female, 40, 47–48; absentees, 42–43, 170, 185–186; single male, 48, 50; numbers of absentees, 198–199

Homesteads, regulations governing, 9, 18–19, 21, 28, 42–43

Inavale post office, 130
Indian Creek neighborhood, 122
Inland towns, 86, 88–89
Inman, George, 96, 97, 204
Interior, 158, 159
Isabel, 137

Jackson brothers, 92, 94
Jackson County, 149, 165, 197, 202
Jeffries, Henry, 147, 158
Johnson, John, 125
Jones, George V., 90
Jones County, 202
Jorgenson, Mrs. Theodore, 157

Kadoka, 78, 82, 87, 90, 92, 95–97, 98, 101; populations analysis, 103–105; material life, 105–106; work patterns, 106; school, 106–108; churches, 108–110; ladies aids, 110–111; secular social groups, 111–117; informal sociability, 117; Opera House, 117–118, 139, 148, 152, 158, 164; postdrought social patterns, 164–165; county seat of Jackson County, 165–166, 167, 175, 192, 193, 194, 195, 196, 197, 198, 203
Kadoka Commercial Club, 164, 165, 166
Kadoka Dramatic Club, 116, 117, 165
Kadoka Kommercial Klub, 95–97, 98, 112, 164, 193
Kadoka *Press,* 95–96, 97, 98, 102, 103, 106, 108, 109, 112, 114, 115, 116, 117, 118, 121, 132, 135, 140, 148, 149, 150, 156, 157, 158, 164, 165, 166

Keith, E. L., 125–126, 134, 135
Keller, H. E., 196
Kjar, Rasmus, 151–152, 153
Klotz, D. F., 148–149
Knights of Pythias, 114
Kohl, Edith Eudora. *See* Ammons, Edith
Kopac, Ed, 25

Ladies aids: role of, 73; United Lutheran, 73; Deep Creek Lutheran, 74; Hilland, 74–75; Kadoka Presbyterian and Methodist, 110–111
Lakeside neighborhood, 76, 122
Lakota, 2–6, 9, 12, 18, 21, 26, 38, 87, 179–180
Lamro, 94–95, 97
Land lotteries, 17–19
Land values, 123, 134, 199
Larsen, Chris, 148
Last great frontier, 14, 15, 22
Leggett, C. H., 124
Lemmon, 37, 86, 88, 92, 128
Lemmon Land Company, 86
Lincoln Township, 124
Liquor issue, 97, 194
Lovald, Harry, 132, 133, 134, 135, 146–147, 148, 157, 161, 201
Lower Brule Reservation, 18, 20, 21
Lutherans, 72–73
Lyman County, 20, 21, 22, 25, 26, 28, 32, 43, 62, 70, 73, 113, 129, 157, 202

McNaboe, Father Thomas A., 109, 110, 197
Malone, Fanny, 26, 62
Marietta Township, 139, 140
Marrington, Sophia, 74
Masons, 112

Maximilian neighborhood, 126
Meade County, 13, 86, 125
Meadow, 91
Mellette County, 19, 31, 61, 63, 64, 93
Methodists, 73, 108, 109, 110, 111, 164, 196
Micheaux, Oscar, 51–52, 127–128
Midland, 36, 72, 76, 81, 83, 84, 85–86, 92, 114, 130, 148, 152, 153, 158, 204
Midland *Mail*, 144, 145, 146, 150, 151, 153, 156, 161, 201
Miller, William and Carrie, family, 52–60, 63, 125, 128–129, 130, 132, 159, 187, 188, 202
Milwaukee Road. *See* Chicago, Milwaukee, St. Paul and Pacific Railroad
Mining frontier, 4–6, 26
Mitchell Creek, 37, 123, 149, 150
Mix, Fred, 123, 124, 125
Modern Woodmen of America, 112, 116–117
Murdo, 73, 83, 89, 114, 139
Murdo *Coyote*, 15, 124

Nellor, Edward, 95
Nelson, James, 148
Nesheim, Grandma, 74
Newcomer, Martha, 115
Newell, 89, 186, 195
Nolting, C. H., 79
Nordlander, Wm., 79
North Star school, 73
Nott, George, 194
Nowlin, 162

Oglala. *See* Lakota
Okaton, 25
Old Settlers and Cowboys Reunion, 112

Oliver, S., 124
Olney, F. E., 79
Olseth family, 132
Ottumwa, 158

Park Embroidery Club, 165
Pascoe, Fred, family, 129
Pease, J. C., 164
Pennington County, 43, 125, 129, 179
Pepper, Jud, 66–67
Perkins County, 21, 48, 71, 86, 88, 91, 92, 125, 128–129, 130, 131, 133, 159, 199, 203. *See also* Miller, William and Carrie, family
Peterson, P. H., 79
Pheba neighborhood, 123
Philip, 92, 158
Philip *Pioneer*, 170
Philip *Weekly Review*, 125, 134, 149
Pierre, 9, 18, 20, 21, 126, 127
Pine Ridge Reservation, 19, 96
Pleasant Hill, 122
Plum Creek school, 76
Population, west river, 21; town of Kadoka, 103–105; loss of, 130, 183; towns, 195
Prairie fires, 29, 37–38
Prairie Homestead, 175, 205
Prairie View school, 161
Presbyterians, 88, 108, 109, 110, 111, 112, 114, 115, 164, 196
Presho, 18, 20, 113

Railroads, 7–8, 14, 17, 21, 82, 84–88; relief efforts, 136–138, 192
Rapid City, 4, 21, 39, 139
Rattlesnakes, 38–39, 54
Reidinger, F. E., 90, 197
Reservation openings, 17–19
Retz, John R., 162

Reutter, Winifred, 64
Robertson, William W., 162
Rohan brothers, 114–115
Root, Fred H., 130
Rosebud Reservation, 14, 17, 18, 19, 20, 22
Rousch school, 73
Russell, J. C., 84, 85, 192

St. Paul's Lutheran Church, 73
St. Peter's Evangelical Lutheran Church, 72
Sansarc, 146, 147, 158, 161
Sansarc Agriculture Association, 158
Schools: rules governing, 48, 75; role of, 75; growth of, 75–76; local control and factionalism, 75–76; fund-raisers for, 76–78; in towns, 106–107; postdrought problems, 156, 160–163, 174, 203–204
Schoolteachers: role of, 76–78, 161–163; pay and status, 190, 191
Scientific farming, 126, 134–135, 156–160, 173–174, 200, 202
Sellars, Albert, 139
Senn, E. L., 98
Serr, America, 115
Seymour, Press, 129
Simek, Frank, 114–115
Sioux. *See* Lakota
Skrove, R. G., 90, 204
Social R circle, 163
Social relations: rural, informal, 63–67; tension and conflict, 79–80; town and country, 102, 195; within towns, 102–103; critique of rural, 188–189
Sod-house or soddy, 28, 30, 53
Soils, 11, 39–40
Solon, J. J., family, 114–115
Sorum, 203

220

INDEX

Stahl, Al, 98

Standing Rock Reservation, 19, 29, 135

Stanley County, 1, 21, 26, 35, 45, 49, 65, 75–76, 77, 79, 81, 85, 92, 95, 101, 107, 120, 121, 122, 123, 124, 127, 130, 132, 133, 134, 135, 139, 140, 143, 146, 149, 150, 151, 153, 157, 161, 165, 167, 197, 199, 201, 202, 205

Stanley County Fair Association, 114

Stearns, Maude Wright, 27

Stevenson, Libby, 115

Stevenson, Nat, 204

Stewart, James, 169, 194

Stuart, Grace, 115, 116

Sturgis, 13

Tar-paper shacks, 27, 28, 29–30, 34, 41, 44, 131, 175

Taylor, Katherine, 37

Teaney, E. E., family, 148

Teter, Clara Bentley, 120

Thorne family, 46

Thrall Academy, 157, 203

Tripp County, 18, 21, 78, 94, 97, 119, 127

Turner, Frederick Jackson, xi, xiv

Twentieth-century America, xv, 14–15, 176–177

Valentine, Vey J., 202

Van Metre, 44

Vera school, 73

Vice, W. D., 204

Wakpala, 29

Warner, W. W., 161

Washabaugh County, 19

Wasta *Gazette*, 129, 130, 139

Water supply, 32–33; in Kadoka, 105, 184

Wellman, Scott, 90

Western Star, 121, 122, 123, 127, 141

Western Townsite Company, 94

Westover, 39

Weta, 67, 163

White River, 31, 93

Wiley, Hugh, 79

Willard, 117, 150, 163, 195

Wiltfang, Albert, 204

Winner, 94–95, 97

Withrow, Myrtle Davidson, family, 186, 195

Wives: farm wives' roles, 54–58; town wives' roles, 106

Women homesteaders, 40; daily routine, 44–47; job opportunities, 47–48; goals and impact, 186–187. *See also* Ammons, Edith; Corey, Bess; Hansen, Erikka

Women's Christian Temperance Union, 115, 116, 165

Women's clubs, 115, 163–164, 165, 166

Work patterns, family roles: on farms, 50, 52; Miller family examples, 52–58; in town, 104–106

World War I, 176–177, 206

Yankton, 8, 17, 18, 19

Zemanek, A. C., 204

Ziebach County, 136, 137, 162, 203